Flight and Migration from Africa to Europe

Gefördert vom DAAD aus Mitteln des Auswärtigen Amts (AA)

 Auswärtiges Amt

Angelika Groterath
Viviana Langher
Giorgia Marinelli (Eds.)

Flight and Migration from Africa to Europe
Contributions of Psychology and Social Work

Verlag Barbara Budrich
Opladen • Berlin • Toronto 2020

All rights reserved. No part of this publication may be reproduced, stored in or introduced into a retrieval system, or transmitted, in any form, or by any means (electronic, mechanical, photocopying, recording or otherwise) without the prior written permission of Barbara Budrich Publishers. Any person who does any unauthorized act in relation to this publication may be liable to criminal prosecution and civil claims for damages.

You must not circulate this book in any other binding or cover and you must impose this same condition on any acquirer.

A CIP catalogue record for this book is available from
Die Deutsche Bibliothek (The German Library)

© 2020   by Verlag Barbara Budrich GmbH, Opladen, Berlin & Toronto
www.budrich.eu

    ISBN   978-3-8474-2349-2
    eISBN 978-3-8474-1479-7
    DOI   10.3224/84742349

Das Werk einschließlich aller seiner Teile ist urheberrechtlich geschützt. Jede Verwertung außerhalb der engen Grenzen des Urheberrechtsgesetzes ist ohne Zustimmung des Verlages unzulässig und strafbar. Das gilt insbesondere für Vervielfältigungen, Übersetzungen, Mikroverfilmungen und die Einspeicherung und Verarbeitung in elektronischen Systemen.

Die Deutsche Bibliothek – CIP-Einheitsaufnahme
Ein Titeldatensatz für die Publikation ist bei der Deutschen Bibliothek erhältlich.

Verlag Barbara Budrich GmbH
Stauffenbergstr. 7. D-51379 Leverkusen Opladen, Germany

86 Delma Drive. Toronto, ON M8W 4P6 Canada
www.barbara-budrich.net

Jacket illustration by Bettina Lehfeldt, Kleinmachnow –www.lehfeldtgraphic.de
Picture credits: photo: Suzanne Koehler
Editing by Máiréad Collins, Belfast, UK
Printed in Europe on acid-free paper by
paper & tinta, Warsaw

This book is dedicated to the memory of Julia Knoke, who died far too young in May 2019. As Head of the International Office of the Hochschule Darmstadt, Julia started this summer school project with us - and without her we would not have started.

Table of Contents

Editorial 9

Renzo Carli, Rosa Maria Paniccia
The Culture of Security and Governance in Italy and Germany: a comparison 13

Christopher Hein
Contemporary mixed migration from Africa to Europe via Italy 30

Giorgia Marinelli, Viviana Langher, Andrea Caputo, Kibreab Habtemichael, Angelika Groterath
The Viernheim study: use clinical psychology to explore integration capacities of a German community 52

Lena Pschiuk, Viviana Langher, Giorgia Marinelli, Angelika Groterath
Resilience and Posttraumatic Growth of Refugee Women – One Study and Two [Types of] Results 68

Denise Filmer, Massimo Sturiale
Trust, identity, and the intercultural mediator's role in the migrant crisis on the South East coast of Sicily 84

Sabine Pirchio, Sara Costa, Rosa Ferri
Language and social integration in multicultural contexts 105

Maria Cristina Tumiati, Andrea Cavani, Laura Piombo, Giorgia Marinelli, Gianfranco Costanzo, Concetta Mirisola
Itineraries of geoclinical psychopathology in Public Institution 117

Katrin Luise Laezer, Marianne Leuzinger-Bohleber
Psychoanalytically based social work with traumatized refugees: implementing the STEP-BY-STEP project 131

Germana Cesarano, Angelika Groterath, Daniela Moretti
The Service System for Victims of Human Trafficking in the City of
Rome 160

Sofija Georgievska
Indicators for identification of victims of trafficking in human beings 173

Giuseppe Mannino, Eleonora Maria Cuccia, Marta Schiera, Erika Faraci
The challenge of recovering trafficked and smuggled humans: new
integration proposals starting from analysis of the old protection
system for asylum seekers (SPRAR) in Sicily 190

David Schiefer
Migration and family: a neglected nexus? 201

Editorial

The issue of migration has become a central focus in global contemporary political discourse. In Europe, it is considered a priority in the current and future European agenda, represented as a matter of urgency and emergency. Since 2015, the European Commission has presented the, regularly updated, document "European agenda on migration" to the European Parliament. This document describes several pragmatic and programmatic measures are described, in order to manage the migration flows inside European territories, but also to control the pressure of migrantion pushing from the outer European boundaries. It seems that one of the main issues related to migration is the possible conflict between EU citizens' legitimate aspiration to feel safe and secure inside European borders and non-EU citizens' right to be hosted and protected when running away from poverty, war, natural disasters, famine, severe political tensions, and so on.

The plain distinction between economic migrants and refugees/asylum seekers cannot be easily claimed, due to the different intersecting factors that can be considered as responsible for the migration process. For example, poverty is associated with migration: does this association explain migration as a process based on economic motivations? It may seem that it does, but it cannot be forgotten that poverty is very often associated with other conditions of vulnerability, which make a person more exposed to social exclusion, segregation, discrimination, and persecution. What we want to state here is that when we consider a migration process, which begins in a poor region not involved in an actual conflict with other regions, we are pushed to explain that process as due to economic motivating factors. This could be an oversimplified thought. What we face, in reality, are the multifaceted consequences of poverty, which always result in different and increasing levels of inaccessibility to the different layers of society, meaning, for those affected by it, a precarious, difficult or impossible realisation of one's own individual rights.

Notwithstanding such complexity, it seems to us that a sort of "simple thinking" dominates the contemporary common opinion on migration. This topic has indeed polarised several political campaigns, causing the presentation of opinions and consensus, which seem to stand in front of one another as counterposed blocks. We are however convinced that the migration issue is too important to be dismissed as a rigid and unproductive contraposition of pros and cons. For this reason, we have decided to participate in the public debate on migration, offering a scientific, multidisciplinary, multi-professional contribution, with the idea that a patient exploration of this phenomenon can be used in order to overcome the militant contraposition, which characterises the current political debate.

We got this opportunity to open this debate when we succeeded in organising a summer school in Rome, in June 2019, named "From Africa to Europe through Italy", which was attended by psychology and social work students, together with academic scholars and prominent professionals, coming from three different European countries.

The first country we have to mention is Germany, which made real the summer school project. The summer school was funded by the German Academic Exchange Service DAAD in the framework of the programme "Hochschuldialog mit Südeuropa" (University dialogue with southern Europe) supported by the German Foreign Ministry. With this initiative, Germany has shown openness and the will to involve young generations in rationally confronting the topic so that better possible solutions can be found.

The second country is Italy, which hosted the seminars. Italy is a place often involved in migration events, due to its 5000 km long coasts, and to the short distance, less than 170 km, severing the small isle of Lampedusa from the Tunisian coast. In Italy, thousands of diverse and disconnected migration experiences can be detected and can serve as case studies, but can also contribute to the attempt of a systematic consideration of migration.

The last country involved in this project is Northern Macedonia, which testifies to the difficulty of realising truly inclusive processes; it is a small section of South Eastern Europe, with the Balkan Route in the background, walked across by families, or lone children, or vulnerable women, all longing for the desired European boundaries.

Although the summer school is enrooted in a multidisciplinary background, a preeminent contribution is due to social work and psychology. Social workers are among the professionals with a higher probability of direct contact with migrant and refugees: they work in the field, they are often involved in emergency situations, they stand in the middle, on the psychosocial, emotional boundary, work in the very sensitive space between strangers and residents. They have to keep in mind that everyone is a stranger to someone else.

As for psychology, we wanted to share a particular theoretical perspective that is offered in some Italian universities: clinical psychology, based on psychoanalysis, aimed at exploring and intervening in social contexts. Differently from what is normally intended by the term "clinical psychology", often focused on psychopathological individuals, this "Italian" theoretical perspective is interested in analysing the emotional dynamics modeling people behaviour and sense-making in a tight relationship with their culture and social contexts.

We wanted to offer our audience the possibility to reflect, with the support of theory and empirical research, on the socialised emotions that can explain some irrational behavior and emotional contagious among individual sharing the same social environment.

The different chapters forming this volume wind through a multicultural and multi-perspective dialogue, where studies and research, as well as descriptions of services to support migrants and refugees and case studies took part in building this common narration.

The first contribution (Carli & Paniccia, 2020) is a psychosocial research study carried out within the psychoanalytical theoretical framework, comparing German and Italian cultures on security and governance fields, with a specific focus on the migration topic. The authors help us to comprehend to what extent the sense of belonging to one's own community allows the individuals and groups to face changes – here represented by the social impact of the migration flows on the host communities – with a reasonable confidence that the changes can be dealt with. Without a sense of belonging, on the contrary, an individualistic tendency, eventually unscrupulous and predatory, may prevail.

The next contribution (Hein, 2020) illustrates an updated and synthetic juridical framework on European laws and regulations on migration, completed with a statistical analysis of migration flows in Europe during the last decade.

The following two contributions help to understand the social representation of the migrant/refugee, with a particular attention to its affective symbolic component. The emotional aspects evoked by the "stranger" and socialised in the host cultures will be discussed in the first of these two pieces of research (Marinelli et al. 2020), through the analysis of narratives collected interviewing people in Viernheim, a tiny town in Assia distinguished for its programmes in supporting the refugees. The other work (Pschiuk et al. 2020) is instead focused on the narratives of women talking about themselves, their journey to Europe, the emotions evoked by the relationship with their country of origin.

The volume continues with several contributions focused on professionals that may play a crucial role in managing and facilitating the relationships between migrant communities and host communities: social workers, cultural mediators, educators, psychologists. Here language is to be considered as an element of one's own identity (we call it "mother tongue") as well as an instrument of communication and construction of relationships with the others (Filmer & Sturiale, 2020; Pirchio et al., 2020).

Finally, we have a set of contributions represented by the chapters describing some services offered to the migrants/refugees provided by the host communities, with the aim to take charge of the apparent fragile situations related to the migration flows. These services can offer health care assistance to migrants and poor people (Tumiati et al., 2020), psychological support to children and families (Laezer & Leuzinger-Bohleber, 2020), or protection to victims of human trafficking and smuggling (Cesarano, Groterath & Moretti, 2020; Georgievska, 2020; Mannino et al., 2020).

The last contribution, again on the topic of the family and its influence on a migration decision, is focused on the analysis of the complex processes of family reunification that, when disregarded, may increase the likelihood of irregular ways of reuniting migrant family members in destination countries or supporting their relatives financially from abroad (Schiefer, 2020).

We decided to publish all the papers presented during the summer school in order to share and make accessible the common effort of all the speakers to offer a meaningful perspective, a rational view and a passionate attitude.

We hope that this book can benefit all the persons, students, professionals, scholars, and volunteers that are trying to help the management of this impressive global phenomenon, studying and researching, as well as carrying on theory-oriented and empirically based actions on the field; persons who are guided and inspired by their sense of responsibility towards human beings who bet on their own life and their future on the precision of the long jump that they will be able to perform, with our help or alone. They already made their decision. We can choose to be silent spectators only, distrustful or even hostile, or can accept to be a stranger to someone else and share solidarity.

Angelika Groterath, Viviana Langher, Giorgia Marinelli

The Culture of Security and Governance in Italy and Germany: a comparison

Renzo Carli, Rosa Maria Paniccia

Aims

This research study intends to show the local cultures evoked by the issues of Security and Governance in two populations: Germans and Italians.

The research was carried out by administering a specific questionnaire for each of the two issues to groups of Italians and Germans whose work was related to each issue. For each issue, young people aged 17 to 25 were also questioned.

By "local culture" we mean the set of symbolic mental dimensions that are evoked in talking about security and immigration, or governance.

The research hypothesis is that the themes elicited by the questions in the two questionnaires will bring out different interrelated symbolic visions. Our aim is to analyse these different symbolic visions and to show how they are related[1]. The data analysis will therefore enable us to describe the whole culture evoked by the issue and the different emotional dynamics making it up.

The analyses of the data emerging from the statistical elaboration of the responses to the two questionnaires will then be presented.

The questionnaire responses were subjected to factorial analysis of multiple correspondences and cluster analysis.

The interpretation of the data will consider the different clusters of questionnaire responses and the relation between them and the factorial space that emerges.

---

1 Usually the questionnaires are read using the range of different individuals responding to the questionnaire, question by question. In the methodology we used, both the range of respondents and the range of questions are "processed" statistically, presuming that the interaction between these ranges defines the local culture evoked by the issue being investigated. The methodology used can pinpoint the interactions between this double source of variability and diversity of data. The diverse range we are talking about is not related to a summation of elements (objects of symbolisation and individuals who symbolise) but to the interaction between these elements.

Security and immigration

Participants in the study

The number of participants in the research was 608: 308 Italians and 300 Germans. The participants overall were subdivided as follows (half Germans and half Italians):

Participants' occupation:
1. Representatives of local administration, for example mayors, town councilors responsible for immigration etc. (22%)
2. Staff in immigrant reception centers and volunteer workers in the immigration field (22.4%)
3. Representatives of security forces (police, army, carabinieri, traffic wardens, finance corps etc.) (22.2%)
4. Young people between 17 and 25 years of age (33.4%):

 - *Age*:
   18-30 years: 38.2%
   31-60 years: 53.9%
   61 and above: 7.9%

 - *Sex*:
   male: 49.3%
   female: 50.7%

The ISO Questionnaire: Security, elaborated by Studio di Psicosociologia (SPS) in December 2017, was administered to the participants in February 2018. From the multiple correspondence analysis and cluster analysis on the data collected, the following factorial plane emerged, showing four clusters:

Table 1: Relationship between clusters and factors in Security research

Cluster	Frequency	Factor 1	Factor 2	Factor 3
Cluster 1	177	.140	591 (+)	.269
Cluster 2	151	-745 (-)		.245
Cluster 3	134	936 (+)	- .063	
Cluster 4	146	- .099	- 861 (-)	- .040
Total	608			

Source: The present research

Figure 1: Factorial plan for Security research

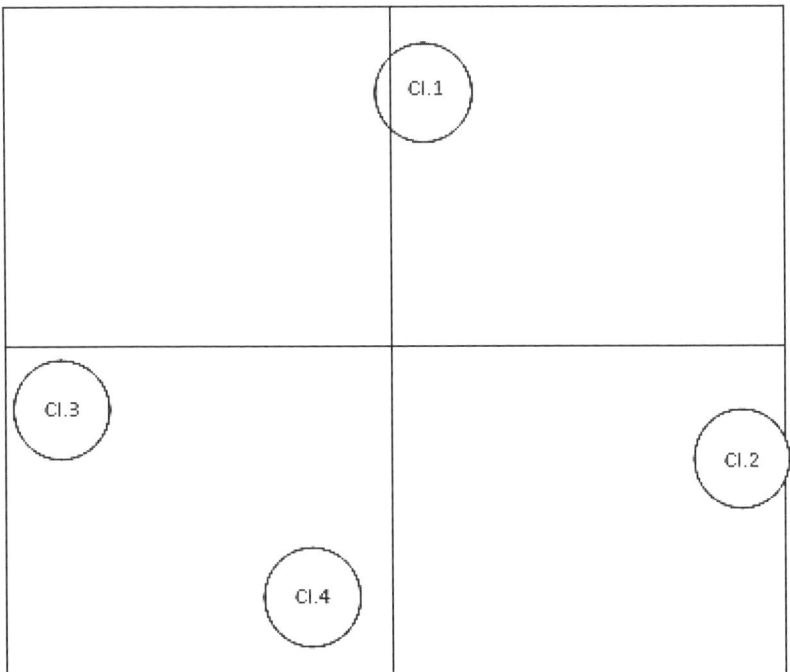

Source: The present research

Clusters 3 and 2 are *significantly* situated on the first factor, while Clusters 1 and 4 are *significantly* situated on the second factor.

Data analysis

On the first factor (Clusters 3 and 2) the issue that clearly separates the German population from the Italian one is civism. Let's look at two definitions of the term:

In an Italian dictionary, civism is defined as: compliance with the rules of civil co-existence, dictated by respect for the rights of others and awareness of one's own obligations (Sabatini – Colletti).

In a German dictionary, the same term is defined as: understanding and commitment to the collectivity, to the *res publica* (Duden Wörterbuch).[2]

As can be seen, when one talks about civism one may think firstly of an individual characteristic. Following the rules, respecting the rights of others and being aware of one's own duties are characteristics that concern the single individual. In the ordinary sense, it is the individual that is endowed with civism.

In our study, however, civism, in the sense of upholding the rules of the game of living together and as the commitment to improve the experience of coexistence, is a "social" event based on reciprocity, i.e. on the confidence that everyone will follow the rules of the game and will make an effort for coexistence.

The first thing we want to underline is this: while the commonly held view of civism contains an individual component, in order to understand the research, it is important to think of civism as an attitude shared by specific social groups.

In other words, civism is not a "normative" phenomenon, tied to the relationship of each individual with the social rules, but a phenomenon based on *collusion*, that is, on the common symbolisation of the rules of the game and of living together. Civism therefore entails reciprocal and collective faith in the rules of the game.

The second thing we want to underline is that individual civism is related to the rules adopted by the single individual; civism as a shared attitude is related to the rules of the game endorsed by specific social groups.

The difference between norms and rules of the game is central in this case: the norm constrains individuals in their behaviour; the rules of the game are the basis of living together and only make sense if everyone accepts them and puts them into practice. For instance, the fact that only some of the players on the pitch in a football game follow the rules, while others ignore them, would make the contest between the two teams meaningless. The very game would not exist.

Let's talk about the data. They show two contrasting cultures: on the one hand a culture that has confidence in the shared rules of the game and, on the other, a culture that has no such faith.

The crucial difference between Germans and Italians, in this context, is the following: The Germans (Cluster 3) have faith in the fact that everyone follows the rules of the game and *therefore* tries to improve coexistence. The Italians (Cluster 1) have no such faith, being convinced that too many people do not follow the rules of the game; living together is marked by a breakdown of

---

2   The difference is interesting: The German definition seems less focused on the individual than the Italian one; recognition of the res publica is the basis of living together.

social values, in the sense of an absence of rules of the game governing social relations.

"Trust" or "distrust" in the reciprocity in following the rules of the game involves different attitudes, which extend to many areas of the social system.

For Germans, the future (in terms of the economy, civism and the structural efficiency of the country's institutions) inspires confidence. Today everything, in general, is going well and will improve in the near future.

This confidence in development entails a valorisation of the differences within the community of living together. Migrants, in particular, are seen as frightened people fleeing from the war and persecution in their countries of origin, and not as grasping individuals out to get hold of the wealth of the country to which they have come; their diversity is seen as a resource, to be integrated into the social system.

By contrast, for Italians, not only is there no confidence in the sharing of the rules of the game, but there is also a deep distrust in the institutional control of infringements of the laws. This entails a failure of both the rules of the game and the control of individual compliance with the rules. The absence of respect for the rules of the game means that the "other", in social relations, inspires distrust and is felt to be a potential or real aggressor. The only way of protecting the social system is therefore normative control, carried out by repressive institutions that have to ensure that norms are followed. However, in this system there is inefficiency in the system of control that should permeate the life of every person, that should intervene in every instance of social interaction. The mutual distrust makes it impossible to apply the system of control to such widespread rule breaking.

The breakdown of social values reported by the Italian culture, neutralises the efficacy of the system of control, which can only work in a less distrustful climate, in a context where law-breaking is less pervasive and more circumscribed, above all, where law-breaking is more clearly distinguished from the failure to uphold the rules of the game.

In this culture, in the same *anomic* dynamics, the migrant is felt to be a dangerous competitor, in the greed that takes the place of the rules of the game and based on which everyone seeks to get hold of the possessions that, albeit illusorily, symbolize wellbeing.

For the Italian culture the absence of civism therefore means widespread distrust towards the "other", seen systematically as different-same. Different but also the same, because it is onto the "other" that people project the divergent connotations which each person thinks he shares since they are unavoidable, but from which they free themselves by believing that it is the other who brings them into play. Hence the emphasis on crime, on the pressure of migrant flows, on the inefficiency of the political authorities, and on corruption as expressions of problems that one would like to see solved by regulatory control, which is however impossible.

In short, in this first juxtaposition, civism, or faith in the mutual compliance with the rules of the game, or the absence of civism, condition two very different cultures. One, the German culture, believes in the rules of the game and seeks to valorise the integration of difference in the social system. The other, the Italian culture, confuses infringing the regulations with ignoring the rules of the game, distrusts the "outsider" as a potential danger, and sees the solution of the distrust in social control, felt however to be impossible. Hence, for the Italians interviewed, the state of anomie disorients people, making them lose faith in any possible development of the economic and social system they live in, fuelling their belief in the powerlessness of all official authority, forcing them to lead a life based on fear and distrust.

On the second factor (Clusters 1 and 4) the compactness of this cultural difference between Germans and Italians is challenged by two other cultures, one belonging to the Germans and the other to the Italians.

The Germans (Cluster 4), in this second cultural area, still have confidence in the *present* of their social system, which they see as based on civism. However, they feel threatened by an uncertain future, at the mercy of dangers outside the German world, reassuring only "for the time being"; the German society is felt to be hanging in a sort of precarious equilibrium because of the looming external world with it extraneousness.

The external threats come from religious radicalisation, international crime, terrorism, migrants (who are here no longer in flight from the dangers in their native land as in Cluster 3 of the first factor, but motivated by envious greed), and from the Islamic world in general. The problem for living together in the community is crime, in all these forms.

The criminal is "different" from the law-abiding citizen engaged in improving coexistence. The criminal does not follow the rules of the game and needs to be kept under control. We are faced with a culture of control, different from the one previously described for the Italians: here control, which should be exerted by the police, magistrates and politicians, has to defend a social system in which people believe, and which would work well if it were not for external threats. Here, crime is evident because the behaviour of those who follow the rules of the game is clear; control is therefore possible. People are willing to see their individual liberties limited and to undergo controls on their private life, in order to improve security and restore faith in the future. Their future is entrusted to control, in all fields of coexistence.

The Italians (Cluster 1) experience the opposite culture. They lack confidence in the country's economy, quality of life, compliance with the rules of the game, development of business and of the country in general, and in the efficacy of politics. This is because the whole country is marked by corruption and this corruption has a two-way relationship with unemployment. Corruption is the only threat to security. However, as we saw earlier, corruption is not a characteristic of the "other", it is not a phenomenon that can be attributed to what is external to the system. It involves all citizens, a sort of epidemic which nobody can or wants to escape. While for the Germans the danger comes from outside, for the Italians the danger comes from within, from the Italians themselves and from the culture of corruption that permeates them.

One of the features of corruption is intolerance for diversity in all its aspects. Membership of familistic groups is the vehicle for corruption, but whoever does not belong to them is dangerous. However, this all concerns the struggle between power groups. The migrant is "too" different to be seen as a danger. The migrant is too unimportant if compared to the "world of crime" that organises, promotes, defends corruption, to be a threat to the community. For this reason, it is hoped that migrants will be integrated. Such integration could, on the other hand, lead to migrants participating in violent power groups and in the process of corruption.

In short, it seems that compliance with the rules of the game, and therefore civism, is the most important factor to generate a feeling of security.

The alternatives to civism are:

a) Anomie as flouting the rules of the game and *failure of control* over crime. The flouters take power; civism loses on all fronts.
b) The *impossibility of control* because everyone, including the controllers, are implicated in the process of corruption that fuels a form of living together opposed to the values of civism. Corruption prevents any development, destroys any control designed to restore civism. When the "different" comes from outside, it can be integrated, although there is the danger that such integration occurs in a system of criminal corruption.
c) The hope that there should be *an effective control* over crime, external to the system: the danger is external and all the members of the social system help the controllers.

In other words, the alternative to civism is violence. It is only in the German culture of cluster 3, where there is faith in civism, that violence seems to be absent from the experience of the interviewees. Instead of violence there is cultural enrichment in the integration of many cultural differences seen as a resource.

In all the other cultures without civism, violence dominates: "external" violence, in the "autarchic" Germans or, in the anomic Italians who don't believe in the possibility of controlling violence, the devastating internal violence of corruption that destroys every aspect of civil coexistence.

It is important to remember that upholding the rules of the game is not an end in itself. It serves to "do" something, to act collectively within the rules of the game. When the rules of the game are upheld, there can be shared production goals. The violation of the rules of the game is an end in itself and its meaning is confined to the act of infringing, directed against the other who will suffer the consequences of this transgression. Breaking the rules therefore unfolds in a dual relationship, where there is a transgressor and whoever is damaged by the transgression. Keep in mind that the greatest damage from the transgression is the collapse of mutual trust, the entry of doubt and diffidence in social relations. Complying with the rules on the other hand serves to engage the social system in all its forms in sharing an interest in what it is believed can be achieved together, thanks also to the sharing of the rules of the game. The inclusion of diversity, in Cluster 3 of German culture, for example, is what the participants in the research think they can achieve together thanks to the valorization of what enriches their community.

Governance

Participants in the study

The participants in the study numbered 606: 305 Italians and 301 Germans.

Participants' occupation:
1. employed in different roles in large or medium sized listed companies with over 100 employees (16.7%)
2. employed in different roles in family businesses (16.8%)
3. employed in different roles in banks or fund management companies (16.5%)
4. independent financial promoters or working for private and public banks (16.5%)
5. young people aged 17-25 years (33.5%)

- *Age:*
  18-30 years: 37.5%
  31-60 years: 55.6%
  61 years and over: 6.9%

- Sex:
  male: 47.7%
  female: 52.3%

The participants were administered the ISO Questionnaire: Governance, elaborated by Studio di Psicosociologia in December 2017, was administered to the participants in February 2018.

Table 2: Relationship between clusters and factors in Governance research

Cluster	Frequency	Factor 1	Factor 2	Factor 3
Cluster 1	231	-.875 (-)	.103	-.021
Cluster 2	91		-.781 (-)	-.218
Cluster 3	185	.191	-.121	.688 (+)
Cluster 4	99	.864 (+)	.108	-.029
Total	606			

Source: The present research

Multiple correspondence analysis and Cluster analysis on the data collected showed the following factorial plane, with four clusters:

Figure 2: Factorial plan for Governance research

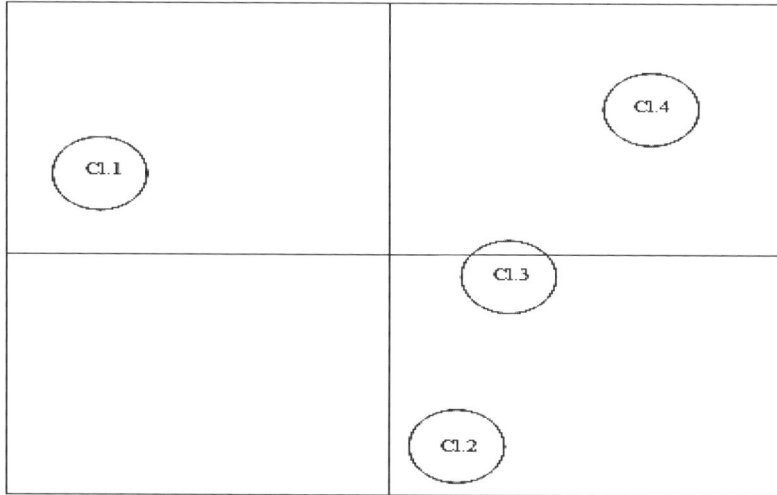

Source: The present research

Clusters 1 and 4 are situated significantly on the first factor.
Cluster 2 is situated on the second factor.
Cluster 3 is situated on the third factor.

Data analysis

On the first factor there are two contrasting cultures, marked by a totally different vision of the neo-liberal paradigm: this paradigm is associated with "success" in Cluster 1, significantly generated by the German participants; it is associated with "crisis" in Cluster 4, characterised by participants working in family businesses (with no distinctive German–Italian features).

The neo-liberal paradigm, in the case of Cluster 1, is associated with a positive vision of globalisation: it leads to a spread of democratic values, a higher quality of life in the majority of the world population and the opening of markets. Globalisation also generates its rules spontaneously, without governance interventions outside the market.

Who belongs to this completely neo-liberal culture? These participants declare secure, extensive wellbeing: in the culture there is profound civism, the economic situation and the quality of life in the social system are high and it is hoped that they will rise further. The protagonists of the social system, magistrates, the police, politicians, are all friendly, efficient and respected. The social structures of the context in which people live are generally reliable. It is a culture capable of planning for development, while membership of power groups is not valorised (in this cultural analysis, the two cultures, planning for development and belonging to power groups, are in contrast to each other). It is a social context where the problems of corruption and unemployment are not present. Citizens enjoy high quality public services, from health to banks and insurance system, from the media to trade unions, from political parties to firms – both large and medium/small – through to the police and the church. Young people's success is based on creativity and professional competence.

In short, it is a culture where compliance with the rules of the game and high quality professional and relational competence help to create an efficient social system capable of inspiring confidence in the citizens.

In this valorisation of the liberal paradigm, it is predicted that in international governance the role of the United States will diminish and that of Germany will increase. Multinationals and large financial groups will be the protagonists of globalization, along with the international organisations. However, they will not need to govern it but simply accompany it, taking advantage of it: the regulator of international relations is the market.

We can sum up the connotation of this culture as "wellbeing": economic and social. In this culture there emerges a two-way relationship between the valorisation of the liberal paradigm and wellbeing: only where there is wellbeing is it possible to appreciate the liberal paradigm; only when the liberal paradigm is appreciated is it possible to live in a situation of wellbeing.

It is a conservative culture, which attributes conservative connotations to the new political groups in Europe. The latter are seen to be consistent with the political climate from which they derive, not intending to change anything but instead to maintain the status quo on a backdrop of wealth; local wellbeing can potentially spread throughout the world.

This conservative vision based on faith in the neo-liberal paradigm does not seem to have great interest in developing the culture, even when it is concerned with changes and crises in the economy, therefore in the liberal paradigm itself. The focus on wellbeing is primarily addressed to economic wealth deriving from good governance of businesses and from mutually fruitful alliances between banks and firms.

At the same time, we are dealing with a culture that is "autarchic" in its blind conservatism, incapable of grasping the cultural and social changes of a world that is deeply critical of the neo-liberal system which ignores the problems spread along its path. Economic security and social stability seem to make it easier to ignore the changing critical phenomena of contemporary life, which removes this culture from any potential confrontation with the cultural processes under way in other cultures in Europe and worldwide.

The German participants, in short, have faith in the liberal paradigm only insofar as globalisation is taking place with a leading role played by Germany. Hence the illusion that neo-liberal development will be totally coherent with the values and cultural traditions of the system to which they belong. This is further confirmation of the "autarchy" marking this German culture and of the fear of the new, if not directly controlled by Germany.

Let us now look at the culture of Cluster 4, where the neo-liberal paradigm is seen in a negative light, as a cause of the crisis.

This is a transversal culture, covering Italians and Germans, where the research participants come from family businesses, generally small to middle-sized. This culture underlines the great change in the context, in recent years. The change has been for the worse, with globalization causing the uncontrollable growth of terrorism, an authoritarian tendency in culture and society, a progressive, irreversible destruction of the environment and an enormous increase in the gap between rich and poor. Uncontrollable deregulation, produced by a system that is inefficient on the international plane, will increasingly alienate the weaker components of international governance, thus marginalizing Europe, while bolstering the role of the strong powers, including that of the USA.

This culture is marked by anomy, indicating the absence of civism. The economy is embroiled in sterile conflicts, like the one between banks and businesses, where greed centered on short-term interests prevails over a longer-term vision of social function. This leads to the lack of confidence in businesses, regarded as not being rational and being incapable of developing in a context that sees the interests of international, multinational finance prevail. The authoritarian climate that is part of the experience of this culture is also manifested in social intolerance towards minorities, seen to be greedy and dangerous.

The only bulwark against the worrying advance of financial *dirigisme* and authoritarianism remains the family business as the refuge where relationships are based by definition on friendly perceptions among the various family members. Family businesses are like the family and are the first victims – for this culture – of globalisation and neo-liberalism without definite regulations.

It is a culture where the difficult assessment of one's socioeconomic situation underlines the negativity of the profound and unstoppable change underway.

Lastly, this Cluster, like the one we looked at above, and to which it is in contrast, pays no attention to culture, in the sense of investment in the knowledge typifying a community, centred on the theme of economic liberalism and its impact on international governance. It is only in this respect that the two cultures present on the first factor are not opposed, but close.

An alternative to the focus on the liberal paradigm of these first two cultures is offered by the third culture, Cluster 2, which we could call "catastrophic localism". The illustrative variables characterising this Cluster include young Italians and Germans, and Italians working in Lombardy.

This culture replaces the neo-liberal paradigm with the family; not the family business of the second culture, but the family as an important social structure, a compact group of individuals, in a private sphere that differs from the public sphere in crisis.

Outside the family nucleus, which is also undergoing a challenge, the general situation, in its economic, political, associative and cultural aspects, is felt to be uncontrollable.

The only hope seems to lie in the new political groupings of one's town, localist groupings capable of triggering a revolution to overturn, at a local level, the hegemony of the financial-economic system. Such a system, at an international level, will cause serious conflicts marked by widespread civil wars.

Globalisation, in short, is not controllable and will not lead to anything positive especially in terms of the economy and quality of life. The only hope lies in local rebellion against a system that is out of control and in the enhancement of the family, in its real and symbolic aspects, as a private place that forms a reassuring affective certainty with respect to the public degradation.

Young people in this culture are seen as lacking hope, with no chance of success in a context where nothing can achieve this goal: nothing can come of belonging to power groups or from the race to assert oneself over others, no chance of success can come from creativity or from professional excellence. For this culture, the only hope lies on the one hand in family groups, seen as the only ones able to promote development in local contexts, and on the other hand, in revolutionary movements.

The localism of the young Italians and Germans and of Lombardy is juxtaposed to a fourth culture, Cluster 3, where the correlated illustrative variable is Italy. In this culture the neo-liberal paradigm is in decline as is the system of coexistence in the hometown. The country's serious problems, underlined by this culture, are corruption, unemployment, the deterioration of political debate and the low quality of services. With its deregulation, the liberal paradigm, also in decline, is associated with corruption and unemployment. The breakdown of values marking this culture can be linked to the lack of faith in cultural system belonged to; the corruption prevents people from looking at an "external" enemy against whom to fight.

"It's all pointless" seems to be the widespread attitude in this cultural repertoire: the new groups in local politics are reactionary, seeking to defend local interests and incapable of modifying the corrupt behavioural model; there is no hope of economic development since the neo-liberal principles are in decline and there is no prospect of new modes of national governance. The country will become less and less influential on the international scene, which will be dominated by Germany with its economic strength and its civism, but also with its self-centeredness, which we have called "autarchy". There is the need for more efficient bodies to control national finance, but yet again the system of corruption will frustrate any initiative of control.

Summing up the theme of Governance, it can be said that the only people that can envisage development in the social system are those who believe in the liberal paradigm and its success. This is supposedly thanks to a form of globalisation capable of self-regulation, and to the contribution made by multinational finance to general wealth. The believers in neo-liberalism therefore represent a culture that "is content" both economically and democratically, and they believe that their approach can strengthen general wellbeing.

On the other hand, those who currently have problems living together in their community, those who experience the lack of civism and the economic hardship as a breakdown of social values, think that things can only get worse. They foresee a drift towards authoritarianism, the increase in social injustice, the excessive power of countries already holding economic supremacy; the future will bring a profound cultural crisis, with revolts, civil wars and an ungovernable situation.

The only alternative to neo-liberal globalisation or to anti-liberal catastrophism is localism based on the family, on the one hand to boost the private sphere, and on the other in the symbolisation of the family-run business. Family-centred localism is thought to be the main target in the clash with neo-liberalism. This clash is described as a matter of life or death for localism. The globalised world, which increasingly characterises liberal financial development, makes the latter invulnerable to attacks from local situations.

Alongside the ideological enemies of economic liberalism we therefore find the supporters of localism as an alternative to globalisation. There is evident ambivalence towards financial development, which many associate with authoritarianism, the strong powers, the United States or Germany as the leading lights of worldwide economic liberalism, with the different cultures that have emerged and with economic cynicism which pays no attention to issues of family, culture and local development.

Remember that only 38% of the interviewees are in favor of neo-liberalism. The remaining 62% belong to cultures that in various ways oppose neo-liberal optimism and foresee conflict and ungovernable situations in the future. Of the latter, 45% support localism as the alternative to globalised neo-liberalism.

The most important argument in support of economic liberalism is its ability to facilitate economic growth in all the countries in the world. However, this extension of the liberal advantages to the entire world is juxtaposed to a strong valorization of localism and of the role that the family and the family businesses can play in the wellbeing of local communities.

It is important to keep in mind that localism, in the representation of those who feel it is the only alternative to globalisation, is seen as a revolt against the hegemony of the strong powers that control multinational and international finance. It is therefore a "violent" localism, capable of civil unrest, of a no-holds-barred opposition; a question of life or death. This violent localism seems to contradict the valorisation of the family where violence certainly is not lacking but where it underlies powerful systems of self-regulation.

Final considerations

The first consideration regards the difference that emerged, repeatedly, in the two studies between Germans and Italians. This difference presents itself recursively, despite the marked variation of the research participants between the studies[3].

The difference in question emerges in particular in two main issues: civism, on the one hand, and the neo-liberal paradigm, on the other.

From the psychosocial perspective adopted here, we define *Civism* as the experience of trust in the compliance with the rules of the game by all participants in the system of coexistence. In other words, civism, in the sense we propose here, is not the "actual" compliance with the rules, but rather the expectation we have that the "others", with whom we share the same system of coexistence, will comply with these rules.

Italians appear to experience a complete and radical distrust in their fellow citizens, as far as the respect for the rules of the game is concerned. This implies the experience of very little civism, accompanied by the belief that corruption is generalised and widespread in their country. If there is no civism, then rules violation reverberates on the organisational and institutional systems of social life; in which, according to the Italian interviewees, corruption is widespread and unstoppable.

It is worth remembering that this finding does not describe the reality; instead, it reflects the way the interviewees think of and experience the other citizens and the Italian social system. Such an experience of widespread rule violation and corruption means for the Italian participants the unravelling of trust in the economy, cultural development, institutional efficiency (control institutions in particular), the management of the systems of production as well as the media, the educational system and healthcare. In summary, in this culture the "enemy" is internal to the system of coexistence, being the "generalized other" to which one confers characteristics which are destructive of the fundamental rules of coexistence.

---

3   We recall here some information concerning the research sample: the two studies involved in total 1,214 participants (Security: 608; Governance: 606) equally divided between German and Italian respondents. Participants in the study on Security included: a) representatives of local authorities (22%); b) employees and volunteers in reception centres for migrants (22.4%); c) representatives of security bodies (police, army, financial police, etc.) (22.2%); d) young people aged 17-25 (33.4%). Participants in the study on Governance included: a) employees in medium-sized and big companies (different roles) (16.7%); b) employees in family firms (different roles) (16.8%); c) employees in banks and fund management companies (16.5%); d) independent investment bankers or working for private banks (16.5%); e) young people aged 17-25 (33.5%). Different questionnaires prepared ad hoc for each research theme were adopted in the two studies.

The German participants, by contrast, show deep trust in the compliance with the rules of the game on the part of all German citizens; they think that coexistence inside German society is founded on mutual trust and the contribution of everybody to the development of the social system. From such an experience of civism and joint work for development, stems a positive evaluation of the economic, cultural and institutional situation in their country. The "enemy", from the German interviewees' perspective, is external to German society and is identified in particular with religious radicalism, growth of the Islamic population, terrorism, international crime, expanding migration. All these are perceived as forms of potential "crime" aimed at upsetting the satisfying system of coexistence of German society. The German culture, in other words, is informed by trust in German people's civism and in their commitment to economic, cultural and civic development, but on the condition that the systems of control keep a firm hold on dangers coming from the "outside", in all their forms. Within such representation, migrants constitute a grave danger for the functioning of the social system, and they are symbolised as moved by envy and greed towards German wealth—the wealth of their host country—and the wish to take possession of it.

The same thing can be said in regard to the neo-liberal paradigm: i.e., only the German interviewees value economic and market globalisation, since they think it might enhance progress worldwide, not only in economic terms. Such a positive view of neo-liberalism, and of globalisation as the most evident expression of the former, is based on the belief that Germany itself will play a leading role in the globalisation process, at the expense of the United States, which will become less and less relevant. Once again, trust in development appears grounded in German supremacy and Germany's capability to push the "stranger" away as well as the dangerous power that the stranger represents.

In summary, these two cultures are based on: a) the experience of distrust in their own fellow citizens, in the case of the Italian respondents; b) the experience of distrust in the "stranger" symbolised as a threat for German people, in the case of the German respondents.

It is important to highlight that these experiences do not derive from "facts", that is from factual reality characterising Italy and Germany. For instance, the distrust towards civism and the experience of deteriorating coexistence institutions, which the Italians manifest, does not correspond to the country's "real state of affairs," at least not so radically. However, this experience is eminently relevant for coexistence in Italy, for example encouraging the violation of the rules of the game and the spread of corruption. Moreover, this experience helps to foster a widespread sentiment of discontent and rage against each and every expression of institutional or organisational authority—especially when coming from the world of politics—, of which the growth of populist and protest movements is an instance.

By contrast, the Germans' experience of "wealth" is menaced by the strangeness and invasion of "outside" components, which German society cannot avoid. This pending menace leads the German interviewees to sacrifice their own privacy, as long as the systems of control—the judiciary, the police and the political system—watch over and protect German isolation from all contamination. This implies hostility towards what is new and the wish for a perpetually self-conserving social system, and the acceptance of change only if governed by Germans themselves.

For example, the German interviewees perceive digitalisation as dangerous, since it can distract the wealthy Germans from their proud autarchy, and create problems for banks and investors by making finance uncontrollable.

It is only when considered as a tool used by individuals —always according to the German interviewees — that digitalisation becomes useful for the life of the mind, especially among senior citizens. In other words, digital progress is acceptable only as an instrument for "health," which fosters the growth of individuals.

The only exceptions to the radical opposition between Italian and German respondents, in the terms above-described, are the two cultures transversal to the opposition itself: One characterised by interviewees who work in family firms and who experience the neo-liberal paradigm as destructive of the family-run small-to-medium production system. This culture also associates neo-liberalism with the growth of terrorism, the authoritarian drift in society and culture, the destruction of the environment and the irreversible rise of income inequality between the rich and the poor in the world. The neo-liberal paradigm gives cause to the experience of being increasingly marginal to the firm in which one is employed, but also to the country one belongs to and to Europe. In the experience of these participants, globalisation implies an unchecked rise of American political, economic and military power — a power which would allow the USA to act as the guardian of the world — and of the revolts that the same neo-liberal system has generated.

Finally, we find a culture that we could call "catastrophic localism", characterising mostly young people and the inhabitants of Lombardy, in Italy. This culture condemns globalising neo-liberalism as the source of all evil, both from a financial and a social viewpoint, and considers family as the only value-driven bulwark. It sees new localist political groupings as a useful chance of rebellion against the global financial empire, namely as a tool to initiate a real revolution that might be able to counter globalisation, which generates anomie since it is ungovernable, and reinstate local powers which actually take care of the people.

Contemporary mixed migration from Africa to Europe via Italy

Christopher Hein

Migration is an ever-changing phenomenon

What we say today about migration statistics, migration flows, destination countries, policies, legislations and other migration related issues will probably no longer be true tomorrow. Fluctuations of the universal migration scenario are extremely rapid. This is even more true if we look at migratory movements in the various regions, sub-regions and countries. A broad variety of political, economic, social and cultural dynamics influence individual as well as collective migration tendencies and trends.

All countries in Europe have been emigration countries at some time and over extended periods during the last three centuries, including those which today are perceived as territories that receive migrants and refugees. Many African countries are being in the recent past confronted with migrants and refugees departing from other African areas. The very distinction between emigration, transit and immigration countries is often arbitrary since the three features are manifest contemporarily. Italy, for example, has been over 150 years a country from which an estimated number of 30 million citizens have gone abroad. Between 1975 and 2000, Italy converted into an immigration country but has remained during the same period an emigration country showing an approximate balance between the numbers of citizens leaving and of foreigners arriving as migrants or refugees. At the same time, an unknown number of migrants and asylum seekers have transited trough Italy on the way to other European countries. After a short period, from 2000 to 2012, during which the number of incoming migrants superseded that of Italians going abroad, Italy is becoming again and increasingly an emigration country, as we will detail in this article.

All North African countries are today simultaneously sending, receiving and transit areas, and the same is true for West and South African sub-regions as well as for the Middle East. The number of international migrants in Africa, the vast majority of whom originated from other African countries, has increased from 17,7 million in 2016, to 20,5 million in 2017 and to 24,5 million in 2018, an increase of almost 40 percent in 3 years (Figure 1). Migration routes are not, as many believe, in first instance on the South to North axe but are, to a major degree, South to South oriented, or even from what in an European view is regarded as the "South" to the "deeper South", e.g. to the South Africa Republic or to Angola.

Figure 1: Origins of migrants in Africa 2018

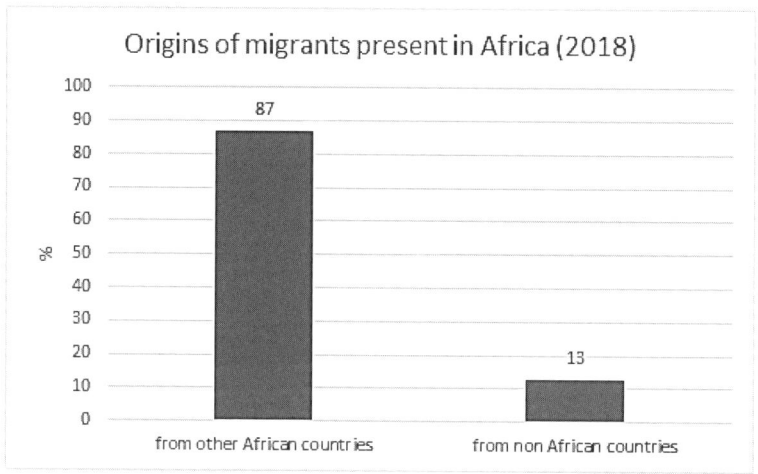

Source: Study commissioned by the IOM

Figure 2: Regions of origin of migrants 2017

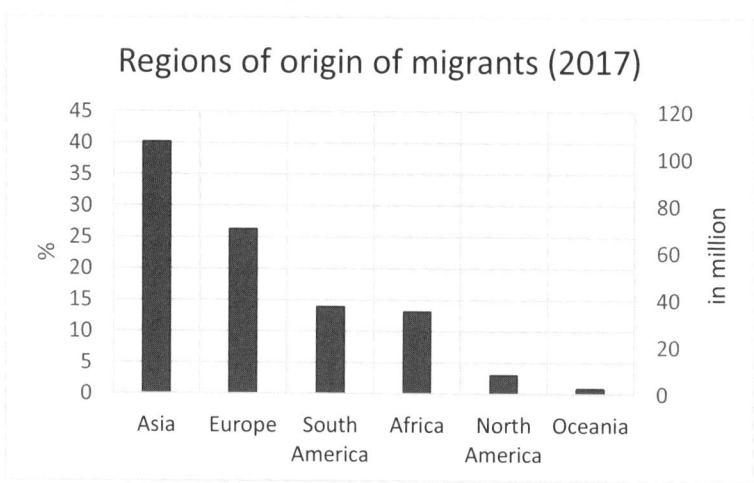

Source: Study commissioned by the IOM

Figure 3: Outflow of African migrants 2016-17

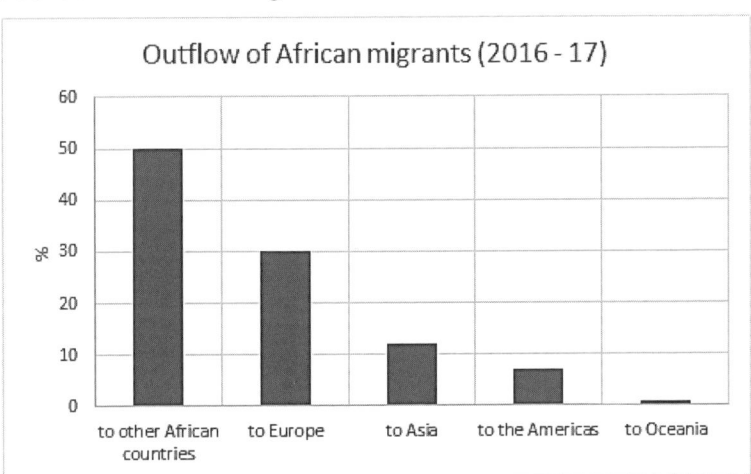

Source: Study commissioned by the IOM

Public and political opinion usually becomes aware of the changes of the migration patterns only with a considerable delay. The perception of the reality and, consequently, the policy responses run behind the development. To take again Italy as an example: it has been only in 1990, after 15 years of steadily growing influx of migrants, that the transformation from a traditional emigration into an immigration country was perceived and a first aliens law[1] adopted.

Today, public and political discourses still highlight the "immigration problem", in spite of the fact that as from 2017 the number of incoming migrants and asylum seekers has come down to a minimum level. The relatively new and steadily growing phenomenon of emigration of, predominantly young and highly educated, Italians is not perceived and reflected in the public debate.

We will attempt to analyse the main variables that determine the fluctuations of migratory flows and render the predictability of concrete future scenarios as well as the planning of policies in this field extremely difficult.

Among the main variables on the macro level are:

a) The outbreak of new conflicts, wars, civil wars;

---

[1] Law no. 39/1990 ("Martelli Law")

b) Coups d´état; taking power of dictatorial regimes; waves of persecutions or severe discriminations of minorities or groups of the population.
c) The demographic evolution.
d) Internal migratory movements, in particular towards urban agglomerations.
e) "Natural" short-outset disasters like earthquakes, floods, hurricanes.
f) Slow-outset disasters like desertification and drought as an effect of the climate change.
g) Economic crisis, increasing unemployment, impoverishment.
h) Legislative, policy or economic variations in receiving countries.

Exodus caused by factors under a) and b) are commonly called "forced migration". Concepts of "early warning" or "preparedness" aimed at allowing for timely preventive initiatives or of planning strategies have shown weak results. The events of the "Arab spring" between December 2010 and spring 2011, and the consequent migration movements, for example, were in no way predicted. Evacuation and reception strategies had to be planned ad hoc.

The cessation of conflicts or of dictatorial regimes may in turn cause returns to countries of origin, whereas, as we will see, an improvement of economic conditions in home countries does not necessarily induce, over a considerable period of time, a diminution of outflows of migrants or stimulate their return. On the micro level, the main factors influencing the individual decisions to leave the home country are:

a) "Push factors" that reflect the general conditions in the country of origin combined with personal and individual circumstances. Among these factors we may enumerate: the individual economic and employment conditions; the effects of disasters and of climate change on the livelihood of communities; persecutions and discriminations for political, religious, ethnic or other reasons; the fear for life and freedom due to general violence, wars or civil wars; the conviction that there is no future, not only in economic terms, in the home country. In many cases, links with family member residing in other countries or the need to sustain economically the family in the home country through the sending of remittances constitute, too, driving push factors.
b) The information available and received individually on migration prospects. Variables are the level of access to media, to internet, to social networks; information received by family members, friends and communities living abroad; the information on travel conditions as well as the impact of information campaigns against irregular

departures conducted by international organisations or embassies of destination States.
c) The individual level of "migration skills". In fact, not everybody has the subjective capacity and pre-disposition to meet the challenge of going away from the home country, of leaving family, friends, the own community and the socio-cultural context of life, even where there are pressing needs and pull factors to do so. This is true even more if the reaching of the envisaged destination country presupposes a travel over long distances, the transit through third countries, the prospect of facing a radical difference of cultural environment compared to the habitual one. At the beginning of each migration project there is, at least in the case of adults, an individual decision and a pre-disposition to meet these challenges. Migration skills are determined by the level of education and of language skills; by the socio-psychological conditions of the individual and of his/her family; by the belonging to a relatively privileged social class; by the availability of funds for the travel. Among the migrants and even among the refugees arriving in Italy or other European countries, we can observe an elevated number of people from urban origin who have been benefitting from a degree of education above the average of people in the home country as well as some knowledge of foreign languages. It has been noted, in addition, that in the case of migrants originated not from metropolitan areas but from villages or small towns, whole groups of persons belonging to the same community have been departing together or are arriving at different moments in the destination country where they re-constitute a community in order to overcome the sense of loneliness and isolation. In these cases, the individual migration skills are re-enforced by the combined skills of the community.
d) Another variable is the facility of travel to the destination country. In the case of regular travel, determining factors are: the conditions for legal departure from the home country and legal entry into the county of immigration or asylum; the availability of travel documents and entry visas; the pre-conditions set for the issuance of an entry visa, in particular in the case of the European Union under the requirements established by the Schengen Visa Code. Among these conditions are: an employment offer; close family links; a concrete study prospect/ scholarship; requisites for the obtaining of a humanitarian visa; inclusion in a refugee resettlement programme, or others. In the case of irregular travel, in absence of any possibility for regular entry,

among the variables are the access to smuggling networks or individual smugglers as well the costs involved.

e) The direction of migratory flows is determined by the pull factors that guide the individual migration projects to a specific destination[2]. For both economic migrants and refugees, the presence of family members, of friends, of communities in a given country constitutes the principal pull factor. The reasons are twofold: firstly, persons already established in the destination country may assist in overcoming the initial material obstacles, may provide temporary shelter, may help in search of employment, and may serve as mediators between the newly arrived migrant and the unknown and even hostile social and cultural environment with which he or she is confronted. Secondly, the presence of people with whom the migrants are familiar alleviates the strangeness and disorientation which they experience in the unknown milieu.

Other pull factors are the language of and the cultural links with the destination country, that are frequently originated from the colonial past, in the case of Western Europe, or from ethnic and/or linguistic links between home and receiving countries, e.g. in Africa, the Middle East or Central Asia.

The geographical location as well as the entry and reception conditions of the envisaged destination country are further factors that determine the migration projects. The general economic conditions, the access to the labour market as well as the level of wages define the "attractiveness" of a given country, not only for economic migrants but also for refugees who, after an initial period where obtaining protection represents the paramount driver, have to look for the material survival of themselves and their families.

In many cases, however, the expectation to arrive at a place of safety and stability where individual freedoms are guaranteed may be even more important than economic and labour conditions.

We may summarise that a very broad number of factors determine migration flows and contribute to rapidly changing scenarios. The decision to leave the own country, the family, the community in whom a person has grown is in any case difficult and includes a sacrifice. In most cases, the underlying reason is

---

2   The "Study on Migrants' Profile- Drivers of Migration and Migration Trends" By Migration Policy Institute and European University Institute, commissioned by the International Organization for Migration has found out that in many cases African migrants have at departure no precise destination in mind.   See https://cadmus.eui.eu/bitstream/hadle/1814/43964/IOM_   Migrants_Study_2016_EN.pdf?sequence=1

that of inequality of living conditions in the own country compared to others, in the various areas of the world, and the sense of not having a future in the place of habitual residence. We do therefore not fully agree to the picture of migration as a "source of prosperity, innovation and sustainable development, a natural phenomenon of mankind", as it is put in the Global Migration Compact of 2018[3]. The Global Compact reflects the rather optimistic view that a better global management of migration as designed in the document would "mitigate the adverse drivers and structural factors that hinder people from building and maintaining sustainable livelihoods in their countries of origin, and so compel them to seek a future elsewhere"[4]. The very distinction between "voluntary" and "forced" migration is questionable. There are certainly different levels of constriction when taking the decision to leave the own country, but the "voluntariness" of this decision is, in our view, rather an exception than the rule.

The term "mixed migration" comprises both "voluntary "as well as forced migration. It is usually referred to a migrant population composed of people with different motivations and need to migrate, as well as to groups of persons who travel together for logistic reasons, irrespective of the motivation to migrate and of the intention to present an asylum request in the destination country. The notion of mixed migration is connected to irregular entry. In the case of legal entry, the motivation for the migration project is already established at the moment of presenting a visa request, or, in case of absence of a visa requirement, at the moment of requesting a residence permit.

Irregular arrivals of refugees and migrants in Europe

Contemporary public opinion in Europe perceives immigration as mostly an irregular phenomenon where people from other countries bypass the rules for regular entry. In Italy, the term "clandestini" is generally used as synonymous with "immigrant". Little public attention is given to the fact that the vast majority of migrants arrive in the EU countries by regular means. For the mass media, irregular group arrivals are an "event", in particular if coming by boats across the Mediterranean, whereas the daily regular entry of thousands of people with a visa for family or employment or study reasons is not a news.

However, it is true that most asylum seekers are indeed obliged to use irregular channels and the services of smugglers for arriving at European shores. The rules of the Schengen Visa Code do not allow for the issuance of

---

3   Global Migration Compact, para. 8
4   Ibid., para.12

an entry visa for the purpose of presenting a protection request nor a specific visa for recognised refugees.

Until 1990, entry of citizens of third countries into a Member State of the European Union did not present particular problems. Many countries of origin of migrants were exempted from entry visas. For others, visas were issued without particular formalities. People originating from Eastern European countries under communist rule were anyhow welcome for political reasons. The various Member States of European Community had different policies and legislations on entry conditions. Countries like Italy were accused by other member States for particularly liberal or "relaxed" entry practices, given the fact that many migrants and asylum seekers moved subsequently on to other countries and regarded Italy more as a transit area. Italy, traditional tourism and pilgrimage country having the Vatican in the midst of its territory, had no particular interest in introducing stricter entry rules and border controls. Moreover, Italy had maintained until 1990 the geographical limitation to the application of the 1951 Geneva Refugee Convention with the consequence that refugees from non-European origin were not able to request asylum.

After Second World War and until 1991, there were no "boat people" in Europe. The notion of "boat people" was associated with Indochinese refugees and migrant crossing the Chinese Sea after the war in Vietnam. At European shores, the phenomenon of group arrivals by ship or boat started in March 2001, when tens of thousands of Albanians crossed the Adriatic Sea and arrived in the Apulia region in South-East Italy. From that time on, irregular Sea arrivals of refugees, asylum seekers and migrants have become a continuous feature over the last 30 years, on an increasing level due to the introduction of ever more stringent conditions for legal entry into the EU.

The construction of the "Fortress Europe" has started with the Schengen Convention of 1990 and the common European visa policy under the Maastricht Treaty that entered in force in 1993. "Schengen" has intended to create conditions for the abolition of border controls at the internal borders of the participating countries, later extended to almost all Member States and even to States that, without being members of the Union, have joined the Schengen agreements: Norway, Switzerland, Iceland and Liechtenstein. The concept of free movement of people within the EU territory, originally not included in the Rome Treaty of 1957 on the foundation of the European Communities, has become one of the most visible advantages of inter-State cooperation in the frame of the Union. This cooperation includes necessarily the harmonisation of a broad number of policy fields between the member States and ultimately the adoption of common and binding rules. Regarding the entry of third country nationals and migrants in particular, the Schengen

Visa Code and the Schengen Borders Code are the most important legislative settings.

Presently (July 2019), an entry visa for the "Schengen zone" is required for citizens of 105 countries. Without exception, all African countries are on the list. Moreover, citizens of the 12 main countries of origin of asylum seekers need an airport transit visa if on the route to a third country a stopover at an EU airport is required. This measures which affects, among others, citizens from the Democratic Republic of Congo, Eritrea, Ethiopia, Ghana, Nigeria and Somalia, has been introduced in order to prevent the presentation of an asylum request at the EU transit airport.

The need to have an entry visa, combined with the restrictive conditions for obtaining a visa makes it virtually impossible for an African citizen to enter the EU legally, with very few exceptions in favour of close family members of persons already residing legally in the EU and eligible for family reunification, as well as for some thousands refugees included in resettlement or humanitarian corridor programmes to whom a visa on humanitarian grounds may be issued. As a consequence, the overwhelming majority of asylum seekers and migrants have no other choice than to resort to irregular means of travel end entry. Irregular air travel, e.g. with false passports or visas has become extremely difficult due to the externalization of entry controls carried out airports of departure in third countries with the support of officials deployed by EU Member States or by Frontex. Thus, for African asylum seekers and migrants there is no realistic alternative to irregular travel by sea, crossing the Mediterranean on boats by making use of the services of smugglers. Subsequent to the implementation of the Schengen system, Italy, along with Spain, Greece and Malta, has become one of the main entry points of asylum seekers and migrants travelling irregular towards the EU territories. The number of sea arrivals is not stable but is determined by two factors: by events occurring outside Europe that create particular push factors and by the results of policies adopted by the Union and by individual Member States.

During the war in the former Yugoslavia and in Kosovo as well as during the political and economic crisis in Albania, the focus of attention in the 90s was on the Adriatic Sea and the main Italian region affected by massive sea arrivals has been Apulia. The scenario changed dramatically at the beginning of the new century. The end of the conflict in the Balkans and the stabilisation of the situation in Albania has resulted in bringing the number of boats crossing the Adriatic Sea towards zero. However, Afghan refugees and other migrants from Asian countries have resorted to a new mode of travel by hiding in regular ferry ships and in trucks carried on these ships directed towards Italian Adriatic ports, namely Venice, Ancona, Bari and Brindisi[5]. But as from 2001, the Central Mediterranean has become the principal maritime route of African asylum seekers and migrants towards Europe.

The conflicts in the Horn of Africa; the protracted dictatorship in Eritrea; the Islamist terror in Somalia; the genocide in the Sudanese province Darfu; the outbreak of civil wars in Ivory Coast and other West African countries; the repression of any opposition in the Democratic Republic of Congo have caused migration movements, principally forced migration from Sub-Saharan African countries, partly directed towards Europe, partly towards other African regions. Natural transit countries have been Morocco on the route to Spain and Libya on the route to Italy. Following the decision of Spain to close militarily the Gibraltar Street and the agreements made by Spain with Morocco, Mauritania and Senegal in 2006 allowing the return of migrants to these countries when they were intercepted on the Western Atlantic on the way to the Canadian Islands, a growing number of migrants and refugees went eastwards towards Libya with the intention to reach Italy. The Spanish policies of closing the borders, pushing back people from the high sea to Western Africa and cooperating with African transit countries has resulted in the decrease of boat arrivals in Spain and a simultaneous increase of arrivals in Italy.

The Italian Government, in turn, has started in 2009 to push back refugees from the high sea of the Canal of Sicily to Libya where they were immediately arrested and detained, for an indefinite period, and deprived of any rights in inhumane deportation centres. The action, carried out by the Italian Navy, has been condemned in February 2012 by the European Court of Human Rights (ECtHR)[6] as a violation of fundamental rights enshrined in the European Human Rights Convention (ECHR). The Court held that the claimants, 23 Eritreans and Somalis, were at risk of being tortured or subjected to inhuman treatment in Libya and not protected against refoulement to their home countries. They had no possibility of a legal remedy against their deportation to Libya. The Court found, too, that the push back represented an indiscriminate mass expulsion prohibited by the Protocol no. 4 to the EHRC. Given that the treatment of refugees and migrants has not undergone any significant change of improvement, the Court ruling that Libya is an unsafe country for refugees and migrants is still valid today. No State party of the ECHR is allowed to send back people to Libya.

---

5   We cannot discuss here the legal implications caused by the fact that sea arrivals in Italy from Greece represent the crossing of an internal EU border where, under the Schengen Borders Code, no immigration control at border points shall take place.
6   Judgment Hirsi Jumaa and others v. Italy of 23 February 2012, Grand Chamber, appl.no.27765/09

EU and Italy's policy responses

As from 2000, Italy has signed a broad number of agreements and treaties with Libya on the fight against organised crime, trafficking of persons, drug trafficking, terrorism and illegal migration[7]. Following the withdrawal of sanctions against Libya and the return of diplomatic relations, strongly supported by the EU, the cooperation on migration issues between Italy as well as other EU Member States and Libya has progressively been intensified.

The revolution of 2011 and the end of the Ghedaffi regime as well as new outbreaks of civil wars in 2014 and 2019 have not substantially changed the EU policies aimed at stemming irregular migration flows from Libya.

Cooperation, including police collaboration, with sending and transit countries of migrants has become an important part of the EU's external action and has been enormously strengthened during and after the "European refugee crisis" of 2015/16. The four principal aims set in the EU Migration Agenda of 2016[8] and in numerous conclusions of the European Council are: firstly, combatting the root causes of forced and economic migration through investment in countries of origin. Secondly, redressing irregular movements of refugees and migrants from transit or intermediate countries towards Europe. Thirdly, inducing third countries to facilitate readmission of their nationals and, where possible, of other nationals who have transited. Fourthly, enhancing avenues for legal arrivals of refugees and migrants, through the promotion of resettlement programmes and visa facilities for high-skilled workers.

The priority area is the African continent. Structural dialogue on migration between the EU and Africa had been on the agenda already prior to 2015, namely under "Rabat Process" of 2006 regarding North- und West Africa, and the Khartoum Process of 2014 regarding the Horn and Eastern Africa[9], with emphasis on the cooperation for the fight against the trafficking of persons. Tackling the root causes, in the frame of the concept "migration and development", is addressed by the Valletta Action Plan of November 2015 and the creation of a Trust Fund for Africa, comprising financial contributions paid by the EU, by individual Member States as well as by the private sector.

The underlying idea that enhanced economic development of home countries would have an impact on the push factors for migration and reduce migration outflows is challenged by many voices of the literature on migration

---

[7] See in detail: Christopher Hein, Migratory Movements to and from Libya. Italian and European Policy Responses, in: I Conflitti in Siria e Libia, ed. N.Ronzitt and E. Sciso, G.Giappichelli Editore, Turin 2018
[8] See https://ec.europa.eu/home-affairs/what-we-do/policies/european-agenda-migration_en
[9] See https://www.khartoumprocess.net/

sociology[10]. Based on solid empirical data, it is argued that, contrary to this expectation, for a considerable period of time development would rather produce an increase of, in particular inter-continental, migration. It would enhance migration skills and enable potential migrants to put their desire in practice. The Graph 4 shows that almost one third of the entire African population has expressed the wish to leave the own country but relatively few actually do so.

Figure 4: Potential migration

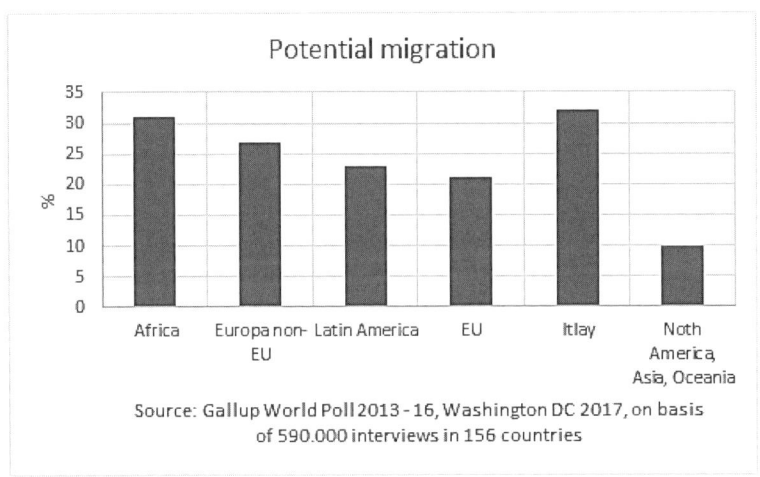

Source: Gallup World Poll 2013 – 16, Washington DC 2017, on basis of 590.000 interviewa in 156 countries.

Migrants in Europe are not normally originated from the poorest countries like the Central African Republic but from areas where a certain degree of development has been reached, like Morocco, Tunisia or Nigeria. Tackling the economic root causes for migration appears therefore to be a long - term process the result of which is not easy to predict. With respect to the more politically motivated migratory movements, the capacity of the international community and of the EU to prevent deteriorating conditions in home countries or to contribute to the cessation of conflicts and of dictatorial regimes has

---

10 See 2017 MEDAM Assessment Report, https://www.medam-migration.eu/en/publication/2017-medam-assessment-report-on-asylum-and-migration-policies-in-europe/; Mauro Zanati and Rainer Thiele, "The Impact of Foreign Aid on Migration Revisited", European University Institute Working Paper 2017/5, https://cadmus.eui.eu/bitstream/handle/1814/46124/MWP_2017_05.pdf?sequence=1

proved to be extremely limited. From countries like Afghanistan, Somalia or Iraq that are among the main countries of origin of refugees, forced migration has occurred continuously over the last decades and international interventions have rather contributed to raising the level of conflicts than to bring them to an end. We are therefore not very optimistic regarding the impact of efforts to combat the root causes, in spite of the great importance given to the matter in the public debate.

From the viewpoint of the declared aim to keep asylum seekers and migrants in the places where they reside, in particular in transit countries, and to discourage them to cross over to Europe, the policies adopted by the EU over the very last years appear rather successful. The Statement signed by the EU with Turkey in March 2016[11] aiming at reducing the flow of Syrian, Afghan and Iraqi refugees to the Greek island and from there to Western Europe has shown immediate and impressive results. As from April 2016, the number of refugees arriving from Turkey has dropped to less than 5 percent of the numbers experienced prior to the agreement[12]. The flow did not significantly shift to other routes.

A replication of this policy regarding the other main transit country, Libya, is facing more difficulties. The agreement with Turkey has been based on the legal assumption that Turkey is a "safe third country" for refugees and the EU would therefore not violate its laws when inducing Greece to return refugees there. Nobody can seriously sustain that Libya is a safe country for refugees. Libya has even not signed the 1951 Geneva Refugee Convention and has no legal regime in place to protect the most basic Human rights. The return of migrants, refugees or asylum seekers is illegal under the ECHR and the EU Charta of Fundamental Rights.

The Italian Government, with full support of the EU, has however signed in February 2017 a formal Memorandum of Understanding with Libya[13] by which the Libyan Coast Guard and Border Guards obtain ships, equipment and training in order to be enabled for the surveillance of their territorial waters, the interception of migrant boats and for search and rescue operations. The agreement foresees, too, the financial and logistic contribution to "temporary reception camps in Libya, under the exclusive control of the Libyan Ministry of Interior" where migrants are kept "pending their repatriation of voluntary return". The terms "asylum", "refugees", "asylum seekers" or "protection" are

---

11   See   https://www.consilium.europa.eu/en/press/press-releases/2016/03/18/eu-turkey-statement/
12   See arrivals in Greece 2015: 857.000; in 2016: 173.000 of whom some 150.000 Jan. to March; 2017: 30.000; 2018: 32.000
13   See the English text under: https://unsmil.unmissions.org/sites/default/files/Libyan%20Political%20Agreement%20-%20ENG%20.pdf

not mentioned in the text. Moreover, Italy promises to contribute to "job creation" and the "substitution of income"[14] in the areas affected by illegal immigration and by smuggling and trafficking of persons.

In subsequent meetings between the Italian authorities and Libyan local representatives and mayors, this latter clause of the Agreement has been detailed specifying that smuggler networks should be induced and financially stimulated to undertake different business. The same approach has been endorsed in the Joint Statement adopted in the Paris Conference on 28 August 1917, in which the heads of Governments of France, Germany, Italy and Spain as well as the European Commission participated on the European side, and Chad, Niger and Libya on the African side. The European participants have promised "support to communities along the migration route in Libya, creating alternative resources of income, increasing resilience and making them independent of human trafficking.[15]" During the first semester 2017, approximately 100.000 migrants arrived in Italy from Libya, a further increase with respect to the same periods of 2015 and 2016, in counter-tendency to all other EU countries who "benefited" from the EU-Turkey agreement and witnessed a sharp decrease of the number of asylum seekers.

Italy had become, again, the principal "gateway to Europe". Due to the implementation of the cooperation with Libya, as from July 2017 the numbers dropped most significantly, as to be seen in following table. According to estimations, more than 50.000 refugees and migrants were intercepted by Libyan forces and forcibly brought back to Libya over the last 24 months. Libya declared, for the first time ever, an own "search and rescue zone" according to international maritime law, initially comprising only the territorial waters and then extended into international waters, in 2018, to 100 miles from the Libyan coast. In principle, Libya has obtained the exclusive competence for coordinating search and rescue operations in this zone, and, thus, international endorsement for carrying refugees and migrants rescued and intercepted in international waters back to Libyan territory.

At the same time, the Italian Government has started to limit the rescue activities carried out in the Central Mediterranean, as from 2015, by non-Governmental organisations (NGOs). The Ministry of Interior elaborated in the first semester 2017 a code of conduct to be signed by these NGOs. Judiciary investigation on the NGO were initiated under the accusation to support illegal immigration.

---

14 In the italian text: "sostituzione del reddito", MoU, art. 2
15 Joint Statement 28 August 2017, see https://www.bundesregierung.de/resource/blob/975244/603824/5c1dee9e40e743517ceb883c98c543d9/2017-08-28-statement-refugee-migration-english-data.pdf?download=1 chapter 2.3-1

Figure 5: See arrivals and asylum seekers in Italy

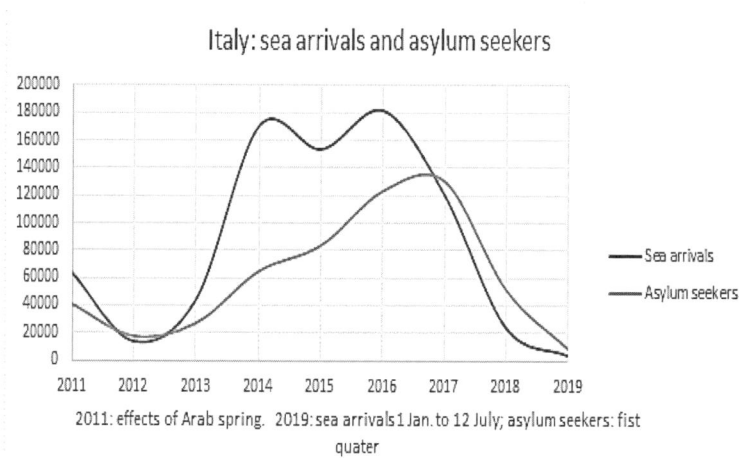

Source: Christopher Hein, "Migratory Movements to and from Libya – Italian and European Policy Responses", in:"Conflitti in Siria e Libia",ed. N. Ronzetti and E. Sciso, G.Giappichelli Editore, Turin 2018

Even if no proof of any collaboration with smugglers has been found[16], public opinion has been influenced by the allegation that NGO ships served as "taxis" for irregular migrants. Following the taking up of office of the new Italian Government in June 2018, the repression of NGO activities in the Canal of Sicily has been endured, in particular by not allowing the disembarkation of rescued migrants in Italian ports. Several ships have been seized and ship captains have been arrested. During the same period, the EU coordinated maritime operations "Themis" and "Sophia" have come to a still stand. At the time of writing, no public rescue operation is in place anymore. As a matter of consequence, the numbers of migrants dying in the sea, which in absolute terms decreased heavily with respect to previous years, has been in the first semester of 2019 four times higher in relation to those who manage to arrive in Italy or Malta[17]. In June 2019, the Italian Government adopted a decree by which the Minister of Interior may interdict the entry of a ship carrying migrants rescued into the Italian territorial waters. The first application of the

---

16 As stated by the Chief Prosecutor of Agrigento in his hearing at the Italian Senate, 1 July 2019

17 See https://missingmigrants.iom.int/

decree has been the case of the ship "Seawatch 3" that has caused worldwide media attention.

The Italian policy of cooperation with the Libyan coast guard of closed sea borders has produced a shift of migratory routes to the Western and the Eastern Mediterranean. As from 2018, the number of sea arrivals in Spain in Greece has significantly increased. Spain has become, too, a transit country, namely towards France. However, comparing the numbers of asylum seekers and migrants in the whole of the EU with those of the "refugee crisis", it has to be stated that the adopted policies have contributed to a dramatic overall decrease. It is likely that migratory movements will take place ever more within Africa and will affect the relatively more developed countries in the North and the South of the continent. At the same time, avenues for regular travel to Europe are expected to be gradually widened. Indicators are the increase of resettlement places[18] that States have put at the disposal of UNHCR for refugees who have no possibility to obtain effective protection in countries of first arrival, as well as of humanitarian admission programmes carried out in collaboration with civil society organisations. In view of the demographic decline in many European countries, the over-aging of the population and the foreseeable shortcomings in the labour market, entry facilities for foreign workers, not only highly qualified ones, will likely be negotiated with third countries, under the condition of cooperation for the quick return of citizens in irregular residence situation and the frame of Mobility Partnerships.

It may be predicted that the phenomenon of irregular migration movements to Europe that has overshadowed the migration debate over the last 30 years is gradually diminishing. We will eventually see in future a change to pro-active migration policies that may even include programmes aimed at attracting migrants to come to Europe, in spite of present tendencies of racism, xenophobia and social exclusion. Environmentally induced migration movements, mainly due to climate change, are supposed to occur predominantly within the countries of origin, in particular to urban agglomerations, as well as to countries in the immediate neighbourhood with cultural, ethic and linguistic similarities.

---

18 Upto 2014, the total number of resettlement places offered by EU member States were less than 5000 per year. From 2015 to end 2018, a total of 44.000 refugees have been resettled under various schemes. In September 2017, The European Commission appealed for 50.000 resettlement places in the EU for the period 2018/19; see https://www.resettlement.eu/page/resettlement-in-Europe

Public opinion and political debate on migration in Italy

Millions of people in Italy have a "migration background" within their own families. The trauma of having been obliged, mainly for economic reasons, over 150 years to seek a future abroad is deeply rooted in minds. The emotional notion of Italy being a small and overcrowded country where there is no space for newcomers is stronger than statistical evidence of demographic decline, of the objective need to "import" foreign populations, and of the contribution migrants are giving to the economic development as well as to the pension funds. As from the moment, end of the 80s, that public opinion became aware of Italy's evolution towards an immigration country, the influx of migrants has been perceived constantly as an "emergency" rather than as a structural fact. Policy responses, with rare exceptions, have reacted *a posteriori* to new immigration scenarios in form of emergency measures. Significant is the Italian policy of "regularisation" of irregular migrants through a number of ad hoc interventions during the period from 1987 to 2012. Approximately 80 percent of the 3,5 million migrants from non EU countries presently residing regularly in the country is composed of "regularised" migrants who had arrived irregularly or had overstayed their sojourn permits, and of their family members who subsequently entered with family visas. Each regularisation law was announced as "the last one". The emergency approach, consolidated in a number of formal "emergency decrees" freezing the normal administrative procedures, has neglected the need to promote integration of migrants and refugees which by definition requires structural interventions and long term planning. The support to integration efforts has largely been left in the hands of civil society organisations.

A pressing emergency situation is also the requirement established by the Italian Constitution for the adoption of a "decree-law" by which the Government can address a specific issue with immediate legal effect, to be converted into a parliamentary law within 60 days. In November 2018 and in June 2019 the Government has promulgated two decree-laws on security and immigration in spite of the fact that the number of incoming migrants has reached an extremely low level and does not represent in any way a threat to security or public order. Again, the perception in the public opinion of immigration as an emergency is artificially fuelled by resorting to emergency legislation in doubtful conformity with the Constitution.

It is interesting to note that electoral campaigns have been dominated by migration issues as from 2008, precisely when the global financial crisis has started to hit the Italian economy. Again, against all statistical evidence, criminality and migration have been used by political leaders as synonyms. Fake news has been published not only in recent times and has contributed to influencing public opinion over years and to creating a hostile approach against migrants in parts of the population.

The almost daily news spread over years in the media on tragedies in the Canal of Sicily, of boats arriving at beaches or at the shores of the Lampedusa island, with pictures of people exhausted, arriving without any belongings in absolute poorness – all this has created the perception that immigrants are equal to" boat people" and has obscured the fact that the overwhelming majority of migrants is living and working "normally" in the country holding a regular residence permit. The more recent – and for Italy unexpected – slogan "Italians first", a slogan not only spread by parts of the media but by some of the most prominent political leaders, has aggravated the situation. Discrimination on grounds of nationality and of colour of the skin has become a constant feature on all levels, including at local policies of municipalities and regions. "Italians first" constitutes as such a violation of basic values enshrined in the Lisbon Treaty of the EU and of precise legal obligations under the EU anti-discrimination law.

On the other hand, an extremely active and broadly anchored social society, formed in particular by Church organisations, NGOs, trade union organisations, committees formed spontaneously by citizens and similar, promote a positive image of immigrants and substitutes for the lack of public interventions in a vast spectrum of social and cultural activities. The migration theme has contributed largely to the deep fragmentation of public opinion and of the society which can also be observed within the catholic community to which the vast majority of the population belongs.[19]

Italy: again an emigration country

Whereas the public debate in Italy is continuing to focus on immigration issues, the really alarming new phenomenon with which Italy is confronted has not entered into the public and political discourse: the statistical fact that Italy has been developing over the past 5 years again into an emigration country.[20] More than half a million of, mostly young and highly educated Italians have left for an extended period and perhaps for ever by going to other European as well as

---

19 See the first page headline of the daily „la Repubblica" of 8 July 2019: "Cattolici a un bivio: il Papa o Salvini" (Catholics at a crossroad: the Pope or Salvini")

20 See The Italian Insider, "Italy has more emigrants than immigrants, study shows", 12 July 2017, with reference to IDOS, Dossier Statistico Immigrazione 2017. For more recent data see: N.Lombardi and F.Pittau, "Italiani all estero'" in: IDOS, Dossier Statistico Immigrazione 2018

to South-and North American countries. The tendency is growing year by year as can be seen in the following figures:

Figure 6: Italian migrants 1960-1999

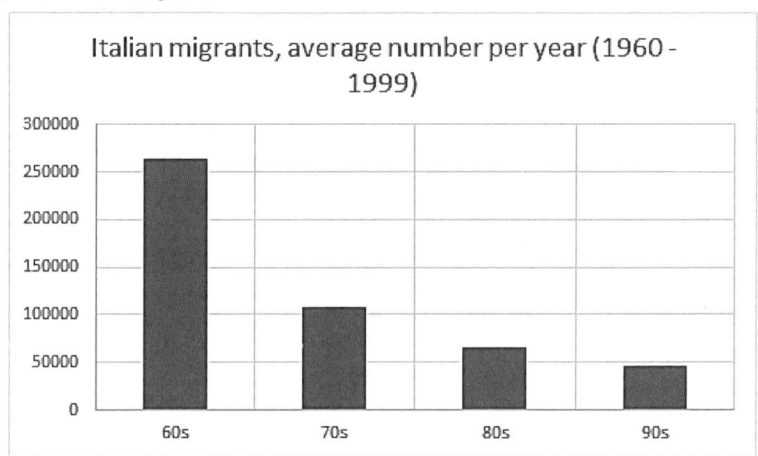

Source: The Italian Inside, "Italy has more emigrants than immigrants, study shows", 12 July 2017, with reference to IDOS, Dossier Statistico Immigrazione 2017

Figure 7: Italian migrants 2010 – 2017

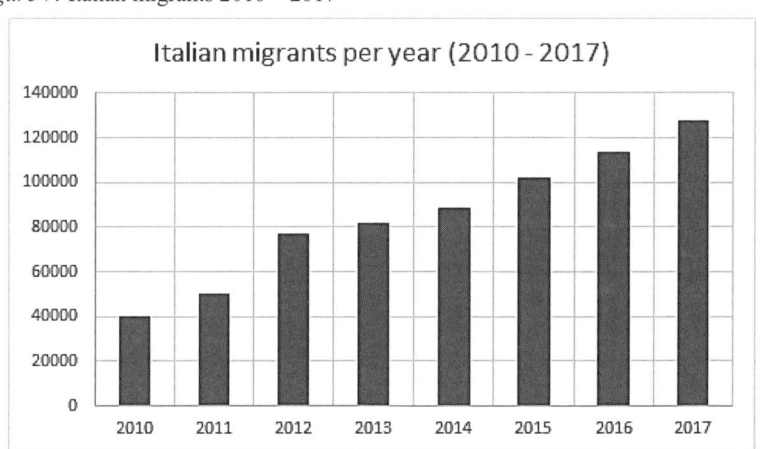

Source: The Italian Inside, "Italy has more emigrants than immigrants, study shows", 12 July 2017, with reference to IDOS, Dossier Statistico Immigrazione 2017

Conclusion and Prospects

We have tried to demonstrate that migration is a social-political-economic phenomenon that undergoes rapid fluctuations due to a broad number of variables determining the individual as well as collective decisions to leave the home country, the routes of migration travel, the envisaged countries of destination, the duration of the life abroad and the prospects for return. In the last few years, the migration scenario in Europa has radically changed. The number of asylum seekers in the 28 member States has dropped from 1.2 million in 2016 to 580.000 in 2018. There is no "refugee crisis" anymore. For many Syrian refugees, voluntary or even forced return will become an alternative to prolonged stay in European countries and in Turkey. Italy, still in 2017 the main country of first arrival, is no longer a gateway for African refugees and migrants to Europe on a significant level. The various policies adopted, in particular regarding cooperation with transit countries in North Africa and the Middle East, have fortified the "fortress Europe". At the same time, legal and protected entry mechanisms for refugees are being increased, however they are still remaining on an extreme modest level[21]. Similar mechanisms will likely be developed for migrant workers. The unexpected crisis in Venezuela has added a new main country of origin to the European as well as to the South American asylum statistics. Spain is, again, in the forefront as country of first arrival of asylum seekers and migrants originated from Latin America and from West Africa.

The recent appearance of China in the African continent in terms of investments, infrastructures and deployment of workers will have an impact on the economies and the labour markets of many African countries. It represents one of the factors that will presumably enhance intra-African migration. Another factor is the creation of zones in which, similar to the Schengen system, internal border controls are being abolished. The Economic Community of West African States (ECOWAS) has been the forerunner and other African sub-regions are following the example.[22] The rapid economic evolution of a number of traditional African emigration countries will in a mid-term diminish the outflow of migrants towards Europe. On the other hand, the protracted armed conflicts in the poorest countries like Somalia, South Sudan,

---

21 According to UNHCR, 1,4 million refugees worldwide need to be resettled, but places are available for less than 5 % of them. See www.europeanmigrationlaw.eu/en/articles/news/unhcr-resettlement

22 It appears that migration within West Africa is roughly nine times larger than movements from the region towards Europe and North Africa: see Dris Ghazounani, "Morocco: A Growing Destination for Sub-Saharan Africans" 2019, http://migrationpolicy.org/article/growing-destination-sub-saharan-africans-morocco

the Central African Republic and others are not likely to produce massive intercontinental refugee exodus but will rather increase inter-regional migration movements and will require the strengthening of international humanitarian and development aid in favour of the receiving countries.

References

European University Institute. *The Impact of Foreign Aid on Migration Revisited.* In: Working Paper 2017/5.

Ghazounani D. (2019) *Morocco: a growing destination for Sub-Saharan Africans.* Migration Policy Institute.

Global Compact for Safe, Orderly and Regular Migration, Dec. 2018. https://www.iom.int/global-compact-migration

Hein C. (2018). Migratory Movements to and from Libya – Italian and European Policy Responses. In N. Ronzetti & E. Sciso, *Conflitti in Siria e Libia (Conflicts in Siria and Libia).* Turin: G.Giappichelli Editore.

International Organisation for Migration (IOM), *Missing Migrants Projects.* http://missingmigrants.iom.int

Migration Policy Institute and European University Institute. *Migrants' Profile – Drivers of Migration and Migration Trends.* In: Study commissioned by the International Organization for Migration.

The Italian Inside, "Italy has more emigrants than immigrants, study shows", 12 July 2017. With reference to IDOS, Dossier Statistico Immigrazione 2017.

UNHCR Libya. https://www.unhcr.org/libya.html

Zanati M. & Thiele R., (2017*) Assessment Report 2017.* Mercator Dialogue on Asylum and Migration (MEDAM).

The Viernheim study: use clinical psychology to explore integration capacities of a German community

Giorgia Marinelli, Viviana Langher, Andrea Caputo, Kibreab Habtemichael, Angelika Groterath

Premise

The present paper is concerned with a case study on the migrant integration process, that began in 2017 thanks to a question and thanks to the efforts of ten advanced students, two passionate professors and a whole or almost a whole small town in the South of Hessen in Germany and its main actors in the field of refugee or migrant integration. In line with the idea and the spirit of the DAAD (Deutscher Akademischer Austauschdienst) of involving young scholars, this study group set about exploring the phenomenon of integration and to answer fundamental questions that moved the whole of Europe in these times right after what has been called "the refugee wave".

In winter 2016/2017, two Italian psychology students from Sapienza University of Rome, Giorgia Marinelli and Fabrizio Passacantilli, went to the Department of Social Work of the Hochschule Darmstadt as Erasmus exchange students. During the exchange, they had the opportunity to work as interns in a German facility, an afterschool service that aims at integrating children with migration background through education. The work experience in Viernheim, the small town where the facility is located, gave rise to a fundamental question in students' minds: "What does integration mean to Viernheimers?". The question came to them because they had observed that "even if the declared goal of the facility is integration, the group of children that takes part in the afterschool activities is composed only of children with a migration background, and there is a complete lack of native German children" (Groterath, 2018)[1]. After her Erasmus semester, Giorgia Marinelli came back to Darmstadt and Viernheim to work on her master's thesis. She wanted to find a possible answer to this question. She could investigate emotions about integration shared among the Viernheimers thanks to the cooperation of two

---

1   A preliminary publication in Germany was possible under the "socialnet Materialien". Angelika Groterath acted as editor, with co-authors Andrea Caputo, Kibreab Habtemichael, Viviana Langher, Giorgia Marinelli and Franziska Blanz, Lennart Esselbrügge, Joanna Kaiser, Christina Katsampouka, Jannike Keil, Claudégio Messias Filho, Clara Neumann, Lena Pschiuk, Gabriel Weber and Sascha Wellmann.

professors of psychology, Viviana Langher from Sapienza University and Angelika Groterath from Hochschule Darmstadt, two scientists, Andrea Caputo from Sapienza University and Kibreab Habtemichael, in parts from Hochschule Darmstadt in these times and in parts from the City of Viernheim, the integration office. Moreover, she had the meaningful help of ten German students from Hochschule Darmstadt. They had a key role in the data collection, conducting interviews in German with the key actors of Viernheim, and in the data analysis because they were with Angelika Groterath the experts in German language and German culture. Viviana Langher and Andrea Caputo, instead, were experts in the field of research in "Italian psychology"[2] and in data processing and interpretation. They consider the knowledge of the context as crucial for understanding human behaviour. Kibreab Habtemichael in his function as head of the Integration Office, gave us access, indeed, not only to the key actors from Viernheim, but to the whole context of the "City of Viernheim".

Integration from the point of view of clinical psychology

The construct of integration has evolved and enriched over the years. It took its starting point in the theoretical framework of *acculturation*. Migration flows lead societies to become *culturally plural*. People belonging to many cultures come to live together in the same place, in a diverse society (Berry, 1997). The encounter between different cultures entails individual and social changes (Graves, 1967) through a process called *acculturation,* a concept widely used in cross-cultural psychology, by which "groups of individuals having different culture come into continuous first-hand contact with subsequent changes in the original culture patterns of either or both groups" (Redfield, Linton & Herskovits, 1936). Against this background, two research streams have developed that look at acculturation as a unidimensional or respectively a bidimensional phenomenon (for a review, see Van de Vijver & Phalet, 2004). For the research field that looks at acculturation as a bidimensional process Berry's model (1997) is central. It focuses on the minority group, with a lack of a view on the wider context and the relationship between natives and migrants. It could be one of the reasons why subsequent researches based on Berry's model, were focused on individual belonging to a minority (Schwartz, Zamboanga & Jarvis, 2007; Neto, Barros & Schmitz, 2005; Zagefka & Brown, 2002). Other scholars paid attention to a positive relation between integration

---

2 As defined in the editorial of the present book.

strategy and psychological well-being (Scottham & Dias, 2010; Ward, Stuart & Kus, 2011).

In a unidimensional understanding, instead, the integration process is viewed from the perspective of a majority, the host population. Research has been conducted on the correlation between natives' social wellbeing and the perceived threat through immigration (Mera et al., 2017). The concordance or discordance of acculturation preferences of migrants and the host population are also largely studied (Ward, 2013).

What stands out from these researches is an integration process seen by an individualistic paradigm, which does not provide an overview in terms of individual-context relationship (Caputo, 2015) because it considers social behaviour as determined by inner psychological processes without taking into account the context. The individualistic paradigm looks at the social dimension as the result of individual characteristics related to each other, without considering the co-construction of social context by people, groups and organisations which are in relationship to each other within the context (Grasso & Salvatore, 1997). Thus, taking the individualistic paradigm as a reference, the understanding of a social process will be partial and not exhaustive about the implication of different actors and aspects involved in the construction of an integrated community.

In our view, a specific social dimension has a meaning based on the socialization of emotions among individuals belonging to the same context. The set of shared emotional symbolisations of a specific context (or relationship) is called Local Culture (Carli & Paniccia, 2003). In the current paper, Local Culture is proposed as the theoretical concept to explore the processes of integration and social coexistence, the symbolic component of human relationships based on shared rules which allows people to exchange and live together (Caputo, 2013). The concept of Local Culture has been chosen because of its ability to explore symbolical and emotional meanings that underpin and organise social relationships, and to open up spaces of reflection and action based on what emerges from community itself. The case study method allows to understand events and relationships within groups, institutions or communities in their specific context (Langher, Caputo & Martino, 2017) and it can provide us with a deep knowledge about the subject of investigation (Giacchetta et al., 2017; Langher et al., 2017).

Theoretical Framework: The Mind's Unconscious Mode of Being and the Local Culture

We propose a psychodynamic perspective to explore social situations, based on the theory of mind's functioning elaborated by Ignacio Matte Blanco and the theoretical concepts of Collusion and Local Culture theorised by R. Carli and R. M. Paniccia.

The mind's theory of Matte Blanco is known as *Bi-Logic*, a system where rational thought and emotion are simultaneously involved in the process of sense-making and organise the individual-context relationship. Matte Blanco resumed and synthetized Freud's theorisation of five characteristics or rules that govern the unconscious in the principle of symmetry. According to this principle, the unconscious mode of thought treats asymmetrical relationship as symmetrical (Matte Blanco, 1975) and all permutations of the terms of any relationship are possible and identical (for instance, if Paolo is the father of Giovanni, then Giovanni is the father of Paolo too). This mind's mode of being is different from the rational modality, based on asymmetry, differentiation and on the Aristotelian principles of identity, non-contradiction and tertium non datur where Giovanni cannot be the father of Paolo at all.

The symmetrical and asymmetrical mode work together at the same time. Without the asymmetric modality, which divides and sets distinctions, we cannot process the reality that would appear instead as a homogenous and indivisible totality, where everything is equal. The asymmetry introduces elements of differentiation in the blurred magma of the symmetrical mode of being that are called "bags of symmetry". These bags are the first classes of emotional meaning that people use to affectively signify the experience of reality, as a guide in the process of interpretation and sense making in the relationship with the environment (Salvatore & Freda, 2011).

The Italian psychologist Renzo Carli and his colleagues developed a hierarchical model of affective symbolisation, the most immediate way to establish relations with objects with which people interact, the context (Carli & Paniccia, 2003). According to this model, the first emotional categories are three different dichotomies: *inside/outside, high/low, in front/behind.* Inside/outside represents the dynamic of inclusion/exclusion because what is "inside" is something good and friendly, while what is out "outside" is bad, threatening and rejected. The high/low dichotomy refers to symbols of power and the in front/behind dichotomy provides to the emotional dynamic of true and false (Carli & Paniccia, 2004). These symbolisations of the context are shared with the others, and they are intersubjectively constructed in processes of communication (Caputo, 2015). Carli names this phenomenon *Collusion,* an unconscious process, which refers to the common way the members of a social group emotionally experience the context to which they belong and react to aspects of the environment, in particular other human beings (Carli, 1993). The set of collusive affective symbolisations, belonging to a specific social group, is called *Local Culture*. The adjective "Local" underlines the dependence of culture on the specific object and target population. In our opinion Local Culture allows us to highlight emotional dimensions of integration processes and the needs linked to them, that may be unexplored because of the value-driven connotations of integration in the political and social discourse.

The Case-Study

The major research issue is to understand, which are the affective symbolisations (Local Culture) of integration that are shared by Viernheim's population, both natives and refugees and detect the possible problems and potential demands of development.

This could provide policy makers with important information about the state of the arts that is the state integration in the collective life to plan local development actions and thus to sustain the multiculturalism.

Method

The inquiry is based on a computer-assisted text analysis (Emotional Text Analysis) of interviews of 21 key actors, and on the multiple correspondence analysis of the texts.

Participants

We interviewed, in the German language, 21 people with a key role in Viernheim's life and actively engaged in promoting integration (13 men and 8 women) across different age classes (2 aged 18-35; 6 aged 26-45; 11 aged 46-65 and 2 aged older than 65 years). Five participants were foreigners. Among the interviewees there were heads of associations (*e.g.,* socio-cultural, political, religious, voluntary organisations), business people (*e.g.,* shopping mall, hotel, cinema) and representatives of institutions (*e.g.,* school, university, police department, church, local administration).

A structured interview was used, with five open questions on integration:
1. What do you think the refugees expect when they arrive here in Viernheim?
2. And what do the people of Viernheim expect from the refugees?
3. What do you mean by "integration"?
4. When do you think someone is fully integrated?
5. How do you think society will change in the future?

Emotional Text Analysis (ETA)

Emotional Text Analysis (ETA) was used to analyse the interviews and detect collusive dynamics, which organise the Local Culture in Viernheim, on the issue of integration. ETA is a psychological tool for the analysis of written texts or discourse, to explore specific cultural models structuring the text itself. Against this theoretical background, "emotions are […] shared categorisation processes, expressed through language, by which people symbolise the reality" (Caputo, 2013). The ETA basic assumption is the *double reference principle*, postulated by the Italian psychoanalyst Franco Fornari (1979), which allows to detect the emotional and symbolic dimensions running through the text.

The infinitive set of emotional meanings that we can attribute to a single word is called *polysemy*, which arises when the word is taken out of the written or spoken text. Thus, words can be divided in two categories: *dense words*, which can transmit well emotional meanings with high level of polysemy and a low level of ambiguity[3]; *non-dense words,* characterised by the maximum ambiguity and thus the minimum of polysemy (Carli & Paniccia, 2004).

Dense words can be detected and grouped, according to their co-occurrence in the same text segment, with the help of a specific software for text analysis, the *T-Lab Plus 2018.* The T-Lab software makes it possible to disambiguate the text and to identify statistical connections between dense words, thus derterminig a few clusters, i.e. groups of co-occurring dense words (Lancia, 2004). The dense words of the clusters are connected to each other according to the collusive dynamics they represent, as it happens in the free association technique where an unconscious process of the patient arises from the chain of words and thought (Freud, 1899. Ita. trad.: 1966). The assumption is that the co-occurrence of words within the same text segments reduces the association

---

[3] Words with a high level of ambiguity are, for example: adverbs, conjunctions, auxiliary verbs, words with different meanings, according to their position in the sentence and their relationship with other words.

of meanings attributable to each word, in other words the polysemy, allowing a thematic domain to be constructed (Caputo, 2014). The software analyses the text corpus, which includes all the literal transcription of the answers to five questions. The second step is the detection of a words list, from which the researcher selects dense words based on word's polysemy, etymology and relevance to the research topic. Then, T-Lab detects groups of words co-occurring in the same text segments (*elementary context units*) with highest probability, as indicated by a Chi-square test (χ^2). Each of these word-groups, or clusters in a statistical sense, represents a different collusive process belonging to thecontext in which the research is carried on. The clusters are labelled by the researchers in a group interpretation process. The interpretation is the qualitative part of data analysis. The process ends with the interpretation of *Cultural Space,* represented by clusters placed on n-dimensional spaces. The relationships between the different clusters within the factorial space represents the Local Culture of the specific context under analysis.

Table 1: Clusters of dense words ordered by Chi-square

Cluster 1	χ^2	Cluster 2	χ^2	Cluster 3	χ^2	Cluster 4	χ^2
Human being	375.31	Help	155.82	Integration	142.65	Work	110.15
Problem	121.2	Living	116.74	Expectations	68.75	Coming	101.1
Seeing	81.47	Side	103.2	Viernheim	62.23	German	94.42
Media	63.43	Refugee	102.1	Believe	39.74	Good	62.07
Foreigners	54.48	Child	85.29	Important	36.12	Women	51.38
Receiving	42.05	House	81.61	Heavy	28.52	Open	37.73
Arrived	31.65	Showing	41.07	Cultures	21.41	Family	35.64
Thousands	20.19	Taking	33.49	Entirely	21.41	Turkey	29.9
Old	19.84	Situation	27.88	Language	19.55	Country	27.15
Difference	18	Habit	20.09	Answer	18.56	Man	26.23
Policy	11.76					Get	25.45
Dangerous	10.65					Money	23.82

Scource: The present research

Results

The detected clusters are presented as follows, including some extracts from interviews. The extracts represent the most typical elementary context units (UCEs) of each cluster.

Cluster 1

> *"You see half-naked people. Or you see people who drink from morning to night on the street." (Int. 21)*
> *"Yes, I think that there are many fears in the society at the moment, which are not considered sufficient by all sorts of institutions, by politics, and even by the society itself, so that people are afraid." (Int. 19)*

Cluster 1 is composed of 36.8% of the overall elementary context units (435 out of a total of 1182).

The first word is *human being* ("Mensch" in German). It suggests the idea of someone without definition, someone who belongs to the human species but without a precise origin and affiliation. In fact, reading this cluster creates an imagine of an alien population landed in an empty city, with hidden people watching at the newcomers from the house's windows, with a deep sense of mistrust and fear. The second word *problem* ("Problem" in German), suggests critical dimension in meeting these new arrivals, which seem to be experienced like threatening and mainly seen (*seeing,* "Sehen") through the lens of the *media* ("Media") as *foreigners* ("Ausländer"), someone who comes from outside of Land (country, state), to emphasise the distance and the different cultural belonging. The cultural identity refers to the emotional set of "being inside" which evokes the warmth of family and the sense of security, that missing here. The word *receiveing* ("bekommen" in German) reminds to a relational dimension, where someone is willing to give something to another person, but it could also remind to predatory phantasies of taking something aggressively to withhold it from a person who has the desired object. The next words underline the preoccupation linked with the perception of refugees as *thousands* ("Tausend"), a number which evokes strength and power, *arrived* ("gekommen") in a town where the population sees itself as *old* ("alt")[4]. The adjective "old" suggests a feeling of weakness and impotence against the

---

4   As we can see on the web site https://it.actualitix.com/paese/eurp/europa-eta-media.php, Germany is in first place in Europe for high average age (46.3 years in 2015), which is twice the average age of Syrian population (22.7 years in 2015).

backdrop of a plethora of vigorous newcomers whom seem to invade the country under the paralyzed gaze of population. The strangeness and the following preoccupation are marked by the association of the word *difference* ("Unterschied") with *policy* ("Politik") and then *dangerous* ("gefährlich"). The term Politik comes from the Greek root Polis and Politikè, which means "what adheres to the city and the art of governing res publica". Its closeness with the words difference and dangerous seems to suggest the idea that differences on living the city and being part of it are felt as dangerous.

Cluster 2

> *"So I think people expect refugees to adapt to their lifestyle habits, or to accept lifestyle habits that are here and without consciously ignore them." (Int. 19)*
> *"But now it has to be slow, like a child. If you have a child, you can still take it on your knees after twenty years." (Int. 21)*

Cluster 2 is composed of 18.44% of the overall elementary context units (218 out of a total of 1182). It starts with the word *help* ("Helfen") whose meaning has a strong reference to the psychological dimensions of care and assistance, following by the word *living* ("wohnen") which has the same etymological root of apartment/flat. This co-occurrence of words lets think about someone who needs help or someone who receives help to rebuild a new safe house where to start a new life. The word *side* ("Seite"), in the light of the following co-occurrent words, seems to picture a child taken by the caregiver's hand, alongside the adult, in a position that does not allow to look into each other's eyes, to see each other and therefore to know each other. The help is addressed to a refugee felt as fragile and needy, emotional dimensions evoked by the words *child* and *refugee* ("Kind" and "Geflüchtete". Geflüchtete is the German word used to refer to refugees in a more respectful way. Instead, Flüchtlinge is the German word for refugees with a negative connotation). The use of Geflüchtete rather than Flüchtlinge underlines the idea of a refugee as someone someone you have to protect, someone you should not be directly aggressive against.

The next word is *house* ("Haus"), symbol of family, security and welcoming. But it is also a symbol of the emotional category of "being part/being inside" which allows to recognize the enemy as the one who is outside. Following the next words, the friend has *to show* ("gezeigt") and *to take on* ("nehmen") new *habits* ("Gewohnheit") and adapt itself to the new *situation* ("Situation") in the host country.

Cluster 3

"*I want to integrate myself, that's what I think is the most important thing that both sides want.*" *(Int.8)*
"*Integration is important. With every stranger, you always have to take care of the culture.*" *(Int.18)*

Cluster 3 is composed of 31.05% of the overall elementary context units (367 out of a total of 1182). It organises the associative chain around *integration* ("Integration), the first word of the list. This word is followed by *expectation* ("Erwartung") and *Viernheim,* which underlines the emotional symbolisation of integration as a goal felt by the community, something that is expected to be achieved. Integration seems to be felt more rather as a mission than as an achievable and realisable goal, a dimension evoked by the German word "Glaube" translatable as *believe* or *faith*. Also, the following words reduce the emotional polysemy of the first word by bringing it under the responsibility to achieve integration at any price, because it is *important* ("wichtig") and at the same time *heavy* ("schwer"), as if integrating *entirely* ("vollständig") different *cultures* is felt as complicated. Moreover, the cluster says that integration between cultures in Viernheim is mainly pursued by sharing the *language* ("Sprache"), the only cluster word with a pragmatic implication, the communication with a common language as principal *answer* ("Antwort") to achieve integration.

In our opinion, this cluster speaks about the values and the social mandate that organize consensus towards the integration aim, the "open-doors to refugees" policy supported by German government. However, organising a process or social action based only on common sense and values, without considering the importance of sharing goals, may lead to ineffective actions (Carli & Paniccia, 2003).

Cluster 4

"*What do I expect from a refugee? Well, I hope for a refugee that he/she integrates him/herself well here, that he/she learns German well. (Int. 8)*
"*You do not have to come here. But if you come to a Christian country, then you have to, to, you have to consider that two men may kiss on the street.*" *(Int. 21)*

Cluster 4 is composed of 13.71% of overall elementary context units (162 out of a total of 1182). It begins with the word *work* ("Arbeit"), the most important value in Germany, a mainly protestant nation. Protestantism enhances the function of work and considers personal success as a sign of God's grace. The next word *coming* ("kommen") refers to move from one place to another, implying an intention. The correlation with the first word supports the idea of a migration with economical purposes. The words *German* ("Deutsch") and *good* ("gut") let think of phantasies about Germany and the German as epitome of the good. A slightly different interpretation of this word co-occurrence would be he idea of finding a good *work* with a good (command of) German. The next word *women* ("Frauen"), in co-occurrence with *good* and *open* ("offen"), refers to the image of the woman as Mother Earth, an earth unexplored and welcoming which is expected to give every good. Moreover, *woman* and *family* ("Familie") lead to the emotional set of belonging. All these words, apart from representing the hopes and expectations of migrants, are the traditional values which give confidence to German citizens. The word Turkey ("Türkei") makes part of this tradition, because the Turkish community has a long story of settlement in Germany and meanwhile is considered as part of the German population. The word *country* ("Land") underlines the above mentioned idea of traditionalism and conservatism embodied in this cluster. Indeed, the image attributed to the forth cultural repertoire by the research group is the German flag. The word *man* ("Mann"), followed by *get* ("kriegen") and *money* ("Geld"), sheds light upon the dimension of professional success, usually perceived as something male or masculine.

Figure 3: Oppositions between clusters in the factorial space

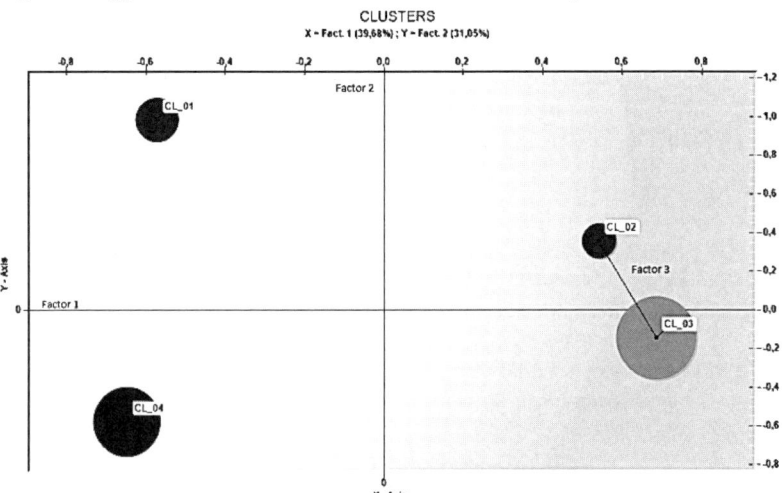

Source: The present research

Factors

The correspondence analysis has detected three latent dimensions or factors, which organise the main oppositions between clusters in the factorial space (Figure 1). The first factor is represented by the horizontal axis and gets significance from the opposition of Cluster 1 and 4, on the negative pole, and Cluster 3 on the positive pole (Cluster 2 does not add any meaning to the horizontal factor). We have called this factor *the tension,* related to the achievement of integration where two pressures push in opposite directions; the negative pole is *the conservation* and the positive one embodies *the transformation.*

The tension is between what is pushing for maintaining the present *status quo* against what is pushing for a change, for integration. But promoting integration without clear steps and without exploring the relationship with an unknown *other* makes the population feel alone in front an important aim, as a lonely athlete in front of an obstacle, imbued with tension. The second factor is the vertical axis, which highlights two different positions on how to relate to migrants.

We have called this factor *the inner conflict* because it represents the indecision between *certainties* (cluster 4 on the negative pole), to remain anchored to traditional values on the one side, and *novelty* (cluster 1 on the positive pole), opening up to migrants and facing the fear of the other that the first cluster highlights, on the other side. This factor, together with the first one, seems to tell us that the interviewed persons do not consider integration as an already ongoing process. It seems that they are wondering, instead, if they are ready to meet this challenge, or if conservative pressure and separation will win. The described situation suggests an impasse fuelled by the ongoing conflict, which does not allow the exploration of the other and of themselves in relationship with him/her, finding together development opportunities. The third factor crosses the factorial space perpendicularly and the clusters that give more meaning to it, are the second one, on the positive pole, and the third one, on the negative pole. We have called it *the solution* because the only choice that has been found to fulfill the social mandate (Cluster 3) is to deny the inner conflict, deleting, at psychic level, each element of aggressiveness and threat felt in the relationship itself. The complaisance arises from the positive pole (Cluster 2) where the phantasy of the refugee as a child emerges. The refugee-child must be needy and dependent to be acceptable and to permit the management of the conflict. Furthermore, the symbolisation of the refugee as a needy child recalls parent-child relationship, where the parent is who welcomes. This collusive dynamic does not request the exploration of the other, neither on the native's, nor on the migrants' side, because the parent knows what his/her child needs and the child is dependent and does not take care of the relationship, since that is a parent's task.

Discussion

The shared affective symbolisations analysis (Local Culture) suggests that migrants are perceived emotionally as an enemy and that the relationship between migrants and natives is unexplored. The relationship appears as based on projections of unconscious frightening feelings that overlap a real exploration of the unknown others. Being integrated was felt as a mission and a value for Viernheim's citizens, it is not possible to avoid a peaceful coexistence and to enact a fight/flight behaviour. Thus, the solution is complaisance by ridding the fear and let it hide. But even if the fear is hidden it works under the citizens' consciousness and it acts as an obstacle to the the possibility of rational thought and impacts the public decision on integration measures. However, the City of Viernheim has accepted and supported this research, and this suggests that there is a wish to overcome the present impasse between clinging on to tradition and facing the fear of the other and knowing him/her.

In conclusion, the study of shared affective symbolisation makes progress from a view of integration as a universal construction, which is strongly criticised (Rudmin, 2010; Andreouli, 2013), to another view possible: the view of integration as a relation where diversity is recognised and diversities are considered as interdependent and in need of collaboration. This view recognises development goals thanks to the exploration of shared feelings, which base the action of each specific social reality (Paniccia, 2012a; Paniccia, 2012b).

References

Andreouli E. (2013). Identity and acculturation: The case of naturalised citizens in Britain. *Culture & Psychology, Vol.19(2) 165-183.*
Berry J. W. (1997). Immigration, acculturation, and adaptation. A*pplied psychology: an international review, Vol. 46(1), 5-68.*
Caputo A. (2013). Cultural Models Shaping Stalking From a Content Analysis of Italian Newspapers. *Europe's Journal of Psychology, Vol. 9(3).*
Caputo A. (2014). I modelli culturali nel discorso sul cybersex: Analisi di un corpus di articoli di giornale (Cultural models in the speech on cybersex: analysis of a corpus of newspaper articles). *Psicologia della Salute*, Vol. 1, 5-28
Caputo A. (2015). The local culture as a means to explore the processes of social coexistence: A case study on a neighborhood in the city of Rome. *Community Psychology in Global Perspective, Vol.1(2), 22-39.*
Carli R. (1993). *L'analisi della domanda in psicologia clinica [Analysis of the demand in clinical psychology]*. Milano: Giuffrè.
Carli R. & Paniccia R.M. (2003). *Analisi della domanda: Teoria e tecnica dell'intervento in psicologia clinica [Analysis of demand. Theory and tecnique of the intervention in clinical psychology].* Bologna: Il mulino.
Carli R. & Paniccia R.M. (2004). *L'analisi emozionale del testo: Uno strumento psicologico per leggere testi e discorsi [The emotional textual analysis. A tool for reading texts and discourses].* Milano: Franco Angeli.
Fornari F. (1979) *I fondamenti di una teoria psicoanalitica del linguaggio [Foundations for a psychoanalytic theory of the language].* Torino: Boringhieri.
Freud S. (1899, trad. ita. 1966). L'interpretazione dei sogni [The interpretation of dreams]. In: *Opere*, vol. 3. Torino: Boringhieri.
Giacchetta A., Martello A., Nannini V., Riglioni A. & Vicanolo F. (2017). La rigenerazione delle comunità in termini di sviluppo produttivo: Un caso-studio sulla cultura locale nell'agro-romano antico [The regeneration of communities in terms of productive development: A case-study on local culture in the ancient agro-Roman]. *(S)radicamenti Società di studi geografici. Memorie geografiche* in Aa.Vv., NS 15, 809-815.
Grasso M. & Salvatore S. (1997*). Pensiero e decisionalità: contributo alla critica della prospettiva individualista in psicologia [Thought and*

        decision-making: a contribution to the individualist perspective in psychology critique]. Milano, FrancoAngeli.
Graves T. D. (1967). Psychological acculturation in a tri-ethnic community. *Southwestern Journal of Anthropology, Vol. 23(4), 337-35.*
Lancia F. (2004). *Strumenti per l'analisi dei testi: Introduzione all'uso di T-LAB [Tools for text analysis. Introduction to the use of T-Lab].* Milano: FrancoAngeli.
Groterath A. et al. (2018). Die Viernheim-Studie. Eine psychologische Untersuchung zur Integration von Geflüchteten in einer deutschen Gemeinde [The Viernheim study: A psychological study of the integration of refugees in a German community]. Veröffentlicht am 24.05.2018. In: *Socialnet Materialien* unter*http://www.socialnet.de/materialien/28146.php*
Langher V., Caputo A. & Martino G. (2017). What happened to the clinical approach to case study in psychological research? A clinical psychological analysis of scientific articles in high impact-factor journals. *Mediterranean Journal of Clinical Psychology, Vol. 5(3).*
Langher V., Ricci M.E., Propersi F., Glumbic N. & Caputo A. (2017). Inclusion in Mozambique: A case study on a cooperative learning intervention. *Cultura Y Educaciòn Vol. 28(1), 42-71.*
Matte Blanco I. (1975). *The unconscious as infinite sets*. London: Duckworth.
Mera, M.J., Martínez-Zelaya, G., Bilbao, M.A., & Garrido, A. (2017). Chilenos ante la inmigración: un estudio de las relaciones entre orientaciones de aculturación, percepción de amenaza y bienestar social en el Gran Concepción [Chile's approach to immigration: a study of the relationship between approaches to acculturation, threat perception and social well-being in the Great Convention]. *Universitas Psychologica, Vol. 16(5).*
Neto F., Barros J. & Schmitz P.G. (2005). Acculturation attitudes and adaptation among Portuguese immigrants in Germany: Integration or separation. *Psychology and Developing Societies Vol.17(1), 19-3.*
Paniccia R.M. (2012a). Psicologia clinica e disabilità: La competenza a integrare differenze [Clinical psychology and disability: the competence to integrate differences]. *Rivista di Psicologia Clinica, Vol.1, 91-110.*
Paniccia, R.M. (2012b). Gli assistenti all'autonomia e all'integrazione per la disabilità a scuola: Da ruoli confusi a funzioni chiare [The assistants to autonomy and integration for disability in school: From confusing roles to clear functions]. *Rivista di Psicologia Clinica, Vol. 2, 165-183.*

Redfield R., Linton R. & Herskovits M. J. (1936). Memorandum for the study of acculturation. *American Anthropologist, Vol. 38(1), 149-152.*
Salvatore S. & Freda M. F. (2011). Affect, unconscious and sense-making: A psychodynamic semiotic and dialogic model. *New Ideas in Psychology Vol. 29, 119-135.*
Schwartz S. J., Zamboanga B. L. & Jarvis L. H. (2007). Identity and acculturation in Hispanic early adolescents: Mediated relationships to academic grades, prosocial behaviors, and externalizing symptoms. *Cultural Diversity and Ethnic Minority Psychology, Vol. 13(4) 364–373.*
Scottham K. M. & Dias R. H (2010) Acculturative strategies and the psychological adaptation of Brazilian migrants to Japan. *Identity: An International Journal of Theory and Research, Vol. 10, 284–303.*
Van De Vijver F.J.R. & Phalet K. (2004) Assessment in multicultural groups: The role of acculturation. *Applied Psychology, Vol. 53(2), 215-236.*
Ward C., Stuart J. & Kus L. (2011) The construction and validation of a measure of Ethno-Cultural Identity Conflict. *Journal of Personality Assessment, Vol, 93(5), 462–473.*
Ward C. (2013) Probing identity, integration and adaptation: Big questions, little answers. International *Journal of Intercultural Relations, Vol.37 (4), 391-404.*
Zagefka H. & Brown R. (2002) The relationship between acculturation strategies, relative fit and intergroup relations: Immigrant-majority relations in Germany. *European Journal of Social Psychology, Vol 32, 171–188.*

Resilience and Posttraumatic Growth of Refugee Women – One Study and Two [Types of] Results

Lena Pschiuk, Viviana Langher, Giorgia Marinelli, Angelika Groterath

Background – a BA thesis

As part of her BA thesis in social work, Lena Pschiuk has conducted a study on refugee women's responses to traumatic experiences caused by war and displacement. Unlike the majority of researchers and practitioners, she has focused on the positive responses of women, a phenomenon she had become aware of in a year abroad that made up part of her studies in social work.

In winter 2016/2017 she spent four months working in a then new refugee housing project in Athens. For many of the refugees, the road to Europe had ended on a Greek island: the doors into Europe had almost been closed in 2016. The former strategy of adult males traveling to a European country with the prospect of family reunion had been interrupted by legal decisions.

Lena Pschiuk and her co-researchers, German students with internship or volunteer experiences in refugee shelters in Germany, were surprised: They realised that they had got used to the picture of a refugee as a young male. In Athens, instead, the large majority of the refugees they met were women and children. Female refugees are often pictured as victims; and in part they undoubtedly are. But the women stuck in Athens and on their own for longer than ever before in most of the cases, aroused the German students' interest in their resilience or even personal growth developed through coping with a life-threatening situation.

Lena's interest persisted over time in her second semester abroad, a semester she spent at the German Jordanian University in Amman where she benefited from the diploma Course "Migration and Refugees" that GJU had set up in view of the need to improve professionalism in social work with refugees and migrants. When she came back to Germany to finish her studies, she was well prepared to undertake an empirical investigation on flight and migration:

- She was in contact with day centres for refugees in Athens.
- She had acquired a basic knowledge of Arabic, mastered simple communication - and had found in Athens as well as in Amman friends who could help her with translation.
- She had not only acquired sound theoretical knowledge on the

challenges and burden of migration and flight, but she had also developed her own resilience and communication skills.
- In winter 2017/2018 she was involved in working on the Viernheim study described in this volume and got to know Viviana Langher, Giorgia Marinelli and the "Italian psychology"[1].

The investigation

The investigation focused on resilience and posttraumatic growth. Evidently, the author reviewed relevant literature on PTSD and resilience to carve out her research questions. One result of this literature review was, as might be expected, that the attention of the research community, which is based more in the north than in the south, on positive adaptation of refugees to their context, is limited, while attention to PTSD and trauma are prevailing.

The research questions

4.3.1. What are refugee women's neutral (resilience) and positive (posttraumatic growth) responses to traumatic experiences caused by war and displacement specifically in the transitional phase?
4.3.2. In which way do their experiences strengthen them?
4.3.3. Is growth after adversity possible?

(Pschiuk, 2018, p. 24)

The sample

The sample was a convenience sample and included seven refugee girls and women between the ages of 15 and 48, residing in in Athens. They could have

---

1   The term "Italian Psychology" has been coined by Angelika Groterath, who has been living in Italy for many years. She had seen how skilfully many Italian psychologists applied theories and findings of psychoanalysis to communities and social groups and how efficient the practical measures arising from them were. It was on Angelika's agenda, to use the methods that have been developed in Italy for such community research and to apply the find-ings to the benefit of communities or society also in Germany – an add-on to the common social work methods, in her opinion.

or have had the plan to move on to a third country to either be resettled or reunited with their families. All participants came from an Arabic speaking country, due to there being only an Arabic female translator available and ready to volunteer in the interviews. Only one translator for Arabic was available for the transcription of the interviews and the translation of the written material into English.
Other features:

Country of origin: 5 women from Syria, 2 from Iraq
Marital status: 4 women married, 3 unmarried
Children: 3 women with children, 4 childless
Educational background: 6 women with ed. background, 1 without

Two of the participants travelled to Greece on their own whereas the others travelled with her families.[2]

Interview procedure and transcription

It took courage, effort, stamina and a good network to find the interview partners and to conduct these interviews in a conbination of English, Arabic and Greek, and the procedures are best described by the investigator herself:

> The interviews were conducted in two Athenian institutions, the Melissa network[3] and the Jafra Foundation for Relief and Youth Development[4]. Interviews came about spontaneously while being on-site, with special help from the responsible psychologist in the case of the Melissa network and the project manager of the Jafra Foundation for Relief and Youth Development. After introducing and discussing the project with them, they supported the research team by finding potential interviewees. Access was eased, as both were perceived as persons of trust in the institutions. The interviews were conducted with the kind support of a female translator for Arabic, English and German, Ms. Alisa Mayer. Firstly, introducing each other in Arabic and briefly describing the research purpose of exploring positive experiences of refugee women lightened up the situation. At the beginning of the interview situation, a consent form in Arabic language was signed by all participants to guarantee confidentiality, the voluntary participation in the project and the use of audio recording.

2   For more information about the sampling and the sample, compare Pschiuk (2018).
3   Melissa Network is a network for migrant women in Greece, promoting empowerment, communication and active citizenship.
4   Jafra Foundation for Relief and Youth Development is an international non-profit organization registered in Belgium, Sweden, Greece and Lebanon. In Greece, the team of volunteers, who are refugees themselves, work on the topics of emergency response, shelter, child protection, capacity building and livelihoods.

The interviews started whenever the women were ready. Despite few interruptions, the interview flow was not disturbed. It was of great importance for the interviewees to feel comfortable and relaxed, knowing that they could express their thoughts and feelings without being judged and perceiving the communication being on eye and heart level. The aim of the study was to gain an authentic and genuine insight into the participants' personal experiences and perceptions on the topic, which is why the interviewer and translator did not give their view on the spoken word but exclusively showed understanding, approval and empathy. While an open attitude in qualitative research is important, avoiding bias is often challenging due to the existing knowledge inherent in the questions of the interviewer. Questions can be leading. Helfferich (2011) suggests conscious awareness, critical reflexion and control over one's selective attentiveness due to the acquired prior knowledge.

The interviews lasted ten to twelve minutes on average. Afterwards, the interviewer, the interviewee and the translator often proceeded with an informal talk, mostly related to the research topic. Afterwards, the interviews were transcribed and translated from Arabic to English by Mr. Deya Debaja. He is a translator based in Jordan who kindly supported the researcher.

(Pschiuk, 2018, 32ff).

Two [types of] results

As the title of this paper suggests, the empirical material that Lena Pschiuk has collected, has been evaluated twice. In her BA thesis, Pschiuk has done what is customary and considered to be appropriate in the Applied Social Sciences in Germany: She collected and evaluated the empirical material with a qualitative research method that has proven to be valuable, the qualitative content analysis by Mayring (Mayring, 2010).

We do appreciate the method and the results obtained by it; but since Lena Pschiuk's investigation can be considered unique, also in the sense of being hardly reproducible, we want to use the empirical material for further evaluation. We want to go deeper, as could be said, and analyse the material from a psychological perspective. With Mayring's approach we remain on the rational side, no matter how many "hermeneutic spirals" we make. This approach considers what is rationally available and does not grasp the unconscious. We are instead interested in the unconscious, in the collusive dynamics, i.e. in the emotional symbolisation of the context that these refugee women in Athens share, analyse what these women have said, by Emotional Text Analysis (ETA) after Carli & Paniccia (Carli & Paniccia, 2004), because central to ETA is Freud's and post-Freudians' conceptualisation of the unconscious. We want to understand the unconscious psychological dimension in the refugee women's flight experience. What drives them? What keeps them upright? What lets them go on, or what pushes them forward?

Hence, we complement the results obtained with the Qualitative Content Analysis with the insights that we gain by Emotional Text Analysis. The theories and the evaluation methods of Carli et al. are described in detail in other contributions to this volume. We restrict our presentation to a brief description of the actual evaluation at the University of La Sapienza Rome in December 2018, and to the results that this evaluation has provided.

Evaluation one: qualitative content analysis by mayring

The method

Mayring's method is used to analyse subjective perspectives in textual material with the aim of reducing the qualitative material to the core message. In this case, a summarising content analysis was applied, which entails the paraphrasing of the content and reducing it step by step to the most relevant information. The categories that are being formed are discovered in the text in an inductive manner.

Still, these categories are developed according to specific criteria, based on the literature, which is why the process is of inductive and deductive character concurrently (Flick, 2009; Mayring, 2010). The focus of this research was on exploring experiences of resilience and posttraumatic growth in refugee women in the transitional phase and probing the validity of both concepts. Hence, the categories were: community perspectives on strength, individual perspectives on strength, sources of strength on the journey and in transit, growth processes.

The results

As Ungar (2008, p.221) states it is crucial to comprehend "[…] the context in which the resources to nurture resilience are found in order to avoid hegemony in how we characterise successful development and good coping strategies". It is therefore relevant to discover the communities' and individuals' understanding of strength and resilience and to grasp people's views on well-being concepts in a more holistic and culturally embedded way (Afana et al., 2010).

Independence and self-reliance

The study revealed that the interviewees perceived independence and self-reliance as being one of the strongest sources of strength in the community as well as on the individual level. The women mentioned educational choices, occupational opportunities as well as financial independence as being relevant and strengthening to them. If we consider Syrian and Iraqi societies as rather collectivist societies where traits such as loyalty, responsibility for and strong interdependence between members of the in-group matter (Hofstede, 2001), then the rather individualistic answers of the interviewees which imply the strive for personal autonomy and self-fulfillment are interesting findings.

Religion

Religion, often mentioned as source of strength in literature, was not perceived as being strengthening by the majority. Religion is understood rather as being culturally inherent and infused into social practices. Besides, religious and spiritual growth was not mentioned as an experience had by the interviewees despite being relevant in the PTG theory by Tedeschi et al. (2004): "One of the women mentioned that war makes you question your belief and makes you forget about religion while the psychological stain through adversity is predominant" (Pschiuk, 2018).

Social support and cognitive processes

The study further revealed that social support and cognitive processes, of note in resilience and PTG literature, were relevant for the women's perception of strength and beneficial for growth. Social support systems could comprise of family, friends or networks such as volunteers working in camps or NGOs. Refugee women's cognitive processes concentrated on hopes for the future and having specific goals in their mind in order to provide for a better future.

Occupation and commitment

Occupation and commitment were aspects repeatedly mentioned as being a source of strength and resilience shaping by interviewees. While information on beneficial impacts of occupation and commitment in transit could not be taken from literature, Silove's (2013) ADAPT model relates to the significance of re-establishing meaningful roles in society. Several interviewees stated the strengthening effect of being able to contribute their knowledge and skills in society in any station of transit.

The research results show that survivor processes are highly individual and distinctive with every survivor showing and applying different coping strategies and protective factors. Focusing on the transit period including experiences made on the way to Greece, gave new insights into the psychological and social impact migration has on refugees.

Furthermore, the attempt to focus on strengths and resources emphasised in the interviewees these strong survivor processes and their acquired skills which are too often blanked out when applying a prevalent medicalised view on people of concern.

Results thus give evidence to the necessity of creating and providing safe, stable and supportive environments for refugees throughout the migration phases. According to Silove (2013), "[...] restoring the psychosocial pillars that have been disrupted through war and displacement as well as internalising a strength-based approach in order to recognize, support and encourage people's resiliency, their inner strengths and resources and their possibility to grow" are of great significance (Pschiuk, 2018, p. 47). This in turn can make a major contribution towards creating healthy, resilient and stable societies.

Evaluation two – Emotional Textual Analysis by Carli and Paniccia (2004)

The actual evaluation procedure

Emotional Text Analysis is a computer assisted statistical text analysis based on psychoanalytic theory of language [Fornari's "double reference" (Fornari, 1979)] and mind [Matte Blanco's "bi-logic" (Matte Blanco, 1980)], which account both for the rational-operative and emotional-symbolic meaning of the language. This analysis requires that a text is fully transcribed so that the software can process its vocabulary according to several parameters (total number of different forms, frequency of each form, indexes of vocabulary specificity, etc.).

Lena Pschiuk provided the English transcripts of the interviews for an evaluation that Groterath, Langher and Marinelli carried out in December 2018 with a Masters class in clinical psychology from La Sapienza University in Rome[5]. We transcribed the interviews in such a way that we were able to evaluate them with Franco Lancia's T-Lab.

The loss of value or meaning, or even the misinterpretation, that results from applying the Emotional Text Analysis to translations, not to native-

---

5 Thanks to Andrea Caputo, post-doc fellowship at the department of dynamic and clinical psychology, Sapienza University.

language texts, must be accepted. Such losses of value are always there, where textual work is done qualitatively. An advantage of using the English texts is that in English much less time has to be spent on lemmatisation than in German and Arabic.

The lemmatisation is a linguistic procedure which reduces the lexical forms to their common root: for example, the words "announcing", "announce" and "announced" can be reduced to the common root [to]announce. Lemmatisation aims at containing the lexical dispersion, as different forms are transformed in the same lemma thus connoting more clearly the specific vocabulary of a given text.

The questions Pschiuk asked were:

1) What gives people in your community strength despite facing difficult situations?
2) How would you personally define strength?
3) When you think of your way to Greece, what kept you strong? What made you strong?

   a) Social support
   b) Religious awareness
   c) Cognitive strategies
   d) Other

4) What have you learned through your experiences in Greece? Do you feel you have grown?

   a) Social (relating to others and belonging)
   b) Individual (personal strengths and new opportunities)
   c) Spiritual & philosophical (religiosity and appreciation in life)

5) Would you like to add anything?

The results

The Emotional Text Analysis, from a statistical point of view, is based on the thematic analysis of the elementary contexts, which performs both cluster analysis and multiple correspondence analysis. The clusters are formed by co-occurrences of words listed by t-lab according their chi-square values, from higher to lower. Normally, we limit our interpretation to the first fifteen words from the list. We treat the co-occurrences of words in terms of "free associations", the classic psychoanalytic technique to gain access to the unconscious of the patients. In our case, the free associations of words help us to understand the interviewees' affective symbolisations of their condition as refugees.

For reasons of space, we limit ourselves to highlighting the clusters in that we identified in the text material with the T-Lab software of Franco Lancia and to present our interpretations of these clusters.

The clusters are showed in table 1, for each one of the four clusters the lemmas and the related chi-square values are showed.

Table 1: Clusters of dense words ordered by Chi-square

Cluster 1		Cluster 2		Cluster 3		Cluster 4	
Lemma	χ^2	*Lemma*	χ^2	*Lemma*	χ^2	*Lemma*	χ^2
Greece	63.22	year	62.67	Allah	13.96	religion	30.98
country	53.47	Germany	51.57	education	13.96	know	21.60
people	21.67	fear	31.85	support	12.29	life	21.28
change	15.99	thought	25.62	_INT_M	12.00	english	19.98
European	13.89	rely	21.19	strong	11.04	talk	12.46
love	9.57	leave	18.89	degree	10.24	aspect	9.96
mind	9.57	old	15.40	job	10.24	good	8.52
nice	9.57	set	15.40	play	10.24	girl	8.42
friend	8.19	family	15.01	child	9.44	learn	7.26
school	7.44	uncle	8.94	ask	8.89	Greek	5.19
know	6.75	brother	8.75	feel	8.89	hard	5.19
hear	6.38	get_out	7.29	work	8.31	Hope	4.82
world	6.38	marry	7.29	reason	8.18	bit	4.24
meet	5.73	son	7.29	study	7.97	area	4.20
turkey	4.88	_INT_A	6.35	_QUE_02	7.90	start	4.20
_INT_S	4.31	travel	6.00	help	7.63	teacher	4.20

Source: The present research

Figure 1: Cluster 1

Source: The present research

Cluster 1 – Odysseus and the Feacis

This cluster seems to represent the hopes that have accompanied the women on their journey to Europe. The verbs and adjectives contain a fantasy of relationship with the other, oriented towards exchange, to listening and friendliness, relationships based on love and kindness. "Greece", the first word, seems to be the container of all hope for the future. This cluster let us think of the joy that women feel, for having achieved their goal, of having arrived where they wanted to arrive, welcomed nicely by the new, the European, world. A new world where one could go to school, make new friends. Also, the theme of the journey emerges, of the path made both physically and psychologically to arrive at all this, the passage from neighbouring Turkey to Greece.

The mythical image that came to our mind was that of Odysseus, welcomed on the banks of the Feacis, a people dear to the Gods, who magnificently welcomed Odysseus and his companions honouring them with every good thing.

Figure 2: Cluster 2

Source: The present research

Cluster 2 – Masculine Germany

This group of associations arouses a sense of anguish and concern, suspended in an atmosphere of expectation and immobility. "Germany" is the country where many refugees have been received and where probably family members have already settled. "Year" let us think of the year to come, of what will await them. Fear in connection with Germany could be the fear of what will happen once you get there. Thinking of rejoining the family seems to evoke conflicting feelings. On the one side rejoining, which is also returning to depend on the family, and on the other side the feeling of leaving old ties, as if there was a desire for independence that could be threatened by family reunification. All the words that are used to refer to family members are masculine words, from uncle through brother to son, suggesting that it is the male component of the family that arouses this kind of fear.

Figure 3: Cluster 3

Source: The present research

Cluster 3 – God with them wherever

God as the first word of the cluster remind us of propitiatory function of this word, as if it were a lucky hat for what we expect in the new country (Insh'allah: "If God wills it"; mandatory when making a prediction or expressing a desire for the future). After God, follow the words education, support, strong, degree and job, and that lets think of career and professional realisation. In the middle of the cluster, among the various educational and professional expectations, the words play and child appear, as if to indicate a child-like element present in these women that in the new country can find its expression, a child-like part eager to grow and experiment, to know the world and have fun doing it.

What we felt when reading these words was a sense of excitement and power, as if this new country gave them energy and a desire to experiment in many different areas, such as work and study, and the possibility of asking for all this. But it also seems to open up an inner reflection on one's condition of dependence on help and having to decide whether to stay or to leave and join their families.

Figure 4: Cluster 4

Source: The present research

Cluster 4: The life of the girls

The word "religion" that opens the associative chain seems to have a more social than mystical meaning, as the whole cluster speaks of exchange with a new context. It is accepted that one has to come into contact with a new society, with its language, Greek or English, with the way of living and talking, with its difficulties but also with its positive sides. Religion appears as a content to be socialised. The verbs of the cluster remind us of a desire for progress and to come into contact with the other, to talk, to have exchanges leading to growth and to a new beginning. The word "girl" suggests that these women can feel small and inexperienced in a big and completely new world, but also that girls are recognised in their individuality and not in a social role such as daughter or wife. The importance of the encounter with the unknown is recognised (with the appearance of "hard") but does not seem to be seen as something insurmountable. It is simply a matter of fact. In fact, "hard" is followed by the word "hope".

Preliminary conclusion – results of the ETA

The text is far from being analysed exhaustively. There would be much to process and to say, starting from an analysis of the factorial space. Here, we do not go much beyond a co-occurence analysis, analysing different kinds of relationships between lexical units – our dense words.

We can, nonetheless, state that our analysis of the interviews with the refugee women confirms Lena Pschiuks initial assumption that personal growth through or against the background of a life threatening experience is possible. The first, the "Odysseus"-cluster, statistically the most stable one, pictures a beautiful arrival. There is anguish and fear in the second cluster, the "masculine Germany". But strength and confidence in their own skills and abilities, the intellectual as well as the emotional ones seem to overcome loss and concern. The self confidence and the trust in life or in the future of these women who have certainly come in touch with death and pain in their past or during their journey, can be considered a sort of manic internal push aimed at overcoming the sense of loss and the consequent mourning. Far from being treated as an "excessive" emotional reaction, this manic internal push has to be considered an emotional resource that gives the women the ability to think forward.

Some "minor" issue or result can even shed light upon two questions about refugees, which, at least in Germany, are a matter of concern:

1) God and religion are not co-occurrent much, but "God"[6] appears in a context of profession, education and studies. Religion, instead, belongs to the girls' life and talks and hopes, to "normal life".

2) There are two gender(ed) clusters among our four clusters; and that speaks for balance. Masculinity is strongly related to Germany, and this corresponds to Hofstede's (Hofstede, 2001) findings about the country. With a score of 66, Germany ranks high in masculinity. The society is driven by competition and success – and even though this cluster 2, the Masculine Germany, is the cluster that speaks about fear and sons and uncles and brothers – could (our) Germany not constitute a great opportunity, particularly for the refugee women?[7]

---

6   The word God.
7   An idea that we, Langher, Marinelli and Groterath, also had in 2018, when we made a follow up to Viernheim study (see Marinelli et al. in this volume) with another group of students. We had constructed a questionnaire and distributed it among refugees in Viernheim. We expected that as men were almost always essentially the only participants in the survey, e.g. the active members of the self-help group "helping hands", it was to our astonishment to find 26 of the 41 questionnaires we received back were filled out by women. We had distributed the questionnaire, which had been translated into Arabic, in the houses where the refugees live in Viernheim (Bode et al., 2018)

Conclusion

The "two types of results" confirm both that self-reliance and self-confidence are almost "characteristics" of the women with refugee experience that have been interviewed. They also remind us to review our European assumptions towards the role of religion among the refugees. And if evaluation number one, the Mayring analysis, calls us to provide social support for the refugees, evaluation number two, the ETA, invites us to 'prepare Feacis' and to welcome those who are arriving. Occupation, jobs, studies, commitment, degrees and learning turn out to be important for the women – in both evaluations.

This study can contribute to better understanding the psycho-social condition of being a refugee, whether female or male. It suggests that not only need to consider the traumatic consequences of escaping one's own country, but we also need to focus on refugees' resilience, self confidence, and to look at their future. We suggest studies like this one should be encouraged in order to better understand refugees' capacity to adjust themesleves to the new situation.

References

Afana, A., Pedersen, D., Ronsbo, H., Kirmayer, L. J. (2010). Endurance Is to Be Shown at the First Blow: Social Representations and Reactions to Traumatic Experiences in the Gaza Strip. *Traumatology*, pp. 1-12.

Bode, E., Höfling, A., Schmahlfeldt, D., & Senz, T. (2018). *Research Viernheim 2.0 "Multikulturalität und Integration in Viernheim", Forschungsbericht.* Hochschule Darmstadt.

Carli, R., & Paniccia, R. M. (2004). *L' analisi emozionale del testo. Uno strumento psicologico per leggere testi e discorsi, [Emotional Text Analysis. A psychological instrument to comprehend texts and discourses].* Milano: Franco Angeli.

Flick, U. (2009). *An Introduction To Qualitative Research*. London: SAGE Publications Ltd.

Fornari, F. (1979). *I fondamenti per una psicoanalisi del linguaggio [The foundadions for a psychoanalysis of the language].* Torino: Bollati Boringhieri.

Helfferich, C. (2011). *Die Qualität qualitativer Daten, Manual für die Durchführung qualitativer Interviews [The quality of qualitative data, manual for performing qualitative interviews].* Wiesbaden: VS Verlag für Sozialwissenschaften.

Hofstede, G. (2001). *Culture's Consequences: Comparing Values, Behaviors, Institutions, and Organizations Across Nations.* Thousand Oaks: Sage Publications.

Matte Blanco, I. (1980). *The Unconscious as Infinite Sets: An Essay in Bi-logic.* London: Routledge.

Mayring, P. (2010). *Qualitative Inhaltsanalyse.* Weinheim und Basel: Beltz Verlag.

Pschiuk, L. (2018). *Resilience and Posttraumatic Growth of Refugee Women: Impacts and Challenges.* Retrieved 11 8, 2019, from socialnet Materialien: https://www.socialnet.de/materialien/28165.php

Silove, D. (2013). The ADAPT model: a conceptual framework for mental health and psychosocial programming in post conflict settings. *Intervention, 11*(3), 237-248.

Ungar, M. (2008). Resilience across Cultures. *British Journal of Social Work*, 218-235.

Trust, identity, and the intercultural mediator's role in the migrant crisis on the South East coast of Sicily[1]

Denise Filmer, Massimo Sturiale[2]

Introduction

This contribution discusses some preliminary findings of a small-scale survey on the linguistic response to the arrivals in Sicily of migrants[3] who cross the Mediterranean Sea. The project, entitled "Sicily - the Backdoor to Europe: the real conditions of mediating and interpreting during migrant emergencies on the South East coast of Sicily", is connected with a broader project on crisis translation (Federici, 2016) and with my postdoctoral fellowship at Catania University's School of Modern Languages in Ragusa.

The study aims to investigate how intercultural mediators, NGO operators working around ports and reception centres in Eastern Sicily, and the "end-users" themselves, the asylum seekers, refugees and migrants, portray their experience of negotiating linguistic and cultural barriers within the context of the ongoing migratory phenomenon. This paper focuses on issues of trust within these interpreting triads, and on the perceptions and practices of intercultural mediation as facilitator of cross-cultural communication. Data was collected adopting ethnographic methods (Crabtree et al., 2012; Rouncefield & Tolmie, 2016) in the form of semi-structured interviews and observations conducted in-situ. A strict process of ethical approval was adhered to in order to protect those interviewees who could be considered vulnerable respondents. The interviews for this part of the project were carried out between October 2017 and December 2017. Following applications to the

---

1   This contribution is based on an article first published in a Special Issue of *MediAzioni* Online Journal http://www.mediazioni.sitlec.unibo.it/index.php/no-24-2019.html
2   Professor Massimo Sturiale was the supervisor for the postdoctoral fellowship entitled "Translation, Migration, and the Sociolinguistics of Migration" (ERC 2016:SH4_8 SH4_12). The research presented here was part of the proposed project, "The migration of meaning: semantic shifts, news translation, and the language of immigration in news discourse on the migrant crisis", which won the award. Sections 1-8 were written by Filmer, who wishes to express her profound gratitude to Prof. Sturiale for all his help and support.
3   No term concerning migration is ever neutral; while some terms have very specific legal meanings (e.g. refugees, asylum seekers, permanent residents, etc.), others, like "migrant" have taken on a pejorative meaning. However, for expediency, we opted for the term "migrant" to cover all categories of people landing on the coasts and at the ports of Italy having moved from their place of origin, and "immigration" for legally specific policies dealing with people movement in the Italian juridical system.

relevant Sicilian authorities and having been granted permission to proceed, the research was carried out in two port areas and in two different types of reception centre.

The first, CARA di Mineo (ordinary reception centre), was the largest reception centre for asylum seekers in Europe until the beginning of 2019[4], and was under the jurisdiction of the Prefecture of Catania. The second, a CAS, (centro accoglienza straordinaria - the so-called emergency reception centres created in 2014 and run by regional cooperatives), is under the jurisdiction of the Prefecture of Ragusa. The study presented here is divided into two parts: the first part contextualises the data in the current Italian socio-political scenario and presents the methodological and theoretical framework for the research. The second part discusses samples of the qualitative data collected in the form of observations and comments from the participants interviewed on the themes of trust and identity. The article begins with a brief update on the migrant situation in Europe and recent developments in the Italian political scenario that have influenced national policy on immigration and the provision of first and second reception, inevitably impacting on linguistic and cultural mediation services.

Migratory flows and current policy – an overview

At the time of writing, the reception system for migrants in Italy is undergoing radical reform. As mentioned above, data collection for this study took place at the end of 2017. Since then, the reduced dimensions of the migratory flow and the Lega-5SM coalition government's aggressive anti-immigration policies have altered the legal and political landscape in which intercultural mediation takes place. Nevertheless, the research and its outcomes are by no means obsolete. On the contrary, what can be evidenced is that the precarious system of linguistic and cultural mediation in place at the time of carrying out the interviews will undergo drastic disruption and reduction due to the new measures introduced with the latest legislation on immigration.

As can be seen from the table below, the numbers of arrivals in Europe have decreased by approximately 35% from 2017 to 2018. The sharpest decline is clearly in Italy where arrivals in 2018 were 85% down on 2017 (see table 1 below). The number of migrants reaching the peninsula in 2017 had

---

4 Since data collection was carried out, the Italian Minister for the Interior, Matteo Salvini, took the controversial decision to close CARA di Mineo by the end of 2019. At the time of writing, the remaining guests are in the process of being transferred to smaller CAS in neighbouring regions in Sicily.

already fallen to 19,369 from a peak of 181,436 in 2016[5] due to the Italian government's pact with Libya. In February 2017 the then minister of the interior, Social Democrat Marco Minniti signed the so-called Memorandum with the leader of the UN-recognised government, Fayez al-Serraj introducing a new level of cooperation between the Libyan coastguard and the Italians, including the provision of four patrol vessels.

Table 1: Arrivals by sea and deaths in the Mediterranean 2017-2018

Total arrivals by sea and deaths in the Mediterranean 2017-2018 (January 2018-1 December 2018)

2018			2017		
107,583 total arrivals by sea			164,908 total arrivals by sea.		
2,133 total dead/missing			3,113 total dead/missing		
Deaths	Arrivals	Country	Arrivals	Deaths
1,285	23,011	Italy	117,120	2,844
681	52,678	Spain	20,043	208
167	29,782	Greece	27,244	61
0	930	Cyprus	501	0
0	1,182	Malta	0	0

Source: The International Organisation for Migration. All numbers are minimum estimates. Arrivals are based on data from respective governments

The statistics seem to indicate, as Salvini and other political representatives have sustained, that Minniti's "Memorandum di Intesa" and the refusal to allow humanitarian vessels to disembark refugees at Sicilian ports are "necessary" tactics that have succeeded in decreasing the number of migrants who land on the Italian coastline. What the political class in Italy and Europe have chosen to ignore, however, is the gravity of the situation in the Libyan detention centres[6], or "lagers"[7], as they have been termed, and the cascading effects in humanitarian terms on those refugees who are forced to remain in Libya for extended periods and then eventually manage to reach European shores (see Filmer forthcoming). Further legislation has been introduced, known as the "decreto sicurezza" (security decree), which provides for "Disposizioni urgenti in materia di protezione internazionale e immigrazione, sicurezza pubblica" (Urgent measures for international protection and immigration, public security) that was approved by the Italian Parliament on

---

5   https://www.iom.int/news/mediterranean-migrant-arrivals-top-363348-2016-deaths-sea-5079
6   http://www.infomigrants.net/en/post/6078/cnn-reporters-show-migrants-auctioned-off-in-libya
7   http://mediciperidirittiumani.org/quattro-anni-assistenza-ai-migranti-sopravvissuti-alla-violenza-estrema/

28th November 2018. The measures aim to curb what Salvini has referred to as 'la pacchia' (the gravy train) for immigrants, operators and cooperatives that provide first and second reception, including the abolition of residence permits for humanitarian reasons. They are substituted with "special temporary permits" that can only be issued for the following motives: particularly serious health problems; natural disaster in the country of origin; acts of civil valour; victims of human trafficking, domestic violence and cases of "serious exploitation".

Foreign nationals may now be held for up to 180 days in the "centri di permanenza per il rimpatrio" (repatriation centres)[8], instead of the 90 days previously in force. Migrants may also be detained in other types of reception facilities if there are no places available in the CPRs: even the hotspots located in port areas can now be used for extended periods. The conditions for international protection have been reduced with the introduction of more offences that would result in the denial or revocation of refugee status. In an open letter to government officials including Salvini and the Health Minister Giulia Grillo, several humanitarian medical agencies operating in Italy such as "Emergency", "Società Italiana di Medicina delle Migrazioni", "Medici contro la Tortura", "Médecins du Monde", "Medici per i Diritti Umani" (MEDU) and, Medici Senza Frontiere expressed their dismay at the serious erosion of human rights and the impact the laws would have on the health of migrants and refugees arriving on Italian shores. This brief overview of the current Italian political scenario with regards immigration serves to illustrate the context in which the research is situated. The next section outlines the research methodology and reflects on the methodological caveats associated with this type of project.

The study, its contexts, and its participants

Access to the ports, to CARA di Mineo, and to the "Centri di accoglienza straordinaria", or CAS, in order to collect data required high-level authorisation that took time and effort to be granted. The Port of Pozzallo, which is under the jurisdiction of the Prefecture of Ragusa, gave me access to the port itself but declined access to the Pozzallo Hotspot, the most important first reception and identification centre in Sicily, and consequently during 2016 and 2017 also in Europe. Arriving refugees and migrants stay for a purported limited period of maximum 72 hours immediately following their arrival on Italian soil. Recently, however, MEDU denounced the fact that 73 migrants had spent over two months in the centre, seriously putting their psychological

---

8 All translations are from Filmer unless otherwise stated

and physical health at risk[9]. The port of Catania, a large and busy commercial port is under the jurisdiction of the Prefecture of Catania. Access to the disembarkation area was granted, under the condition that I only observed and did not interrupt disembarkation. I witnessed two disembarkation processes and approached prospective participants whom I subsequently contacted in order to carry out interviews.

CARA di Mineo, also within the jurisdiction of the Prefecture of Catania but requiring separate authorisation, has frequently been in the national news. Due to its size, its isolated location, and the institutional complexity of its organisation, it has often been prey to alleged associations with the Mafia and accusations of corruption (Latza Nadeau, 2018) due to the lucrative contracts tendered by the Prefecture for its management. Reports of the centre's frequent overcrowding since it was established in 2011 have also aroused media attention, with guests peaking at nearly 4,000 in 2016 at the height of the landings in Sicily.

At the time of data collection, of the centre's 380 staff, 30 were intercultural mediators. Since then, the harsh anti-immigration policies of the new Italian government have had a drastic impact on the number of migrants reaching Italian shores[10]. From January 1st to December 1st, 2018, there were 23,011 arrivals in Italy by sea, compared to 117,120 in 2017. For the first half of 2019 the numbers have dropped further to 4,897. These reductions in arrivals have given the minister for the interior the pretext for completely closing the centre. At the time of writing the compound still houses approximately 1,500 asylum seekers. Recently, the centre has witnessed protests by the guests against the budget cuts that have reduced services. According to the Palermo edition of the newspaper *La Repubblica*[11], the new management are provided with 15.60 euro per guest to guarantee the provision of "food, accommodation, medical, sanitary and psychological needs along with activities essential for integration for asylum seekers such as Italian lessons, sport, and training courses". Previously, the sum was almost double. What is interesting in this calculation, however, is that no mention is made of the need for cultural mediators or the role of intercultural mediation in preparation for the ensuing integration process.

All my attempts, via official and unofficial means, to establish just how much Salvini's cuts have translated into redundancies for the 30 intercultural mediators that were previously employed by the centre when I went there in October 2017 were met with Sicilian "omertà", or a conspiracy of silence,

9
    https://palermo.repubblica.it/cronaca/2018/10/03/news/pozzallo_da_2_mesi_73_migranti_restano_nell_hotspot_a_rischio_la_loro_salute_psico-fisica_-208084389/
10 https://italy.iom117,120.int/index.php
11
    https://palermo.repubblica.it/cronaca/2018/11/21/news/catania_in_rivolta_i_migranti_del_cara_di_mineo_bloccata_la_statale_per_gela-212209681/

possibly due to fear[12]. However, given the scarce consideration of the intercultural mediator as evidenced by this study, it is reasonable to assume that professional linguistic and cultural support for migrants is low on the list of the present government's priorities and that local authorities will make significant reductions in the numbers of personnel engaged in mediation activities.

In order to gain first-hand accounts of those involved in the mediating triad in the context of the migratory crisis and arrivals to Sicily, face-to-face semi-structured interviews were carried out with the social actors. To date, the only national survey of intercultural mediators was conducted in 2014 and sampled 579 respondents to assess the practitioner's perception of the importance of a professional association and the role of qualifications in obtaining it. Only 81 respondents worked in the 8-region geographical category "Mezzogiorno" including Sicily; only 10.7% of the total respondents had experience working in CARAs (Catarci & Fiorucci, 2014). Interviewing 6 intercultural mediators specialised in first points of contact and reception centres is a significant sample in relation to data currently available. Before beginning the interviews, participants were given a consent form, which they were asked to read, complete and sign before the interviews took place. They had the opportunity to ask questions about the study and their participation before signing the form, as well as at the end of the interview (with recorder off). The semi-structured protocol started with a general question on the informant's background and experience. Specifying gender has been avoided where it could be a decisive indicator as to the informant's identity. It has been included in cases where gender impacts on the discussion and the informant's identity is not at risk.

Table 2 (below) summarises anonymised details of the participants in the interviews.

Table 2: Informants for the study

Intercultural mediators (IM)	**Operators (O)**	**Migrants (M)**
IM1: Tunisian female. Age: 30-40. Role: IM at CARA Mineo. Languages: AR, FR, EN. IT	O1. Age: 40-50 Role: Paramedic for Frontex6	M1. Nigerian female. Age: 20-30 Place: CARA Mineo, interview in English
IM2: White Italian female. Age: 30-40 Role: IM for ASR (Regional Health Service) province of Syracuse.	O2. Age:30-40 Role: Medic and Red Cross volunteer working inside CARA Mineo	M2. Moroccan male. Age: 40-50 Place: CARA Mineo, interview in Arabic

---

12 https://www.lasicilia.it/news/cronaca/179839/cara-di-mineo-ora-gli-operatori-hanno-paura-meno-ospiti-meno-lavoro.html

Languages: AR,FR, EN, IT		M3. Malian male
IM3: White Italian female Age: 40-50 Role- self-employed IM. Languages: FR, EN, IT	O3. Age:30-40 Role: Red Cross Volunteer	Age: 20-30 Place: three years in CARA Mineo, interview in Italian
IM4: Eritrean male Age: 30-40 Eritrean male Role: self-employed IM and interpreter working at CAS, with the police and judiciary in the province of Ragusa. Languages: IT, EN (very little) Tigrigna	O4. Age:40-50 Role: Prison Psychologist	M4. Gambian male Age: 30-40 Place: CAS Filotea, interview in English
IM5. Eritrean male Age: 30-40 Role: IM, employed by UNHCR. Languages: IT, EN, FR, and Tigrigna [permanent resident with refugee background]		M5. Senegalese male Age: 30-40 Place: CAS Filotea, interview in Italian
IM6 Italian female Age: 30-40 Role: IM at CARA Mineo Languages FR, EN, IT,		

Source: The present research

Methods and Methodological caveats

On the very issue of trust, undoubtedly the biggest obstacle in carrying out research of this type is obtaining the necessary collaboration from the institutions. The sample does not include social actors from the law enforcement agencies. Despite concerted efforts to include opinions from institutional actors (coast guard, police, carabinieri, or members of the judiciary registering the migrants), I was unable to secure authorisation so that those participants were backed by their institutions. Individual operators working in these sectors whom I contacted were willing to speak on an informal and anonymous basis but were reluctant to make their participation official; the stumbling block was often signing the consent form.

For the purposes of the study institutional collaboration is essential. More time would therefore be needed to gain the trust of the said institutions. On the other hand, as is discussed in what follows, a significant sample of those working across the medical field has shed valuable insight on multilingual interaction and issues trust in the interpreting triad in which they are involved.

Language difficulties

While the first and second categories of participants were initially reticent and a little wary of my questions, the migrants themselves were quite willing to share their experiences. In transcribing the interviewees' narratives, however, one obvious drawback became apparent: the intercultural and linguistic difficulties that must be overcome for comprehension and understanding to take place. I had assumed before embarking on the interviews that most of the guests at Cara Mineo and at the CAS would be willing to do the interview in English, which for many of them would be a second language. Only a couple whose second language is French preferred to do the interview in Italian, for example, M.3, who had been resident at the CARA for three years. I found Pidgin English as spoken by Nigerians challenging in terms of comprehension; on occasion I had difficulty understanding what the interviewees were saying.

This consideration was also brought to the fore by two young intercultural mediators I subsequently spoke to, one of whom suggested that on a degree programme for intercultural mediation more attention should be placed on world Englishes rather than British English. Cultural assumptions were, however, on both sides. Some of the guests were surprised that in Italy people do not speak English; the Nigerians and Gambians interviewed commented that Italians, who are "white and European", do not know English. They had supposed that in Europe everyone should know English. Some guests did not know where they had disembarked in Sicily. All of them arrived with rescue ships but there are several ports: Augusta, Pozzallo, Messina, Catania, Agrigento, and Palermo. All of them were transferred by bus to CARA di Mineo, which is in the middle of nowhere, a non-place. Geographically, these people have no idea where they are, nor do they have contact with the indigenous population. After six months of being on Italian soil, M1 does not speak nor understand Italian and says that it is pointless to go to Catania on the Mineo bus (which visits the city once a week) in order to go shopping, as her language of communication is English and many Italians she encounters do not speak English.

The CAS visited hosts 75 residents, all male. It has six Italian cultural mediators who work in shifts round the clock, covering English, French and Arabic. Non-Italian intercultural mediators are called upon as and when needed to cover some African dialects such as Tigrigna and Wolof – this information was provided by the accompanying officers who acted as the official source of information during the interviews. The interviewees themselves claimed it was actually very difficult to find a mediator when needed, especially for meetings with lawyers and asylum hearings. For day to day requirements broken English would suffice on both sides.

The question of trust and advocacy in mediating multilingual crisis situations: moving towards source or target culture?

In situations of emergency, Wray (2006, p.45) affirms that "trust is essential to effective communication". More specifically, when lives are at stake "trust plays a vital role in establishing the conditions for effective coordination among otherwise separate organisations in the humanitarian relief environment" (Stephenson Jr., 2005, p.343). The issue of trust, then, is essential to communication and collaboration under crisis conditions; even more so when communications take place in multilingual contexts. Within the discipline of translation studies, the sociological turn has redefined translators and interpreters as social agents that may (or may not) exert power and influence in situations of conflict, injustice, power inequality, and advocacy (Olohan & Davitti 2015). From this perspective, along with issues of ethics and neutrality, trust becomes a crucial factor to all translational acts (Chesterman 1997: 180–83; Pym, 2004), particularly in interpreting and mediation (Angelelli, 2004; 2016).

Political economist Francis Fukuyama (1995, p.268) has defined the concept of trust as "the expectation that arises within a community of regular, honest and co-operative behaviour based on commonly shared norms". The rather slippery yet fundamental notion of trust presents a challenge to researchers because "it is bound up conceptually with notions of confidence, leaps of faith, familiarity, dependence, cooperation, commitment, expectations and risk" (Olohan & Davitti 2015, p.391). Yet for interpreting and intercultural mediation it is extremely significant: Angelelli (2004) identifies "establishing trust between the parties" as one of the five cardinal tasks of the interpreter, along with alignment with the parties, communicating affect as well as message, explaining cultural gaps/interpreting culture as well as language, and finally establishing communication rules during the conversation. In a translation network context Koskinen (2007, p.677–678) observes that in order to build trust, "perspectives are addressed, knowledge is shared, and information is clear, accountable and legitimate as far as all parties are concerned".

In an ideal world that may well be the case; however, this level of trust would also entail a symmetrical power balance that is rarely achieved in an interpreting triad where, for example, legal recognition of refugee status is the object of the communicative act. Asymmetrically weighted against the power of institutional representatives like the police, jurists, or even medics, the mediator, who could also be of immigrant origin, attempts to reconcile her/his past with the situation at hand, while the asylum seeker seeks to curry favour with both. The interpreter's, or in this case, the mediator's "zone of uncertainty" (Inghilleri, 2005; see also Merlini, 2009; 2015), relates to the dichotomy between the need to "define a role for themselves that corresponds to 'who they are' rather than to an already established notion of 'who they must be'" (Inghilleri 2005, p.52). This is reflected in the discussion presented in section 6. Merlini (2015) sustains that effective communication in medical interpreting depends on the interpreter's ability to "cue read" from the context rather than merely transfer the text as spoken. According to the perceptions of the intercultural mediators interviewed here, this would certainly fall within their remit.

It is beyond the scope of this paper to examine the professional qualifications and experience required to become an intercultural mediator (see Katan, 2015; Spinzi, 2015; Spinzi & Rudvik, 2014. See also Filmer forthcoming). For our purposes here, however, it is appropriate to mention that in Italy there is no national legislation regarding the minimum requirements, abilities or skills that would identify the professional figure of the intercultural mediator. Regional governments are responsible for laying down definitions and guidelines. They are also in charge of designing training courses that are specifically connected to their own local needs and requirements within a specific socio-geographic context.

Although hard-pressed to deal with migrant arrivals, the Sicilian regional government has only recently published (2018) its definition of the intercultural mediator and a set of ambitious competencies pertaining to the role in line with the national "repertorio delle qualificazioni" (directory of job profiles). Training programmes provided by regionally authorised bodies are, however, "non-regulated". Furthermore, although the competencies listed are many, there are no guidelines as to how such a course should be structured in order to acquire the necessary skills and knowledge requirements outlined in the job description[13].

Due to Sicily's strategic geographical position, its coastline has been the most frequent access route for migrants crossing the Mediterranean Sea. In 2016, at the height of the so-called "Migrant Crisis", the existing linguistic, cultural and interpreting services had already proved inadequate and were stretched beyond their limit despite the 'emergency' measures that were implemented (Filmer & Federici, 2018). Applications for refugee status and asylum, rescue missions at sea or on arrival at Sicilian ports, and the soon to be dismantled second reception system (SPRAR system of protection for asylum seekers and refugees) are some of the contexts that are linguistically

---

[13] https://repertoriodellequalificazioni.siciliafse1420.it/Mediatore+Interculturale/aWRwcm9maWxvPTM1MQ==

negotiated by the "hybrid multifunctional figure" of the [inter]cultural mediators (Merlini 2015, p.31), "who are *entrusted* by policy-makers with the task of bridging communication between immigrants and public service providers" (ibid. my emphasis). Intercultural mediators working in Sicilian ports and reception centres are among the first-line responders to the arrival of vessels (of "hope", "fortune", "death" in the journalistic collocations) to Italy. In the next section, we will focus on the perspective of medics regarding intercultural mediators.

Trust in doctors – views from the operators

Interviews were carried out with official operators in diverse fields in order to understand their experience of health-related communication and the interpreting triad in the context of the humanitarian migratory crisis: an NGO paramedic, a prison psychologist, and a volunteer medical doctor are a sample of the many professionals that migrants encounter before and soon after disembarking. Moving from fundamental and immediate needs on board the rescue vessels from the paramedics (O1), to medical support on arrival and in first reception centres (O2; O3), and medium-term support to mental health (O4), the sample provides evidence of the essential role of trust in this context. Clearly, the central issues pertaining to emergency communication are the ways in which doctors and medical teams cope with multilingual exchanges; how the migrants who encounter medics relay their needs; and, crucially, what role the mediators themselves play in the interactions between the parties.

The first contact between rescue teams and migrants is on board the rescue ships, before disembarkation, should medical assistance be necessary. When asked if s/he had ever had difficulty communicating in an emergency at sea, informant O.1., who is a paramedic for the European Border and Coast Guard Agency, Frontex, responded: "Yes, yes, yes. The very nature of what we do is difficult. But from an emergency point of view it is no more difficult for me than working in West London". What O.1 means is that in a multicultural city like London the language differences that need to be bridged in a hospital environment are neither different from nor more complex than those encountered in an ostensibly perilous situation such as a ship bringing migrants to the coast of Sicily. O.1 maintains that in a real medical emergency, language mediation is relatively unimportant. "[the patients] put a natural amount of trust in you because you're a doctor". O.1 goes on to say that "There's a sort of unspoken agreement that you don't need a language immediately to mitigate the medical problems; they are mitigated by my actions and my gestures that explain what I am doing". He then admits, however, that he takes the help of the friends and family of the patient for granted in order "to explain to them in their language – 'no it's ok, let them do it'". Therefore, there is a certain amount of reliance on the unofficial, natural interpreting going on around the emergency that would aid the medic in her/his work. On reflexion O.1. admits that linguistic mediation would make such situations easier to deal with but "it's not necessary to get the job done". S/he demonstrates reluctance to admit that a mediator would be helpful. S/he does not mention the presence of either translators or interpreters on board the Frontex ships, so from the point of view of the triangle of trust, according to the paramedic it is more a dialogic relationship between the medic and the migrant/patient without any official intercultural mediator. Parallel to the situational contexts described by O1, IM5 reported difficulties in mediating on rescue vessels that arrive at the port due to a lack of trust, or perhaps a lack of professional esteem for the mediator by the medics: "I have been thrown off the ship loads of times. They won't let me on the ship, and I was supposed to work with the doctor – it's protocol but he refuses […] he thinks he understands the whole world and he can't even speak English". Here reference is made to a protocol, which was negated by O.1. But the prevalence of a discourse on continuous "emergency" empowers operators to render intercultural mediators subservient in role, illustrating the asymmetrical power relations between mediators and medics. Angelelli notes that "Every communicative event involves power differentials. Every cross-linguistic/cultural communicative event includes (or *should* include) an interpreter. Interpreters play a significant role in brokering these power differentials, constantly striving for excellence." (2004, p.98-99).

A Red Cross volunteer and a physician by profession, O. 2 does voluntary work at the Red Cross walk-in surgery within CARA Mineo. S/he supports the view expressed by O.1 that there is an automatic trust in medical professionals, but s/he suggests this trust goes beyond medical advice and treatment. S/he notes that often the guests come to him/her to ask for help with a variety of issues that are not strictly related to health. Having worked at the centre for five years, the volunteer affirms that guests seek him/her out when they need language and mediation support instead of the official mediators. S/he has a B1 competence in English, certified with a Cambridge ESOL certificate. S/he recounts that s/he has even been called upon to mediate between other operators at the centre "who perhaps don't understand the culture of the guests", and the guests themselves. When asked why people come to her/him rather than to one of the official cultural mediators s/he says, "because they trust me". This might lead one to suspect that the guests have little faith in the mediation services provided, or like M.1, are oblivious to their existence. When asked if during her six month stay at CARA Mineo she had ever asked for the assistance of a cultural mediator (one of whom was sitting in the interview room with us at the time), M.1. looked blank and repeated "Cultural Mediators? What?" When the question was repeated using the word "translators", M.1. replied "No, I speak English". To my question: "So does everyone speak English here?" M.1. replied: "No. The social workers don't but if I need a doctor I go to the Red Cross, they all speak in English. Yes, yes they all speak in English. I don't understand Italian". This comment would appear to confirm O.2's assertion that the professional status of a doctor confers trust, beyond linguistic or cultural borders. S/he is entrusted with the role of mediator by the guests and asked to intervene in situations of verbal conflict mediating across linguistic and cultural barriers.

O.4, the prison psychologist seems to be the only medical professional to whom I spoke that sees the triangle of trust as mutually constructed between the operator, the refugee and the mediator. S/he sees it as a fundamental premise for his/her work. O.4 observes that although English is a lingua franca, s/he speaks very little and prison guards even less ("they hardly speak Italian, let alone English"). S/he affirms that although the non-European inmates "have the legal right to a mediator who speaks their own language", this is very often overlooked, and in relation to appointments "non-European immigrants are absolutely the last in the queue". A psychologist is likely through the course of his/her work to spend more time in dialogue with his/her patients. For this reason, the relationship of trust that can be established with a certain intercultural mediator is likely to be a strong bond if continued over time. O.4 considers this a fundamental issue in establishing a productive environment in which to work and ultimately benefit the patient.

Views from the migrants

Interviews selected for this sample study include three guests at CARA Mineo and two at the CAS. The data show that interlingual communication is often "crowd-sourced" and organised unofficially amongst themselves; the presence, role, and even the title "intercultural mediator" seemed unknown to many of the guests interviewed. Instead the term "translator" is more easily understood. Conditions for data collection at CARA Mineo were controlled by the presence of mediators during the interview process, which means some of the data is likely to be self-censored by the interviewees.

Nevertheless, regarding self-sufficiency, M1 provides insight into the collaboration that takes place within the CARA with regards to language, translation and mediation: "Since I arrived here, I have been helping people who do not know Italian. [...] I help refugees here and sometimes I help at other places. They ask me to translate sometimes. I know Arabic, Italian, and French." This attitude draws on an unsatisfactory personal experience with an intercultural mediator who misrepresented him in court during his asylum application: "Yes, I stopped the translator many times during the session in court and corrected him by explaining to him what I meant exactly. The translator [sic] should be from the same country and there should be understanding between the person and the translator," a position reminiscent of the recurring discussion among the IM interviewees regarding building bridges of trust. M5, on the other hand, had little faith in the Italian language competences of an intercultural mediator who shared his native language, Wolof, during his asylum application. M5 explains, "I asked him if he could translate my words. He said 'yes, it's perfect!' But still I don't trust. No. Because you stay here in Italy for three or four years… you say you can speak perfectly this language, but you are not born here. It's not possible. What I say to you in Wolof you cannot say all in Italian".

Levels of trust in the institutions who process asylum applications is, however, generally very low. As the waiting time is long and language support may come after initial processing, M4 who has been at CARA Mineo for three years, well beyond the stipulated maximum stay of six months, now speaks Italian. In his interview, he states "I have never needed a mediator. I don't go around asking for help. I try to solve the problem by myself. I don't want to bother anyone", a position of self-sufficiency that also implies a lack of trust in institutional solutions to language barriers.

Identity and trust – ethnicity and the role of the intercultural mediator

One of the liveliest points of discussion with the mediators relates to the opposition interpreter/mediator[14] and their purportedly different functions. Three of the six interviewees said that professionally they performed both roles but in different settings. Yet, all maintained that the two figures require completely different approaches and competences. IM6, for example, highlights the lack of understanding of what mediating actually entails among other operators: "colleagues should be made more aware of our role [as mediators] and that we are not just simple interpreters…they tell us 'you have to tell him this, this, and this'. But it doesn't work like that. I'm not just a simple translator". Working for the CARA and CAS, Italian IM2 accumulated experience during the migrant arrivals in 2009-2014, which were constellated by tragic events; she observes differences in the roles: "Often there is a huge

---

14 The dichotomy between the roles of mediator and interpreter has instigated lively debate within academia, which is still ongoing (see Katan, for example, 2015, p.365-391). It is too vast a topic to be broached in any depth in this contribution, however, briefly it can be noted that intercultural mediators interviewed for this study tended to perceive the "interpreter" as a conduit performing literal simultaneous interpreting with minimal intervention on a cultural or empathic level, akin to the work of a conference interpreter. See Hale and Liddicoat, 2015; Martin & Phelan, 2010; Zorzi, 2007 on the differences and similarities of the two figures.

difference in knowledge between the two parties, especially when the institution is talking to the migrant who does not know the Italian state, the Italian laws, the Italian rules, the Italian culture", in these situations she emphasises that interpreting the words without mediating the content "is plain useless". Non-Italian IM4 sees "the mediator [as] a very important figure […] because it doesn't just mean speaking different languages. You also have to be a mediator of people. Because to be a mediator you have to be a listener". Both these skills are designated as subject-specific in the proposed survey of the profession of cultural mediator (Melandri, Carbonari & Ricci, 2014). IM4 has experience working as an interpreter for the police as well as mediator within the CAS. Despite the possible conflicts of loyalty and the different approaches required, he feels he is able to carry out both tasks but with a written translation he was absolutely categorical: "A written text? I don't want the responsibility. If I make a mistake I could ruin someone's life". Nevertheless, he describes a process whereby he simultaneously interprets intercepted phone conversations from Arabic to Italian while a police officer writes down what he says — a practice whose inaccuracies and unreliable construal are more akin to Chinese Whispers than interpreting.

The interviews also revealed tensions regarding the juxtaposition between "native speaker" mediators (meaning those whose mother tongue is not Italian and have a migratory background) and mediators who are native speakers of Italian. It would appear that ethnicity plays a significant role in the dynamics of trust. In response to the question "Do migrants prefer white Italians or co-nationals to mediate for them?", Italian IM6 replies "Yes, many guests may prefer to have their co-nationals because they think that a person of their same culture will defend them, be less impartial". This perception of the co-national, or at least non-Italian, mediator could also give rise to disappointment on the part of the migrant in asylum cases and certainly present an existential dilemma for the mediator. As Merlini (2009) explains: "mediators are bound to feel torn between rivalling needs: empathy for their fellow people; allegiance to the institution employing them; compliance with the neutrality principle of professional ethics" (p.59). On the other hand, IM6 affirms that it is equally possible that the request on the part of the guest could be for a European mediator: "Sometimes for the psychological sessions the guests ask for an Italian". This might be due to a sense of shame or embarrassment in front of someone of their own culture when discussing intimate psychological issues (see Merlini, *ibid.*). Italian IM2 looks at the longer-term implications on integration if the preference is for a co-national: "A mediator from the same ethnic background can be a comfort, a sort of refuge, you see your co-national and you feel safe, but, in my opinion, this is a doubled-edged sword because this way leads to isolation and ghettoisation". On the other hand, IM3 who has a migrant background and is a mediator for the UNHCR, sees his ethnic origin as a distinct advantage in his work: "Sometimes I take full advantage of this fact to win over their trust. Sometimes I tell them about my personal experience as a migrant to say, 'I am just like you'. In that moment you have to use every instrument available to you". Here then, the lines might blur between empathy and advocacy producing what Inghilleri (2005) has termed a "zone of uncertainty". Italian Red Cross Volunteer O.3 has often assisted at the disembarkation procedures at the ports. He comments on the power that mediators have to determine the lives of the people for whom they are mediating.

> They [native speaker mediators] should tend more towards mediating regardless of their nationality…I ask myself also if some mediators really have the ability to mediate. The figure of the mediator is one that can decide your fate so they must be chosen with extreme care.

Pressed to say if s/he thought the mediators where too biased s/he declined to respond but said "there are some very ambiguous situations with mediators".

Identity and trust – gender trouble

Beyond ethnicity the equally thorny issues of gender and respect are significant components in the dynamics of trust-building. IM1, who is Moroccan and speaks Arabic, in response to the question: "Is it difficult to be a woman and do your job?" brusquely asserts "No. I am recognised and respected here". On the contrary, Italian IM6 explains that when conflict occurs between the male guests, she attempts to mediate to calm them down. She feels however that her gender is a disadvantage due to the "lack of respect because I am a woman". She explains their behaviour thus:

> Everything is relative and in their culture, for many of them it's normal to think of women as having a secondary role…I didn't take it personally because I put myself in their shoes…if it had happened outside of these confines my reaction would have been different. Here I have a role as mediator and I cannot overstep the mark.

IM6's reasoning can be viewed from two perspectives: on the one hand, she confirms what Merlini (2015) refers to as the "Empathy Zone". By saying she puts herself in their shoes, i.e. by trying to identify with their culture, she accepts that she is treated with less respect and is therefore mistrusted because she is a woman. On the other hand, for the IM whose task is to prepare guests for integration in the host country we should also consider as part of the mediator's remit to point out the differences indicating the cultural norms in the receiving context. If we acknowledge that in Italy, at least from a legal point of view, women and men are treated as equals it is also the task of the mediator to explain that outside of the compound, sexist attitudes would not be tolerated and, if evidenced in a migrant, may even be an excuse to further denigrate him. If the mediator's role is precisely that of bridging cultures, then explaining to male guests that women do not (or at least should not) play a secondary role in European societies is just as important as attempting to explain bureaucratic procedures and long waits for their court cases to be heard. IM3 also asserts that:

> as a woman in certain contexts you are not recognized. What you say is not considered reliable...when you are talking to the big groups, for instance, or else, maybe when you are talking about health. In the medical context, you have problems with certain things that are left unsaid because they get embarrassed because you are a woman.

What IM3 refers to is mediating as a woman for a male patient. She confirms on the other hand that this can be an asset in the medical context when mediating for female patients. She points out however that even in a European context gender plays a role in medical care preferences. On the positive side, as a woman over 40, she feels her age is also an advantage. Bearing in mind that most migrants are young men, she says:

> The male migrants take you as a mother, and women take you as a sister so this is good because there is some sort of family relationship, family recognition because especially African countries often have a much wider idea of what a family is. It is not just blood.

Therefore, trust between mediator and migrant within the interpreting triad seems to be attained where bonds are created that go beyond the functional. However, having achieved that level of trust between these two parties might create an imbalance with the third party, the medic or institutional representative, who feels excluded from this relationship thus creating tensions. It would seem that the old adage "three's a crowd" may be applied to mediating situations fraught with emotional intensity such as during the ongoing migratory phenomena in which human ties are inevitably formed.

Conclusions: The intercultural mediator must be a figure of trust

Intercultural mediators have been described as "a new breed of linguists" (Amato & Garwood, 2011) whose working environment and scope of responsibility are still very much open to discussion. The multi-faceted concept of trust with all its shades of meaning and ethical and practical implications within the interpreting-mediating triad is central to any definition of the role of the intercultural mediator.

While the humanitarian crisis is still unfolding in the Mediterranean, in the Italian context the "demand" for "emergency" mediation on rescue ships, at Italian ports, and for language and cultural assistance during asylum applications is on the decline due to a drop in the number of migrants arriving in Italy[15]. Many of those migrants who manage to leave Libya are now heading for Spain instead. In a longer view, while the immediate geographical location may have shifted, the issues and dilemmas relating to language policies that support multilingual communication in migration to Europe remain the same. From immediate humanitarian needs to complex legal issues, the intercultural mediator should be a crucial figure in trying to explain what happens at medical, institutional and legal levels so that the asylum seeker or refugee is clearly informed on what is taking place. This figure should surely also represent the human face of cross-cultural understanding.

In this scenario, the data presented here appears to demonstrate that current praxes reflect the impossibility of neutrality in intercultural mediation while confirming the dangers of any implicit or explicit forms of advocacy in favour of one or other sides of the "interpreting triangle". Intercultural mediators in Italy are not trained to become "invisible" interpreters but are used to practicing interventionalism (Merlini, 2009), which may encourage trust-building on the part of the migrant but arouse suspicion of non-neutrality from an institutional perspective. The mediator must walk a tight-rope. In an ideal world, the highly charged multilingual situations that arise from immigration might benefit from a collaborative approach with two mediators with different linguistic and cultural backgrounds: an "interpreting square" rather than a triangle. This might balance out the "trust" conundrum and alleviate fears of undue advocacy. This, of course, would be in an ideal world. As the political climate in Italy stands, intercultural understanding at any level, be it first reception or long-term integration, are not on the agenda of the governing powers. In fact, current immigration policy is likely to bring even more instability to the 'interpreter's habitus' (Inghilleri, 2005) within the already uncertain and fluid sphere of cultural mediation.

---

15 https://frontex.europa.eu/media-centre/news-release/number-of-irregular-crossings-at-europe-s-borders-at-lowest-level-in-5-years-ZfkoRu

References

Amato, A. & Garwood, C. (2011). Cultural mediators in Italy: a new breed of linguists, *inTRAlinea* Vol. 13. http://www.intralinea.org/archive/article/ 1673

Angelelli, C. V. (2004). *Revisiting the Interpreter's Role A study of conference, court, and medical interpreters in Canada, Mexico, and the United States.* Amsterdam/Philadelphia: John Benjamins Publishing Company.

Angelelli, C. V. (2016) "Looking back: A study of (ad-hoc) family interpreters" *European Journal of Applied Linguistics,* 4(1):5–31.

Catarci, M., & Fiorucci, M. (2014). Indagine nazionale sul profilo del mediatore interculturale [National inquiry on the profile of the intercultural mediator]. In E. Melandri, L. Carbonari, & A. Ricci (Eds.), *La qualifica del mediatore interculturale. Contributi per il suo inserimento nel futuro sistema nazionale di certificazione delle competenze* [The qualification of the intercultural mediator. Contributions for its insertion in the future national system of certification for the required competences] (pp. 41-54). Roma, Italy: Centro informazione e educazione allo sviluppo.

Chesterman, A. (1997). *Memes of Translation.* Amsterdam / Philadelphia: John Benjamins Publishing Company.

Crabtree, A., Rouncefield M., & Tolmie, P. (2012). *Doing Design Ethnography.* London: Springer.

Federici, F. M. (2016). Introduction: A state of emergency for crisis communication. In F. M. Federici (ed.), *Mediating Emergencies and Conflicts. Frontline Translating and Interpreting* (p.1-29). Houndsmill, Basingstoke: Palgrave Macmillan.

Filmer, D. A. (2020). Cascading effects: mediating the unutterable sufferance of gender-based violence in migratory flows. In F Federici & S. O'Brien (Eds) *Translation in Cascading Crises.* London, UK: Routledge.

Filmer, D.A, & Federici F.M. (2018). Mediating migration crises: Sicily and the languages of despair. *European Journal of Language Policy,* 10(2): 229-251.

Fukuyama, F. (1995). *Trust: The social virtue and the creation of prosperity.* New York: The Free Press.

Inghilleri, M. (2005). Mediating zones of uncertainty. Interpreter agency, the interpreting habitus and political asylum adjudication. *The Translator,* 11(1), 69- 85.

Katan, D., M. (2015). La mediazione linguistica interculturale: Il mediatore culturale e le sue competenze[Intercultural linguistic mediation: The

cultural mediator and his/her competences]. *Lingue Linguaggi,* 16, 365-391.
Koskinen, K. & Abdallah, K. (2007). Managing Trust: Translating and the Network economy. *Meta,* 52(4), 673-687
Latza Nadeau, B. (2018, 1 February). Migrants are more profitable than drugs': how the mafia infiltrated Italy's asylum system. Crime families have cashed in on the 'refugee industry'. *The Guardian.* Retrieved from https://www.theguardian.com/news/2018/feb/01/migrants-more-profitable-than-drugs-how-mafia-infiltrated-italy-asylum-system.
Melandri, E., Carbonari, L., & Ricci, A. (2014). *La qualifica del mediatore interculturale. Contributi per il suo inserimento nel futuro sistema nazione di certificazione delle competenze.* [The qualification of the intercultural mediator. Contributions for its insertion in the future national system of certification for the required competences] Retrieved from Roma: http://www.integrazionemigranti.gov.it/Documenti-e-riceche/DOSSIER%20DI%20SINTESI%20QUALIFICA%20MEDIATORI_28_07.pdf.
Merlini, R. (2015). Empathy: A 'zone of uncertainty' in mediated healthcare practice. *Cultus,* (8) 27-49.
Merlini, R. (2009). Seeking asylum and seeking identity in a mediated encounter. The projection of selves through discursive practices. *Interpreting,* 11(1), 57-93.
Olohan, M. & Davitti, E. (2015). Dynamics of Trusting in Translation Project Management: Leaps of Faith and Balancing Acts. *The Journal of Contemporary Ethnography,* 46(4), 391-416.
Pym, A. (2004). Propositions on Cross-Cultural Communication and Translation. *Target,* 16(1): 1-28.
Rouncefield, M., Tolmie, P., Ashgate, A., & Aroles, J. (2016). *Ethnomethodology at Work (Directions in Ethnomethodology and Conversation Analysis).* London, UK: Routledge.
Rudvin, M. & Spinzi, C., (2014). Negotiating the Terminological Borders of 'Language Mediation' in English and Italian. A Discussion on the Repercussions of Terminology on the Practice, Self-perception and Role of Language Mediators in Italy, *Lingue Culture Mediazioni – Languages Cultures Mediation,* 1(1–2), 57–80.
Spinzi, C. (2015). The multifaceted nature of language mediation and Interpreting A personal case of disempowerment. *Cultus,* 8 113-125 http://www.cultusjournal.com/files/Archives/cultus%20_8_final%202015.pdf#page=113.
Stephenson Jr., M. (2005). Making humanitarian relief networks more effective: operational coordination, trust and sensemaking. *Disasters,* 29(4), 337-350.

Wray, R. (2006). Public Perceptions About Trust in Emergency Risk Communication: Qualitative Research Findings. *International Journal of Mass Emergencies and Disasters*, 24(1), 45-75

Zorzi, D. (2007). Note sulla formazione dei mediatori linguistici [Notes on linguistic mediators' training]. *Studi di Glottodidattica*, 1, 112–128.

Language and social integration in multicultural contexts

Sabine Pirchio, Sara Costa, Rosa Ferri

Introduction

This chapter aims to discuss an important topic for the development of European societies: the development and integration of children with an immigration background and native children in educational multicultural context. Cultural diversity is, in fact, a current normative feature of European society and being in relationship to people coming from other countries, showing different ethnicities and speaking the country's language as a second language is a more and more common experience for any European citizen.

However, these changes do not come without difficulties and imply a challenge to face. How this challenge will be addressed, which resources will be used and developed, will determine how harmonious the civil cohabitation will be, and the level of personal and social wellbeing of native and immigrant citizens.

Therefore, in the following sections we discuss the situation of immigrant children in educational institutions in Europe and Italy, we review the relevant literature on specific factors influencing social integration and we describe a European project which aimed at fostering social integration in primary school immigrant children through language learning activities.

European and Italian immigrant students' situation

In the last 10 years, the proportions of immigrant students have increased from 8 to 10% in most European countries. The Organisation for Economic Cooperation and Development (OECD) analysed students' school achievement and their general wellbeing by comparing native students and those with immigrant backgrounds across a wide range of countries. A recent report has shown that across OECD between 2003 and 2015, the number of students with an immigrant background largely increased: children represent a significant portion of global migration flows, especially within refugee populations (OECD, 2019). According to a 2016 UNICEF report, 1 in 8 immigrants worldwide is a child (UNICEF, 2016).

In Italy, in the 2016/2017 school year, students with migratory background were 826 thousand, 9.4% of the overall student population, with an increase of over 11 thousand compared to the 2015/2016 school year (MIUR, 2018).

The percentage of boys (52%) is slightly higher than girls (48%). 61% of them were born in Italy, therefore they belong to the so called second generations, a share that has increased by 35.4% in the last five years.

The most represented nations are Romania (19.2%), followed by Albania (13.6%), Morocco (12.4%), China (6%), Philippines (3.3%), India and Moldova (both 3.1%), Ukraine, Pakistan and Egypt (all at 2.4%).

The incidence of students born in Italy on the total of pupils with non-Italian citizenship is 85% in nursery school, 73.4% in primary, 53.2% in first grade secondary school, 27% in the second grade (MIUR, 2018). Thanks to these data we can say that it is now a consolidated fact that students of migratory origin are an integral part of the national school population, making the Italian school increasingly multi-ethnic and multicultural.

According to previous surveys (OECD 2010, 2012, 2015), immigrant students with similar socioeconomic status, coming from the same country, perform very differently across different school systems. For example, immigrant students from the Russian Federation living in Finland, Germany and Israel perform around the OECD average in reading, while those in the Czech Republic score about 30 points below the OECD average. Moreover, immigrant students living in Greece score more than 50 points below average. Similarly, immigrant students from the Former Yugoslavia living in Denmark score about 40 points below the OECD average, while those in Luxembourg score more than 80 points below average. Likewise, immigrant students from Turkey living in the Netherlands score 45 points below the OECD average, whereas in Belgium, Denmark, Germany and Switzerland they score between 70 and 80 points below average. Finally, Turkish students show the worst outcome in Austria scoring 115 points below the OECD average.

These findings show that immigrant students' achievement varies considerably across countries, but we need some caution in interpreting cross-country comparisons. In fact, when considering immigrant students' achievement, it needs to take into account a larger set of background variables, which could explain different as well as incoherent data across countries. However, immigrant children sometimes show difficulties academic achievement and in acquiring the new language, as well as in certain conditions a lack of motivation towards the schooling path (Iba ez et al., 2004).

The issue of early dropout among foreign students aged between 18-24 years old appears particularly relevant precisely in the countries of immigration in southern Europe, particularly in Italy, Spain and Greece, which register proportions of around 40 percent. In Italy, immigrant students show lower school achievement, especially in first generation. A high percentage of immigrant students' in Italy chose a technical and a professional education or decided to not continue their studies (approximately 17%) (MIUR, 2018). Greater school dropout, lower level of academic achievement, very frequent school delay and the tendency to choose training devoted to immediate insertion into the labour market are the evident signs of the problems of integration of immigrant children in the Italian school (Strozza, 2015). Some disadvantages seem to have been slightly reduced over time, but such progress goes hand in hand with the increasing of the number of children born in Italy, and therefore with the increase of Italian speakers.

In some cases, linguistic proficiency explains almost the entire gap in academic performance between native students and students with an immigrant background. In fact, language fluency is associated with students' proficiency in all academic domains, even those with less language content like mathematics (OECD, 2019).

The role of the school appears to be strategic for all migratory generations but in particular for those immigrants who arrive at school age and for whom actions are needed in order to facilitate the rapid learning of the Italian language, thereby reducing the risk of scholastic dispersion. Moreover, lack of language skills can have a negative impact on the lives and integration of immigrants. It is well-known that children with an immigrant background who face language barriers are more likely to experience bullying, discrimination and emotional problems like depression and low self-esteem (Padilla & Perez, 2003; Romero & Roberts, 2003). Thus, language learning could be crucial in multicultural classes, especially for the acculturation process of children from families with migrant background (Miller, 2010).

Acculturation, integration and inclusion

Migrations and multicultural societies imply the notion of acculturation. Eventhough acculturation is a bidirectional process and implies changes and adaptations both in the host society and in the immigrant individuals and groups, most of the research focus the phenomenon on the side of the immigrants trying to identify risk and protection factors for the development of an acculturated social identity. From this perspective successful acculturation has been found to be linked to features of the migratory experience such as the voluntary decision to move, optimistic expectations about the life in the new country, the mastery of the language of the host country, and the capacity to accept external support (Escobar & Vega, 2000).

When analysing the immigrant children's school adjustment and achievement, as an indicator of acculturation, we should adopt an ecological perspective allowing us to consider the child as part of a cultural, relational and interactional system where each component is influenced by and influencing the others (Bronfenbrenner, 1979). In fact, school variables and child's individual factors alone could not determine the way the child will adapt to and develop in her school community and society but also their interaction with the home culture and community, represented by the child's family.

Immigration represents an important challenge for all the family members: the difficulties parents may experience in organizing their new life, in creating a social network, to learn the language and to adapt to the new culture may create changes in their parenting practices affecting the relation with their child. This interacts with child's eventual difficulties in learning the new language and to make friends with native people (Ibañez et al., 2004). Protective factors for the children school adjustment include parents' education that is positively related to academic outcomes (Portes & Rumbaut, 2001; Suárez-Orozco et al., 2008) and by parents' employment (Perreira et al., 2006).

However, educational adjustment may be difficult if the school social environment does not meet the immigrant students' emotional and learning needs, which may be higher than in native students (Ruiz-de-Velasco & Fix, 2001) and require schools to be specially equipped. Peers interactions with immigrant children may be more difficult (Rosenbloom & Way, 2004), but social exchanges and friendship seem to be facilitated in multiethnic schools (Bruegel, 2006): in these cases, friendship across different classrooms is less common than friendship across different ethnicities (Vincent et al., 2017). This finding calls for the opportunity to promote the creation of a common social identity based on the belonging to the same classroom or school, which may help the acculturation process of immigrant students while supporting the creation of interpersonal social relationships among children with different ethnicities (Gaertner & Dovidio, 2000). This is true especially in primary school when individuals are daily engaged in negotiating diversity and differences as a routine activity in environments that can facilitate disclosure and understanding (Noble, 2009).

Which is the role of language in the acculturation process? A long tradition of research shows that language is a main component of ethnic identity: it activates the processes of social comparison and differentiation between groups (Giles & Johnson, 1987; Gumperz, 1982). By speaking a language and due to the level of language mastery, individuals are categorised by others as members of the same social group (in-group) or as members of other groups (out-group) and this belonging is used as a drive for attitudes and behaviours. At school, language influences learning and functions as a symbolic mechanism for activating stereotypes that influences social inclusion and academic performance of immigrant children (Esser, 2006; Riggs & Due, 2011).

Prejudice at school

The ethnic composition of schools and classrooms plays an important role in the interethnic relations among students and between them and teachers. Studies that explore the relationship between ethnicity and educational outcomes often find that ethnic minority students experience disadvantages during their educational careers. As discussed above, their achievement levels are lower than those of ethnic majority students (Borgna & Contini, 2014), and they are much less than the native in higher education levels (Lewis & Cheng, 2006; Kristen & Granato, 2007; Van Houtte et al., 2012). Some of these disadvantages can be explained by cultural and linguistic barriers, but biases in teacher judgement also play an important role. Even among peers, some recent research has shown that young people often do hold negative attitudes toward immigrant youth in school settings (Brown & Lee, 2015). For example, Brown (2011) examined European American children's attitudes toward immigrants and found that while most of children were relatively positive about legal immigrants, they also believed illegal immigrants should be imprisoned.

Children's ethnic prejudices are expressed in their social behaviour. Since infancy, children show clear ethnic preferences: in tasks where they are required to choose among ethnically different people, they tend to choose members of their own ethnic group and they show to master some kind of ethnic awareness (Aboud, 1988; Nesdale, 2001). An Italian study found that most of the children in day-care centres and kindergarten would prefer to play with a white than with a black child (Castelli et al., 2007). In schools, peer influence also contributes to youth attitudes in important ways: longitudinal studies (Van Zalk et al., 2013; Sinclair et al., 2005; Blanchard et al., 1994) have shown the effect of peers' anti-immigrant attitudes on changes in adolescents' prejudice over time and in opinions on interracial attitudes.

Whether they are aware of it or not, teachers are part of a community that defines their cultural identity, shapes their beliefs and attitudes (Rogoff, 2003), and guides their behavior. Teachers' cultural beliefs can influence their interactions with students, among whom they can make a distinction according to cultural dimensions such as ethnicity, social class, religion and language (Passiatore et al., 2016). Researches demonstrate that in some cases teachers evaluate ethnic minority students more negatively (Glock, 2016; Sprietsma, 2013) and expect lower performance (Tenenbaum & Ruck, 2007).

Plus, differences in teacher expectations might not only explain teachers' subjective judgments of their students' academic abilities, but they are also important because when teachers hold different expectations for particular groups of students, they may engage, support, and teach their students differently.

These differences depend, among other things, on biased attitudes. That is, people with low and high prejudices have different representations of a minority ethnic group, which can lead to different beliefs and different expectations about the behaviour of a member of a minority ethnic group. People with high prejudices will attribute more negative stereotypical characteristics to the minority group, while people with low prejudices will attribute more positive stereotyped characteristics. Faced with an ethnic minority, teachers can therefore react more or less automatically, depending on the representation they have of the minority group and on the prejudicial attitudes that have shaped their representation.

Teachers are also influential adults in children's attitudes toward immigrants, so the relationship between teacher and student might also explain youth attitudes. For example, Thijs and Verkuyten (2012) found that ethnic minority students who shared a closer relationship with their ethnic majority teacher had more positive attitudes toward the ethnic majority group in general. Geerlings and colleagues (2017) studied the role of student-teacher relationships on attitudes towards ethnic minorities. Their research showed that student-teacher relationships were associated with more positive outgroup attitudes and that this association was mediated by students' desire for intercultural openness. Consequently, when considering school influences on student attitudes, ethnically diverse classes and forms of multicultural education are important, but the relationships that teachers develop with their students also count for the development of positive ethnic attitudes.

Promoting school integration in children with immigrant background: the SOFT project

The analysis of the literature and the observation of the many problems schools still face in coping with the inclusion of migrant students and in promoting positive social relationships among students with different ethnicities (for a detailed discussion of this topic see Passiatore et al., 2016) led to the design and implementation of the SOFT project. The project was funded by the Education, Culture and Audiovisual Executive Agency of the European Union, and it is called "School and family together for the integration of immigrant children" (SOFT). The SOFT project was realized in five European countries (Italy, the UK, Germany, Spain, and Switzerland) by a consortium of seven academic and non-academic partners. The SOFT project consisted of a series of events, activities and materials promoting awareness raising about multiculturalism and multilingualism, changes in the school and home practices for language learning and increasing home-school partnership. All the activities were realised by the project's partners in the five involved countries, including cooperative learning activities, foreign language inclusive learning, and collaborative activities shared by parents and teachers.

The project aimed to enhance the social integration of immigrant children by a series of activities targeting the children, the teachers, and the parents separately, but also teachers and children together as well as teachers and parents together. Language activities were at the core of all the project targets, together with additional support activities: a) seminars for teachers and for parents about multilingualism issues, explaining the benefits of cultural diversity and multilingualism in children and adults; b) teacher training in intercultural issues, in the Narrative Format model for teaching languages to children and in strategies to get families involved; and c) coaching the joint teacher-parent activities to assure they are carried out in a positive social climate of cooperation and positive attitudes. The Narrative Format approach (Pirchio et al., 2019) is implemented through a series of acting-out activities performed by the teacher and the children at school and through additional support activities that can be carried out at home by the children with their parents. The Narrative Format approach is based on the creation of positive relationships in the learning group and on the use of positive communication strategies and previous researches showed that it allows every child in the class (native, immigrant, with typical development or special educational needs, younger or older, linguistically more or less experienced) in the language learning experience (Pirchio et al., 2015; Taeschner et al., 2016). The same format activities (the acting out with the adventures of Hocus and Lotus) were used for teaching both the host country language (e.g. Italian in Italy) and a foreign language (e.g. English in Italy) that is new to all children (native children and children with an immigration background). This was aimed at promoting positive attitudes in immigrant and native children towards language diversity, and at creating a common identity framework in the children playing the same positive activity together in the same new language.

With the aim of evaluate the impact of the project's actions on the targets in primary schools participating in Italy, the outcomes in children's language learning and social interaction were measured and assessed comparing them with the same measures collected in control classes of the same schools which did not participate in the intervention. The results indicated that the intervention increased the relationships between native Italian pupils and their immigrant classmates. On the contrary, in the control group, where no specific intervention was implemented, along the school year the relational rejection of immigrant children by their native Italian classmates increased. In terms of foreign language learning outcomes, children who participated in the Narrative Format intervention showed a higher production of English words in a storytelling task compared to students in the control group where English is taught with standard methodologies (for more details on this study see Pirchio et al., 2019). This finding suggests that the narrative format language activities could impact not only on language learning but also, and at the same time, on social identity and relationships in the group of learners.

Conclusion

The peaceful cohabitation of an ethnically, culturally and linguistically diverse population and assuring equal opportunities of personal development to all citizens are one the main goals of European national societies. Even if migration from within and from extra - European countries is not a new phenomenon, most European countries still need to increase their capacity of providing structural, social and educational resources in order to include non-native citizens.

The Italian educational system assumes inclusiveness as a main drive, but teachers and schools still struggle in find strategies to be used to welcome and include students with an immigration background and to set them up as systematic and stable resources (Passiatore et al., 2016). To help this process, by the SOFT project we worked in a systemic ecological framework of individual development, pursuing the goal of social integration of preschool and primary school students with an immigration background by proposing educational activities and strategies that could take into consideration three main factors, which literature showed to be relevant: positive interpersonal relationships (between teachers and pupils and among pupils) as the most important drive for social integration; language as a factor for developing social identity; home-school partnership as a resource for supporting the child's school adjustment. The outcomes of the project were positive in terms of its applicability and of positive changes in language learning and interpersonal relationships, however some limits must be acknowledged. In fact, we observed a resistance in teachers who participated in the project to continue focusing on the same issues and performing the same type of activities for longer than a few years due to the pressure they feel from the wider social environment and by the higher levels of the educational institution (e.g. school directors, ministry, etc.). This issue calls for the need of an even more systemic approach including macro-system and policymakers.

References

Aboud, F.E., (1988). *Children and prejudice*. Oxford, UK: Basil Blackwell.

Blanchard, F.A., Crandall, C.S., Brigham, J.C., & Vaughn, L., (1994). Condemning and condoning racism: A social context approach to interracial settings. *Journal of Applied Psychology, 79, 993–997.*

Borgna, C., & Contini, D., (2014). Migrant achievement penalties in Western Europe: Do educational systems matter? *European Sociological Review, 30, 670–683.*

Bronfenbrenner, U. (1979). *The ecology of human development*. Harvard university press.

Brown, C.S., (2011). Elementary school children's attitudes about immigrants, immigration, and being an American. *Journal of Applied Developmental Psychology, 32, 109–117.*

Brown, C.S., & Lee, C.A., (2015). Impressions of immigration: Comparisons between immigrant and nonimmigrant children's immigration beliefs. *Analyses of Social Issues and Public Policy (ASAP), 15, 160–176.*

Bruegel, I., (2006). *Social capital, diversity and education policy*. London: South Bank University.

Castelli, L., De Amicis, L., & Sherman, S. J., (2007). The loyal member effect: on the preference for ingroup members who engage in exclusive relation with ingroup. *Developmental Psychology, 43, 1347–1359.*

Escobar, J.I., & Vega, W.A., (2000). Mental health and immigration's AAAs: Where are we and where do we go from here? *The Journal of Nervous and Mental Disease, 188(11), 736-740.*

Esser, H. (2006). *Migration, language and integration*. AKI Research Review, 4. (Wissenschaftszentrum Berlin, www.wz-berlin.de).

Gaertner, S., & Dovidio, J., (2000). *Reducing Intergroup Bias*. New York: Psychology Press.

Geerlings, J., Thijs, J., & Verkuyten, M., (2017). Student-teacher relationships and ethnic outgroup attitudes among majority students. *Journal of Applied Developmental Psychology, 52, 69–79.*

Giles, H., & Johnson, P., (1987). Ethnolinguistic identity theory: A social psychological approach to language maintenance. *International Journal of the Sociology of Language, 68, 69-99.*

Glock, S., (2016). Does ethnicity matter? The impact of stereotypical expectations on in-service teachers' judgments of students. *Social Psychology of Education, 19, 493–509.*

Gumperz, J.J. (Ed.). (1982). *Language and social identity*. Cambridge, UK: Cambridge University Press.

Ibaez, G.E., Kuperminc, G.P., Jurkovic, G., & Perilla, J., (2004). Cultural attributes and adaptations linked to achievement motivation among

Latino adolescents. *Journal of Youth and Adolescence, 33(6), 559–568.*
Istat (2018*), Vita e percorsi di integrazione degli immigrati in Italia* [Lives and paths towards integration of migrants in Italy] Report. Roma.
Kristen, C., & Granato, N., (2007). The educational attainment of the second generation in Germany: Social origins and ethnic inequality. *Ethnicities, 7, 343–366.*
Lewis, T., & Cheng, S.Y., (2006). Tracking, expectations, and the transformation of vocational education. *American Journal of Education, 113, 67–99.*
Miller, J.F., (2010). Language use, identity, and social interaction: migrant students in Australia. *Research on Language and Social Interaction, 33, 69–100.*
MIUR(2018).
    http://www.miur.gov.it/documents/20182/0/Principali+dati+della+scuola+-+avvio+anno+scolastico+2018-2019.pdf/fb3e7b10-e2bc-49aa-a114-c41ef53cacf9?version=1.0
Nesdale, D., (2001). Language and the development of children's ethnic prejudice. *Journal of Language and Social Psychology, 20(1-2), 90–110.*
Noble, G., (2009). Everyday cosmopolitanism and the labour of intercultural community. In A. Wise & S.Velayutham (Eds.), *Everyday multiculturalism* (pp. 46–65). Basingstoke, UK: Palgrave Macmillan.
OECD (2019). *The Road to Integration: Education and Migration, OECD Reviews of Migrant Education.* Paris, France: OECD Publishing.
OECD. (2015). *Immigrant students at school: easing the journey towards integration.* Paris, France: OECD Publishing.
OECD. (2012). *Untapped skills: realising the potential of immigrant students.* Brussels, Belgium: OECD Publishing.
OECD. (2010). *PISA 2009 results: what students know and can do: student performance in reading, mathematics and science, volume I.* Paris, France: OECD Publishing.
Padilla, A. & Perez, W., (2003). Acculturation, social identity, and social cognition: A new perspective. *Hispanic Journal, 25(1), 35-55.*
Passiatore, Y., Pirchio, S., & Taeschner, T., (2016). L'interculturalismo a scuola: un'analisi delle credenze di insegnanti di scuola dell'Infanzia e Primaria e dei fattori che le influenzano [Interculturalism at school: an analysis of pre-school teachers' beliefs and of the factors affecting the beliefs]. *Psicologia dell'Educazione, 1, 53-70.*
Perreira, K.M., Harris, K.M., & Lee, D., (2006). Making it in America: high school completion by immigrant and native youth. *Demography, 43, 511–536.*
Pirchio, S., Passiatore, Y., Carrus, G., & Taeschner, T., (2019). Children's

interethnic relationships in multiethnic primary school: Results of an inclusive language learning intervention on children with native and immigrant background in Italy. *European journal of psychology of education, 34(1), 225-238.*

Pirchio, S., Taeschner, T., Colibaba, A.C., Gheorghiu, E., & Jursova Zacharová, Z., (2015). Family involvement in second language learning: the Bilfam project. In S. Mourão & M. Lourenço (Eds.), *Early years second language education* (pp. 204–217). Oxon: Routledge—Taylor and Francis.

Portes, A., & Rumbaut, R.G., (2001). *Legacies: the story of the immigrant second generation.* Berkeley, CA: University of California Press.

Riggs, D.W., & Due, C., (2011). (Un)common ground?: English language acquisition and experiences of exclusion amongst new arrival students in South Australian primary schools. *Identities, 18, 273–290.*

Rogoff, B., (2003). *The cultural nature of human development.* Oxford, UK: Oxford University Press.

Romero, A., & Roberts. R., (2003). Stress Within a Bicultural Context for Adolescents of Mexican Descent. *Cultural Diversity and Ethnic Minority Psychology, 9(2), 171–184.*

Rosenbloom, S.R., & Way, N., (2004). Experiences of discrimination among African American, Asian American, and Latino adolescents in an urban high school. *Youth & Society, 35(4), 420–451.*

Ruiz-de-Velasco, J., & Fix, M.E., (2001). *Over-looked and underserved: immigrant students in U.S. secondary schools.* Washington, DC: Urban Institute.

Sinclair, S., Lowery, B. S., Hardin, C. D., & Colangelo, A,. (2005). Social tuning of automatic racial attitudes: The role of affiliative motivation. *Journal of Personality and Social Psychology, 89, 583–592.*

Sprietsma, M., (2013). Discrimination in grading: Experimental evidence from primary school teachers. *Empirical Economics, 45, 523–538.*

Strozza, S., Serpieri, R., De Filippo E., & Grimaldi E., (2004). *Una scuola che include. Formazione, mediazione e networking. L'esperienza delle scuole napoletane* [An inclusive school. Training, mediation, and networking. Experiences in Neapolitan schools]. Milano, Italy: Franco Angeli.

Strozza, S., (2015). *La presenza straniera in Italia.* Relazione presentata al convegno "L'integrazione delle comunità immigrate e l'imprenditoria straniera" [*The presence of foreigners in Italy*. Paper presented at the congress "The integration in immigrant communities and the foreign entrepeneurship], Neodemos, Firenze.

S rez-Orozco, C., S rez-Orozco, M., & Todorova, I., (2008*). Learning a new land: Immigrant students in American society.* Cambridge, MA: Harvard University Press.

Taeschner, T., Destino, K., & Pirchio, S., (2016). The onset of story comprehension and production in young Italian children learning English as a second language. *International Journal of Psychology*, 51.

Tenenbaum, H. R., & Ruck, M. D., (2007). Are teachers' expectations different for racial minority than for European American students? A meta-analysis. *Journal of Educational Psychology*, 99, 253–273.

Thijs, J., & Verkuyten, M., (2012). Ethnic attitudes of minority students and their contact with majority group teachers. *Journal of Applied Developmental Psychology, 33, 260–268.*

UNICEF (2016), *Uprooted: The growing crisis for refugee and migrant children*, UNICEF.

Van Houtte, M. V., Demanet, J., & Stevens, P. A., (2012). Self-esteem of academic and vocational students: Does within-school tracking sharpen the difference? *Acta Sociologica, 55, 73–89.*

Van Zalk, M., Kerr, M., Van Zalk, N., & Stattin, H., (2013). Xenophobia and tolerance toward immigrants in adolescence: Cross-influence processes within friendships. *Journal of Abnormal Child Psychology, 41, 627–639.*

Vincent, C., Neal, S., & Iqbal, H., (2017). Encounters with diversity: children's friendships and parental responses. *Urban Studies, 54(8), 1974–1989.*

# Itineraries of geoclinical psychopathology in Public Institution

Maria Cristina Tumiati, Andrea Cavani, Laura Piombo, Giorgia Marinelli, Gianfranco Costanzo, Concetta Mirisola

Introduction

Since the dawn of times people have moved through the world. Mankind was initially largely nomadic, and much of it remained so, even after the advent of settled agriculture. Looking at more recent history, we can identify the prelude to the globalisation process in the timespan between 1860 and 1940. At that time, there was a massive population movement across the world's continents: it is estimated that there was a transmigration of around 140 million people, including Europeans, possessed by a drive to go somewhere else and experience new worlds in search of adventure, riches and other destinies. Starting from the "great geographical conquests" of the sixteenth century, over fifty million moved to new territories and then, from the beginning of the 19th to the beginning of the 20th centuries, around 60 million Europeans went to Canada and the Americas by sea. Of that amount, 26.7 million Italians emigrated to other European countries, the Americas and Australia (Ingles & Cardamone, 2010). Only after the two World Wars did European migration flows start an inversion of the route that accelerated its course in the late 1980s, after the demise of the communist regimes and the subsequent opening of East-West migration flows. Until the end of the seventies, Italy was a land of emigration; although there were Italians emigrants returning, women from ex-colonies or other countries like Cape Verde, Tunisian fishermen and refugees from various backgrounds arriving in Italy (Colucci, 2018). It is only from the eighties that Italy, as has happened in other European countries, has progressively and inexorably become an immigration destination, with migrants now into their third generation.

But there are differences from past migrations. The opportunity to travel by plane, high-speed trains, large ships or other means, has made the world more viable and its inhabitants more mobile than before. This faster mobility has given more possibilities of reversibility to immigration. The different settlements of migrants, whose ethnic identities have become stronger in the last centuries because of different factors, such as the birth of nationalist ideologies, have acquired a more assertive attitude and they are opposed to the concept of integration based on assimilation to the host country's culture as the only solution. Nowadays, it often happens that migrants serve as a bridge between two worlds: their world of origin and the one in which they are located. Consequently, they are not willing to deprive themselves of their own cultural traditions and affiliations (deculturalisation and depersonalisation) in order to be accepted. It has been suggested that we should start considering migrants as "human beings moving through existential territories which foster multiple affiliations to different multicultural communities, which call for the action of long-distance social and community networks and which promote the intentional use of flexible identities"[1] (Inglese & Cardamone, 2010). Following this thought and the knowledge acquired in the last fifty years regarding mental health in migrant populations, it is now necessary for the discipline of psychology to address the complexity of otherness by following a geographically-oriented approach – that is to say, by adopting a perspective based on "geoclinical psychopathology."[2].

Social marginality and public service

In November 2007, the INMP[3], Italian National Institute for Health, Migration and Poverty, was established as management project, and later, in 2012, stabilised by the law as public body of the National Health Service, supervised by the Health Ministry. The INMP is now also the Reference Centre of the National network for social and healthcare problems of migrant and poor people as well as Reference Centre for transcultural mediation in healthcare[4].

1 Authors' translation.
2 Term supported by Salvatore Inglese (2014), *Geopolitica e geoclinica dei popoli in fuga* Congress of 29 March in Florence. http://www.exagere.it/follia-per-sette-clan-elementi-di-psicopatologia-geoclinica/
3 Among important steps that were taken, were the restructuring and transformation of a large part of the Institute's spaces into multispecialist ambulatories and high-level research labs, as well as the hiring and stabilisation of personnel in the National Health System, a sign of recognition by the State of a cooperative model between regions and the renewed role of NIHMP on the national territory.
4 The INMP's mission is to develop innovative systems and patterns with the aim to fight inequalities within the ambit of the Italian health care, to facilitate access to the National Health Service (SSN) for disadvantaged population groups and to ensure high quality services to Italian and foreign citizens. In particular, the Institute provides health care services to specific populations (the poor and disadvantaged groups, regularly and irregularly staying foreigners, victims of violence and slave trade, international protection applicants), by implementing its holistic social-health care system with a transcultural approach. Services are provided both daily at health care centres, and within the ambit of specific projects also with international cooperation. It works in synergy with regions and the autonomous provinces of Trento and Bolzano in defining national public policies aimed at answering the emerging health care needs, fighting inequalities, and containing costs at the SSN's expense. https://www.inmp.it/eng/About-Us

The birth of the INMP strengthened the socio-medical approach for poor and migrants in public institutions, which previously was provided mostly by religious associations. In the nineties, some of the pioneers of ethnopsychiatry have contributed to develop the ethnopsychiatric approach as one of the most relevant in mental health care at the INMP. One of the pioneers of that passage was Tobie Nathan who developed the theory of his mentor Georges Devereux and, within the University of Paris VIII Vincennes - Saint-Denis, founded a clinic for migrant people. The clinic was named after his mentor and it was ethnopsychiatrically oriented. It triggered a theoretical effort and promoted an interest toward foreigners, thrilling many psychiatric operators across Europe. Also, in Italy, migrants started to knock on the door of health centres throughout the national territory and revealed to psychiatrists the complexities connected to cultural, symbolical, social and historical differences that were apparent in their psychic distress. So, some physicians, in sympathy with the issue, decided to familiarise themselves with ethnopsychiatry.

Ethnopsychiatry

Ethnopsychiatry can be defined as an "intentional act of an authorised technician to take care of the 'Life Principle' (a mental and body instance) in well-defined geographical regions and human groups" (Inglese & Cardamone, 2010). As initiated by Tobie Nathan and later redefined by his assistants, ethnopsychiatry may be considered as a culturally-informed psychology, an approach that does not oblige the foreigner to present him/herself according to the codes of the hosting country and culture. Within the clinical setting, migrants are welcomed and treated with due respect for their differences, feelings and intentions. Being aware of foreigners being tied to other powers, other commitments of loyalty, is a precondition for ethnopsychiatric clinical work which does not aim to provide messages on the meaning of life nor on duties relating to traditions; ethnopsychiatry is a positive and constructive way to enter into a relationship with patients.

Ethnopsychiatry does not only focus mental disorders, but above all, the competencies, strengths and resources of people. Ethnopsychiatry works for people's development (Sironi, 2005), it has been described as "a motor that generates the possibility of thinking the thoughts" (Inglese, 2014).
In the last few years, the founders of the ethnopsychiatry lab have taken the first steps into a sort of "no man's land" that, although located in the hospital, did not yet receive a formal mandate. They were animated by a great clinical passion for foreigners and gave a substantial contribution to the construction of diagnostic and therapeutic tools in subsequent years. The significant amount of work of the Institution and the daily theorisation and practice made a

comparison between cultural and professional diversities possible, mainly between psychologists and transcultural mediators.

Cultural mediation

As Tobie Nathan (1996) writes, the transcultural mediator working in a mental health context is a psychologist coming from the same country of the patient of which he/she knows local knowledge and at least one mother tongue. In Italy, cultural mediation started to develop around the nineties and is characterised by multiple training courses, most of which does not concern the health field; although Gutierrez says that cultural mediators where originally introduced in mental health systems.

First of all, cultural mediators perform translations at both linguistic and cultural levels in clinical settings that are more or less flexible depending on the psychotherapist. Their presence in a clinical setting has inevitably brought out oppositions and perplexity in some professionals. The inclusion of this extraneous figure in a therapeutic setting highlights several, also epistemological, issues, such as the need to change the leading principle of psychological intervention: the non-contamination of the field of intervention (Gutierrez, 2018). This has led to a debate between ethnopsychiatrists and psychotherapists, who do not agree on the role of mediation. The former believe that cultural mediation is not only a strategic tool to obtain compliance, but is a critical device introduced within the therapeutic system for questioning its own assumptions, organizations and praxis (Pussetti, 2013). The latter prefer to give the transcultural mediator the function of a translator and, at most, an informant about culture-related issues.

Those who embrace the ethnopsychiatric approach see in cultural mediation an opportunity to build a bridge between two worlds, two sets of representations: "the culture of origin must be considered as something that pertains to both sides of the communication and not only as something brought by immigrants or ethnic minorities members. Instead, the concept of cultural mediation must give full significance to cultural aspects in an anthropological perspective, giving value to religion, tradition and experience of the cultural identity. The linguistic aspects and all the forms of communication, including body language, are of paramount importance"[5]. In 2013, a multidisciplinary and multicultural team drew up a manual entitled *Guidelines for Training and Quality of Social and Health Services* which specifies that "The transcultural mediator, preferably a person sharing the origins and/or the migration experience of the patient, is neither simply a translator nor a sort of (fictitious)

---

5   idem

"cultural expert": with her or his active and critical presence, the transcultural mediator introduces a "difference" in the setting, representing the possibility to reformulate the meaning of stories, experiences and symptoms in a new productive form"[6].

Cultural mediation in the mental health field would require a joint training programme shared by clinician and transcultural mediator, in order to enhance cooperation and to develop synergies in the work they perform.

Transdisciplinarity

In 1970, during an international seminar in France, the Swiss psychologist Jean Piaget introduced an interesting perspective stating that: "we hope to see in the future the development of interdisciplinary relations at a superior level, which could be called "transdisciplinary", i.e. which will not be limited to recognise the interactions and or reciprocities between the specialised researches, but which will locate these links inside a total system without stable boundaries between the disciplines" (Piaget, 1972, p.144).

Continued clinical practice with migrant populations underlines the need for exchange between experts who can contribute to diagnostic/therapeutic work and theory development. Ethnopsychiatry, as proposed by Devereux, has a complementary methodology, which provides two languages, an anthropological one and a psychopathological one. The transcultural mediator rarely has the anthropologist's academic qualification that, in some cases, can be very useful to understand the geopolitical aspects of the patient's history and to guide diagnosis and therapy. He or she knows and evokes the world and the intangible feelings lived by the patients because of common origins and/or common experience. After many years of clinical experience shared by therapists and transcultural mediators, it it considered to be appropriate to insert the anthropologist's competence within the ethnopsychiatric service in order to continue working for the creation of a transdisciplinary and transcultural group.

Anthropologists, having culture as an object of study, can contribute to the development of the method, the orientation of the setting and the research. The introduction of additional profiles in an already functioning device has raised questions such as: what is the new positioning of the different workers? What are the differences between transcultural mediator and anthropologist in giving indications regarding the way of life and behaviour connected to the patient's culture? Can the anthropologist have access to the setting? If yes, when and

---

6   idem

how? Does the anthropologist stay for all the interview or not? How must we behave in multicultural and transdisciplinary settings and interviews?

The introduction of the anthropologist's expertise in a clinical institution of the national health system is an unprecedented event. Such an experiment has caused controversy and difficulties related to the authority and differentiation of roles, especially with regard to transcultural mediators who perform functions that overlap with the anthropologist's. The conceptual premise of ethnopsychiatry is to develop clinical and research structures where professionals have the same authority. This was difficult and created conflicts in relation to the management of responsibilities. Everything needed to be rearranged: What are the feelings and the phantasies? What behaviours and expectations did people have towards their position? What should they do and what were the objectives? What were the methodologies, tools and procedures? With whom did they need to interact? What were the available resources?

The transdisciplinary project, in which doctors and social workers gradually took part, has considerably enhanced and enriched the ethnopsychiatric structure and, at the same time, increased the complexity of ethnopsychiatry. Sometimes, the level of conflict has been hard to manage. However, the ambitious project to create health and social services which will address inequalities has always fueled the original spirit and, after difficult times, every branch of knowledge has moved towards a specific definition and redefinition of behaviour and roles. The roles have become more centered on efficacy, contents, conflict management and strengthening relations among professionals.

Service for international protection seekers: INMP

Between 2001 and 2004 three norms were approved in Europe and Italy and they have provoked a shift from economic immigration towards requests of international protection. The norms are:

- The Dublin Convention that defines which state is responsible for examining applications for asylum lodged in one of the Member States of the European Communities (2003)
- The law n.189 (Bossi-Fini law) that ties the residence permit in Italy to work, so economic migrants can enter Italy only if already in possession of an employment contract (2002)
- The ratification of two amendments in **Sar** (International Convection on Maritime Search and Rescue) and **Solas** (International Convention for the Safety of Life at Sea) conventions for which the obligation to supply a safe harbour for the shipwrecks falls on the Contracting

Government responsible for the Sar region where survivors were recovered (2004)

In the space of a few years, as a result of these provisions, most of the people who arrived in Italy for economic reasons have been induced to apply for asylum as the only solution, hoping to get a humanitarian residence permit. The accommodation centres for international protection seekers have become overcrowded, thus increasing the latter's psychological suffering. Meanwhile, in 2001 the San Gallicano Institution participated in a European Project entitled "Italian Network for the rehabilitation of the victims of torture," as a centre specialising in psychophysical and social rehabilitation of victims of torture, mobilising a team of dermatologists, interns, psychologists and cultural and linguistic mediators. Starting from this project, a certification of the health condition of intentional violence victims has been created. This certification, in conjunction with the increase of asylum seekers, has become more and more important, taking on challenging proportions for the whole clinic and health professionals working in it. At the same time, this experience has been extremely useful because it indicated a viable path to carry out health promotion for migrant populations. At this stage, it was decided to open a reception desk for persons seeking international protection and to enrich the culture of transdisciplinarity within the center. The desk still today provides to each applicant:

- Reception and orientation provided by transcultural mediators with specific competences in asylum field
- Analysis of the needs conducted by psychologists, transcultural mediators and then by anthropologists, in order to decide what intervention project is adapted to each individual beneficiary's situation,
- Medical screening with a first internal medicine check-up, followed by a personalised diagnostic and therapeutic process,
- Psychological interviews in transdisciplinary setting (psychologist, transcultural mediator and anthropologist) to monitor the state of the mental health of the person, to collect traumatic memories, to diagnose and engage in psychotherapy
- Orientation towards social services, social cooperatives, employment centres, Italian language schools, lawyers who can provide advice and centres of aggregation available on the territory
- Drafting of bio-psychological and anthropological certificates in support of international protection seekers requested by the territorial commissions and the court

The psychological interviews with international protection seekers reveal that psychic suffering often is often one of the heaviest pieces of "luggage" that they bring with themselves from the migration route. Its weight is aggravated by the difficulty of the "state of suspension" in which they live, waiting for the call of Territorial Commissions or the call of the courts, which process international protection requests. Before the positive or negative answer to the international protection requests, they cannot start planning the future. Continuous waiting becomes an obstacle to planning and reorganising their lives. The social health path offered to asylum seekers seems to represent a time to "cure" the uncertainty they live in and the certification seems to represent a "supportive object" for that passage. As an object requested by lawyers, commissions, courts, the certification represents the first sign of attention by the public institutions of the traumas found on their bodies and minds. The list of signs on the skin, body and their psychological consequences retell what happened, gathering the painful wounds of the victim. The raw constellation of signs and disturbances, revealed by experts, represents an important passage on the path of legalisation and gives the victims an unusual levity. This could raise many perplexities in the workgroup. The multiple dimensions inscribed in the certifications are of professional, human and political nature and this multiplicity demands reflections and discussions that could lead to disputes.

However, there is no doubt that certification and the path to social health are an important act of health care prevention and they assist the people during their request for the residence permit. For these reasons, they are still a substantial social health activity of the San Gallicano Institution.

Geopolitical clinic

The DSM (Diagnostic and Statistical Manual of Mental Disorders) drawn up by the American Psychiatric Association is used to prepare the certificates. The DSM is described as a statistical manual without a theory of reference; however, it is possible to recognise the American medical culture that organises its contents. The DSM has been adopted by most of the international scientific community and this makes it a common language among healthcare professionals. It is an authoritative device, accredited in the legal and forensic field. The DSM seems to be the most appropriate tool to present instances to commissions and courts.

Ethnopsychiatry was born during a time of interesting philosophical reflections and was influenced by the thought of Michel Foucault and Gilles Deleuze, positioning itself as part of the "nomadic theory". Françoise Sironi says that in the nomadic theory, disciplines are fluid, complementary, integrative, placed on borders; they are an interface, a passage. They are inscribed in the multiplicity because they deal with the multiple (Sironi, 2007, 2014). "A theory is exactly like a box of tools. It has nothing to do with the signifier. It must be useful. It must function. And not for itself. If no one uses it, beginning with the theoretician himself (who then ceases to be a theoretician), then the theory is worthless or the moment is inappropriate. We don't revise a theory but construct new ones; we have no choice but to make others" (Deleuze & Foucault, 1972).

The DSM diagnostic codes are suitable for the certification requests and the DSM is only used for them. Ethnopsychiatry uses other theoretical frameworks for clinical and therapeutic intervention. Most international protection seekers were victims or witnesses of intentional violence, in their countries of origin as well as during the migratory journey, therefore they have lived through traumatic experiences. "Intentional trauma" is characterised by the fact of being deliberately caused by a human being or an invisible entity, as in the case of a system or a group, with the aim to dehumanise, physically or psychologically break, the subject, reduce to subservience, deculturalise and/or humiliate the person. Ethnopsychiatry, like traditional cultures, involves the unveiling of the other's intention in treating victims of torture[7]. The unveiling can be done through the personal history of each patient and through the awareness of the collective story, as proposed by Françoise Sironi at the George Devereux Centre. She speaks of the "political emotion" experience, i.e. emotions caused by historical and collective events that are displaced and turned into individual experiences. Françoise Sironi has called ethnopsychiatrical therapy a *geopolitical clinical psychology*:

> The violence of collective history has a great impact on the individual's psychology. It generates psychological sufferings, psychopathologies and sociopathologies, full of individual and social consequences. The subsequent disturbances are not referable to the usual psychopathologies that derive from intrapsychic conflict linked to early childhood. They are deliberately induced by a political dimension. This entails a need, on the one hand, to better understand the specificities of intentional trauma (voluntarily provoked by humans) and, on the other, to introduce a geopolitical dimension in clinical psychology" (Sironi, 2007, p.11. Authors' trans.).

Ethnopsychiatrically-oriented psychotherapy for victims of intentional violence aims to free the person from his/her internalised aggressor where this latter is considered a "fragment of otherness" (Idem.) that owns the victim. The therapy starts establishing reciprocity during the sessions, focusing the intervention on trauma and identifying with the victim the influence of the internalised aggressor (to disconnect the fragment of otherness). It puts the patient in a position of examiner of his/her own suffering, promoting thought

---

7 Most of the traditional care system base the diagnosis on finding what is the cause of the disorder, either a person or an event.

processes. The therapy works on the positive symptoms, the ones that fight against the internalised aggressor, and on the negative symptoms, the ones linked to the malicious otherness. It works also with dreams, rituals and cultural acts (when it is possible), political emotions and with past experiences (like trauma, deficiency in childhood, wounds) and intrapsychic life that are displaced, transformed and acted out in social, political and economic life.

Geoclinical psychopathology

If Sironi's proposal to define clinical geopolitical psychology as the work with people (who are) victim of intentional violence (Sironi, 2007) has, on the one hand, received much acclaim, it has also, on the other hand, given rise to some concerns. Around the term "geopolitics", coined by the Swiss geographer Rudolf Kjellen in 1899, many theories have been elaborated and all of them have been approved or disapproved from time to time. Likewise, ethnopsychiatry has often generated misunderstanding and incomprehension. For example, the "iatry" suffix seems to qualify the discipline as an exclusive specialty of psychiatry, whereas it is a field of study and therapeutic intervention on immigrant populations started within the Paris 8 Vincennes - Saint-Denis University and its chair of Clinical Psychology and Psychopathology. The word "ethno" is also a cause of disagreement, mainly because of its relationship with identity (Fabietti, 2013). Similarly, Sironi's proposal to consider the theme of "mestizo identities", identities with an interface between worlds, as identities that must deal with the multiplicity of the world and often must change or go through a metamorphosis, has given rise to disagreements because of the ambiguity of the term mestizo (Amselle 1999; Clifford, 1993). So, the Caminanti Italian group of ethnopsychiatrists, confronting itself with the terminology issue, considered it appropriate to redesign ethnopsychiatry on the basis of a Geoclinic concept (Inglese, 2014).

The term **Gea** or **Geo** or **Ge** (Γῆ, *Ghê* in ancient Greek) or **Gaia** (Γαῖα in Ionic and Homeric Greek) brings to one's mind Mother Earth and the Greek myth of the origin of the world. The term appears to answer the need to attenuate disputes regarding the name of the approach. Geoclinical psychopathology:

> intends to study the mental disorder, often undiagnosable because of the uncertain nosology (is it a psychopathology or something else?) and nosography (what disturbance is it?), as a product of social history and politics of a specific cultural world. This product is not merely accidental, it follows specific and predictable laws of construction: anxiety, panic, terror, prostration, collective depression, fury, hate, explosive or brutal violence, distrust, hostility,

persecutory ideation, feeling of inferiority, devaluation, social shame, torture, prostitution and exploitation of the bodies, are emotional, behavioural and ideational phenomena found in specific historical-political and socio-cultural times. They are not just individual phenomena nor phenomena that happened only to people at risk with specific personality configurations. Moreover, the variety of phenomenological expressions, their intensity and pervasiveness, their contamination, overlapping and recombination suggests not reducing the multiplicity, variety and differences to a similarity for mere nosography convenience. (Inglese, 2019, p.4., Authors' trans.).

Conclusion

Special merits must be given to religious associations and the private social sector that take care of migrant population and social marginality. It is thanks to them that Italy was able to take care of poor and excluded people, to develop competences in this field and to share this knowledge with the wider scientific community. However, as laid down in Art. 32 of the Italian Constitution: "The Republic protects health as a fundamental right of the individual and the interest of the community, and guarantees free care to the indigent"; themes of overriding collective interest must be carried out and protected by state. It is important that public policies, with their refined tools and fundamental principles identified by sector authorities and European laws, keep on transferring the INMP's knowledge and experience over the entire National Health Service; it would be a sign of responsibility towards the most vulnerable people, such as migrants and poor.

The birth of the INMP marked a fundamental step in health policy against inequalities as well as in "skillful" management of the most vulnerable populations. In fact, it is not only a local, multidisciplinary and multicultural outpatient clinic; it is first and foremost an atelier of public health where professionals work to define and experiment methodologies and epistemological reflections on research, diagnosis and therapy in an innovative geoclinical perspective to be then shared with the Italian Regional health authorities. The clinics are about, audiology, audiometry, otorhinolaryngology, cardiology, dermatological surgery, dermatology, laser therapy, gastroenterology, haematology, gynecology, obstetrics, infectious diseases, pediatrics, internal medicine, travel medicine, ophthalmology, dentistry and gnathology, ultrasound examinations and nursing; furthermore, interviews by leading Italian lawyer associations in studies on migration and street lawyers are implemented into the OPD as well as anthropological researchers and social workers' activities.

As regards the mental health unit, where three psychologists and a psychiatrist take care of patients alongside transcultural mediators, anthropologists, social workers and specialist doctors, in 2018, there were 600 initial psychological examinations registered, 6.500 psychodiagnostic, psychotherapeutic and counselling interviews and psychiatric examinations as well as 500 psychological reports and multidisciplinary certifications. The patients mainly came from Sub-Saharan Africa, Eastern Europe and Asia (Bangladesh, China and Pakistan), and one third of them were women. The patients' mental disorders vary from year to year, depending on the migratory flows. In 2018, using the DSM diagnostic criteria, it emerged that depression, PTSD and adjustment disorders made up one third of the diagnoses. Other widespread mental illnesses were somatisation syndromes and anxiety disturbances. Lastly, a low percentage of disorders was attributable to psychotic and dissociative disorders, often linked to culture-bound suffering. Among Italians, there are predominantly people suffering from severe socio-economic deprivation and/or homelessness. There is also a proportion of Italians who are referred to the mental health unit because of the readiness, quality and proximity criteria. Requests for help mainly come from applicants for international protection but also from economic migrants from Eastern Europe, Latin America, Asia, or students, mixed couples, second- and third-generation young people, nomads, homeless, women and men who are going through difficult junctures or facing work or relational difficulties.

The INMP's vision is the realisation of the right of all people to universal health and it moves daily in this direction. The data collection is valuable but also highlights the importance of reflection and discussion to systematise the acquired experiences. The biomedical model, which can count upon an evidence based process, may result as less prone to a transdisciplinary discussion that is, instead, often proposed by professionals who have a humanistic education. The experience of INMP in transcultural and transdisciplinary social-health care has evidenced both the powerful relationship between different professionals and the conflicts between cultures and society. It has also shown the substantial contribution of such a confrontation between different professionals and of the common commitment towards ethnopsychiatry and geoclinical psychopathology; a confrontation based on a constant search for contradictions to open a new path of growth and knowledge. The geoclinical psychopathology touches theoretical, professional, identity and geographical boundaries; it swings and grows between the gaps in boundaries, frees up spaces, makes connections and transmits transformative energy to physicians and patients, on the worlds of Gea. Let us never forget what Katharine Clifford says in the "The English Patient" movie: "We're the real countries. Not the boundaries drawn on maps or the names of powerful men".

References

Amselle J. L. (1999). *Logiche meticce [Mestizo logics]*. Bollati Boringhieri, Torino.
Bacchetta P., Cagliano De Azevedo R., (1990) *Le comunità italiane all'estero [The Italian communities abroad]*, Giappichelli, Torino.
Clifford J. (1993). *I frutti puri impazziscono. Etnografia, letteratura e arte nel secolo XX [The Pure fruits go creazy: Twentieth-Century Ethnography, Literature, and Art]*. Bollati Boringhieri, Torino.
Colucci M. (2018). Storia dell'immigrazione straniera in Italia: dal 1945 ai nostri giorni [History of foreign immigration in Italy From 1945 to the present day], Carocci editore, Roma.
Deleuze, G., & Foucault, M. (1977). Intellectuals and power. *Language, counter-memory, practice*, 205-17.
Devereux G. (1978). *Saggi di etnopsichiatria generale [Essays on general ethnopsychiatry]*, Armando Editore, Roma.
Fabietti U. (2013). *L' identità etnica. Storia e critica di un concetto equivoco [Ethnic identity. History and critique to an equivocal concept]*, Carrocci, Roma.
Gutierrez A. (2018). *Mediazione culturale nei servizi di salute mentale. Considerazioni e riflessioni [Cultural mediation in mental health services. Considerations and reflections]* in https://www.nuovaciviltadellemacchine.it/wp-content/uploads/2018/05/Chiara-Bodini-sistema_salute-61-3.pdf
Inglese S., Peccarisi C. (1997). *Psichiatria oltre frontiera, viaggio intorno alle sindromi culturalmente ordinate [Psychiatry across the border, travel around culturally ordered syndromes]*, UTET, Milano.
Inglese S., Cardamone G. (2010). *Dèjà vu, tracce di etnopsichiatria critica [Dèjà vu, traces of critical ethnopsychiatry]*, Edizioni Colibrì, Milano.
Inglese S. (2014). *Geopolitica e geoclinica dei popoli in fuga [Geoclinic and geopolitic of refugee]* in Congress of 29 March 2014, Florence.
Inglese S. (2019). Follia per sette clan: elementi di psicopatologia geoclinica [Madness for seven clans: elements of geoclinical psychopathology], in *Exagere Rivista*, n. 7 - 8 anno IV.
Nathan T. (1996). *Principi di etnopsicanalisi [Principles of Ethnopsychoanalysis]*, Bollati Boringhieri, Torino.
Piaget, J. (1972). Intellectual evolution from adolescence to adulthood. *Human development*, 15(1), 1-12.
Pussetti, C. (2013) *Competenze transculturali per la salute e la cura. Linee guida per la formazione e per la qualità nei servizi socio-sanitari (Transcultural skills for health and care. Standards and Guidelines for Practice and Training)*, Edizioni di ARACNE, Napoli.

Sironi F. (2005). La torture et son traitement psychologique. Approche contemporaine des émotions politiques [The torture and its psychological treatment: Contemporary approach of the political emotions], *Revue Stress et Trauma*, 5 (1), 21-26.

Sironi F. (2007) *Psychopathologie des violences collectives: Essai de Psychologie Geopolitique Clinique [Psychopathology of collective violence: Clinical Geopolitical Psychology Essay]*, Feltrinelli, Milano, 2010.

Sironi F. (2014). Les métis culturels et identitaires. Un nouveau paradigme contemporain [Cultural and identitary « métis ». A new contemporary paradigm], *La Pensée sauvage, Vol 14, Num 1, pp 30-42;* Grenoble.

Psychoanalytically based social work with traumatized refugees: implementing the STEP-BY-STEP project

Katrin Luise Laezer, Marianne Leuzinger-Bohleber

In this chapter, we, as psychoanalytic clinicans and researchers, report on our experiences in working with traumatised refugees, the model project STEP-BY-STEP in an "initial reception center", its theoretical assupmtions and concepts, and its implementation in a second "reception center" in Darmstadt (Germany) between 2015 and 2019. Given the substantial problems that society faces in response to the refugee crisis, the authors consider their project and the committment of many volunteers a mere drop in the endless ocean of pain, despair, and suffering of thousands of refugees who have escaped war, terror, and poverty in their home countries and are hoping for a better life in Europe and elsewhere.

Refugees and refugees helpers as "human beings"

In her much-quoted article "We Refugees" Hannah Arendt (2007) gives an impactful description of the loss of refugees' "private lives" from a first-person perspective in the year 1943.

> We lost our home, which means the familiarity of daily life. We lost our occupation, which means the confidence that we are of some use in this world. We lost our language, which means the naturalness of reactions, the simplicity of gestures, the unaffected expression of feelings. We left our relatives in the Polish ghettos and our best friends have been killed in concentration camps, and that means the rupture of our private lives. (Arendt, 2007, 264-265)

The following paragraph is quoted less frequently:

> Nevertheless, as soon as we were saved—and most of us had to be saved several times—we started our new lives and tried to follow as closely as possible all the good advice our saviors passed on to us. (Arendt, 2007, 265)

Hannah Arendt describes an immediate new beginning, which compels the refugees to adapt to the circumstances as quickly as possible and the "saviours" and those helping to offer "good advice".

The following paragraph is quoted even less frequently, perhaps because Arendt touches a sore spot in the current refugee debate:

> ...since we actually live in a world in which human beings as such have ceased to exist for quite a while, since society has discovered discrimination as the great social weapon by which one may kill men without any bloodshed; since passports or birth certificates, and sometimes even income tax receipts, are no longer formal papers but matters of social distinction. (Arendt 2007, 273)

"Birth certificates" and "passports" holding the stamp "Jew" set a social distinction, which resulted in Jewish citizens being persecuted, killed and robbed of their civil rights during the Nazi era. The home countries of the Jewish citizens and the League of Nations failed as political models. They were not able to protect the Jewish citizens from being assaulted by the National Socialists. Having the "wrong" stamp and being part of an undesired group or ethnicity are causes of flight and persecution until today. Arendt describes in just a few words how "citizens" become humans, who "cease to exist". This topic continues to be an issue and dilemma for refugees until today. According to Arendt, refugees move in a "no man's land of lawlessness" and are "guests from no-man's-land" (Arendt, 1989; Kristeva, 1991, 2016; Christoph Hein in this volume).

We would like to describe what this currently means for refugees and refugee helpers in the following case vignette.

A Young Afghan Man without Birth Certificate

Mr A. is an Afghan, 21 years old, who belongs to the Hazara ethnic group. He has been a refugee in Germany for 5 years now with the status "temporary suspension of deportation". He has been in psychoanalytical psychotherapy for one year with me. He suffers from anxiety and sleep disorder, nightmares, depression, an unquenchable desire to be with his parents and siblings, and feelings of guilt. He fears being deported. In one of his nightmares, which he told in therapy, he was followed by men wearing black masks who chase him through the streets and in which he screams so loud, that his flatmates wake him up. In another nightmare he was sitting on a carpet. To his left and right were men with long beards but without faces sitting in a circle. They were passing him bowls of delicious food, which was standing in the middle. He did not want to take the food, but felt compelled to try it. Mr A. associated to the dream: "If my parents had stayed in Afghanistan I would have been dead or would have been forced to work with the Taliban". Both realities are very present in his manifest dreams.

Everything was better than being dead and having to live with the Taliban. However: the story of his flight which had lasted half of his life as well as the separation from his parents and siblings for more than five years now, never seemed to take an end. His efforts to receive a residence permitting him to finally settle in, although building a future and plans to visit his parents were shattered again and again.

In Iran, where the family was forced to flee when Mr A. was 10 years old, he worked from dawn to dusk, Monday through Friday, first in a glass workshop, then in construction – without papers. He only has a copy of his father's ID as a testimony of that time. At age 16 he had already four years of experience in mosaic tiling and was a master of his trade. However, he had to flee again without papers and without a certificate–this time to Europe.

In Germany Mr A. was taken into custody by the police. Having entered the country as an unaccompanied minor, he experienced institutional protection and attended school for the first time in his life, completed lower secondary education and started an apprenticeship programme. When he turned 21, he lost his temporary protection status with the youth welfare office and had to leave his shared apartment, which had been a place of retreat to him, where he was able to connect with others who shared a similar fate and had the same language.

He finally found an accommodation in a refugee centre ouside of the city centre, where 20 male asylum seekers share a floor with a small kitchen, two toilets and two showers. In this accomodatuon everyone kept to themselves. Mr. A. withdrew into his sparsely furnished room feeling anxious and depressed[1]. How can a young "human being live like this", I thought during a therapy session when he told me about this situation. Therefore, I supported him and assisted him to find a room in a shared apartment in the city centre, which is payed by the local department of social services. Without an advocate, he would have had little chance on the housing market. Many of the landlords let him feel his uncertain residence status and his financial dependence, a painful experience for Mr A.

The immigration office insisted on seeing his birth certificate, which he did not have. He was able to obtain it via middlemen in Afghanistan, but it was not accepted due to a missing stamp. The valuable document was sent back to Afghanistan via Iran and further middlemen, more stamps and a sticker with a number were added to the document. The delivery back, which lasted several weeks, kept Mr. A, as well as myself in suspense.

---

1   This seems as an example for us that his depressive retreat is a reaction to his external situation. One could even say that it is the system of the host country which can be seen as causing this psychic reaction in the adolescent refugee.

When he had the document, he still could not apply for his residence permit. Mr A. was now requested to apply for an Afghan passport as a next step. The same burocratic process with the Embassy of Afghanistan started all over again. Mr A. drove to Bonn five times in vain. His passport application was rejected each time for different reasons. During the therapeutic session I felt intensive anger in my countertransference. Mr A. in contrast – reacts more or less in a depressive way to these devaluating, inhuman ways of being treated. Mr A. was left with no choice other than to face this arbitrariness. I asked myself: Do the faceless men with the long beards in his dream only represent the dangerous Taliban or did Mr A. – in his manifest dream – also symbolise his experience with the faceless bureaucracy that he has to surrender to? Was it an expression of his feeling of powerlessness?

Even though Mr A. is not a refugee in a "no man's land of lawlessness" (see Arendt above), the rights and protection as a refugee in Germany are extremely fragile. The protection which is given to him is limited to a (human?) minimum. It goes hand in hand with financial and legal dependency, which stands in the way of the young man's striving for autonomy during late or post-adolescence. However: Mr A. has developed a sense of survival in coping with bureaucracy, but the ground which he is standing on is quite insecure.

When we carefully consider what Hannah Arendt already vocalised so directly in 1943, it also means that we as "helpers" are acting on the borders of legality and rule of law. It is in the nature of things that the interpersonal contact between refugee and refugee helper (when it is focused on the refugee and his well-being as is the case in social work or therapeutic approaches) has the effect that we as helpers no longer see "the" refugee as a mere number but as an individual, idiosyncratic "human being". Therefore, we start caring for him as a "specific human being".

Following the global definition of social work to "promote the empowerment and liberation of people"[2] according to principles of social justice and human rights, we as helpers are moving into a grey area where we are hitting the boundaries of the institutional framework imposed on us, and to some extent even overstep them for the benefit of the "specif human beings", who were forced to flee.

---

2   Global definition of Social Work, approved by the International Federation of Social Workers (IFSW) in July 2014: "Social work is a practice-based profession and an academic discipline that promotes social change and development, social cohesion, and the empowerment and liberation of people. Principles of social justice, human rights, collective responsibility and respect for diversities are central to social work. Underpinned by theories of social work, social sciences, humanities and indigenous knowledge, social work engages people and structures to address life challenges and enhance wellbeing. The above definition may be amplified at national and/or regional levels" (see: https://www.ifsw.org/what-is-social-work/global-definition-of-social-work/)

Migration and flight are invariably connected with departure and the hope for a better, safer life. However, migration is also accompanied by experiences of loss or even severe traumatisation. In Germany, three out of four war refugees are traumatised (Schröder, Zok & Faulbaum, 2018). As we know from psychoanalytical trauma research (e.g., from Holocaust survivors in the camps for displaced persons), the first experiences following acute, life-threatening traumatiaation proved essential for traumatiaed people: meeting the urgent need for security and stability but also for empathetic human beings willing to open up and listen to witnesses of the "incomprehensible", namely, what people are capable of doing to others in man-made disasters and acts of genocide. We know from many psychoanalytical case reports and impressive novels that initial contact with others after having escaped the Shoah was of existential significance for many of the survivors, sometimes even preventing total depression and suicide (see, e.g.: Laub, 2005; Krell, Suedfeld & Soriano, 2011; Bodenstab, 2015; Parens, 2018; Leuzinger-Bohleber, 2015).

As Leuzinger-Bohleber and Parens (2018) discussed: To turn empathically toward traumatiaed refugees and immigrants, it is necessary to counteract an ubiqitous impulse meeting the traumatiaed to look away. Jovi states:

> This first empathetic contact is needed to confront the overwhelming power of dehumaniaation, a destructive process that forms the basis of interpersonal violence and which is ingrained in many supposedly democratic institutions. (Jovi , 2018: 193; Varvin, 2015, 2018; Neumann, 2018; Pschiuk, 2018)

This has proven to be particularly difficult because the current situation reminds people that severe trauma in the context of so-called man-made disasters not only burdens or even destroys the lives of one generation but is often transmitted to children and grandchildren.

STEP-BY-STEP - a Pilot Project Supporting Refugees[3]

The psychoanalytic and interdisciplinary knowledge on the shortterm and longterm consequences of man-made disasters, trauma and its transgenerational transmission was one reason why the Ministery of Social Affairs of the State of Hessen approached me as director of the Sigmund-Freud-Institut (SFI) during the peak of the refugee crisis in October 2015. We were asked to

---

3 This chapter is based on former publications (Leuzinger-Bohleber 2016; Leuzinger-Bohleber & Lebiger-Vogel 2016; Leuzinger-Bohleber et al., 2016a, 2016b; Leuzinger-Bohleber & Hettich, 2018; Leuzinger-Bohleber & Laezer, 2019).

conceptualiae a pilotproject for supporting refugees in the first reception institution "Michaelisdorf" in Darmstadt. The pilotproject (main applicants: Marianne Leuzinger-Bohleber, SFI, and Sabine Andresen, Goethe University Frankfurt a.M.) was successful and was realiaed from January 2016 till April 2017. We are summariaing some of the main concepts and experiences here.

The "Michaelisdorf" (The Michaelis-Village)

The German Red Cross established the initial reception center 'Michaelisdorf' during the acute refugee crisis in September 2015. At first, it was a tent camp before former barracks complemented the refugees' accommodation. After some months, new small houses and a big catering tent broadened the barracks. Depending on the number of refugees arriving, 400 to 800 people live in the village (maximum capacity: 1000 people).

As is well known, in 2015 violence and even rape had been frequently committed in different initial reception centers. This was mainly because several hundred young men (most of them between 20 and 30 years of age) had been accommodated in tents or preliminary buildings together with only a few young women or families. To prevent this situation in Hesse, especially vulnerable groups of refugees (mothers with infants, families, pregnant women, women travelling alone as well as severely traumatiaed refugees) were sent directly to 'Michaelisdorf' in Darmstadt. Within 'Michaelisdorf' the project STEP-BY-STEP together with the teams on-site provided professional support for vulnerable refugees as 'first steps' of assistance. In individual cases, further and long-lasting steps supporting severely traumatiaed families after the transfer to Darmstadt or the local area supplemented those 'first steps'. In future, further or 'second steps' will be improved by the cooperation of the newly established psychosocial centers in Hesse which have been established in October 2017 based on the final report of the pilotproject "STEP-BY-STEP".

Psychoanalytic and interdisciplinary trauma research as conceptual basis

Conceptually, the basic principles of STEP-BY-STEP were derived from psychoanalytic and interdisciplinary trauma research (for details, see Leuzinger-Bohleber & Hettich, 2018; Leuzinger-Bohleber, 2016; Leuzinger-Bohleber & Lebiger-Vogel, 2016; Leuzinger-Bohleber et al., 2016a; Leuzinger-Bohleber et al., 2016b) and can be seen as aspects of psychoanalytically based social work with refugees. The facilitated principles, which are easy to understand even for non-psychoanalysts and have proven to be highly effective, are the following.

Establish secure and reliable structure

Due to traumatic experiences in the countries of origin as well as during flight refugees living in initial reception centers at first need the experience of reliable, predictable and secure daily structures. Therefore, in 'Michaelisdorf' pictograms were used to explain a weekly schedule to newly arrived refugees. The schedule showed offers of STEP-BY-STEP (weekly psychoanalytic-psychosocial consulting hour, therapeutic paining group for children, FIRST STEPS group for pregnant women and mothers with infants, three different youth groups, pedagogic children's groups, adults' group) as well as other offers of the staff and volunteers of the 'Michaelisdorf' (language courses, sports groups, medical consultation hours etc.). Additionally, the schedule accounted for the transparency of the cooperation between different teams as well as volunteers in the center.

Figure 1: Pictogramm as first orientation for the refugees in the Michaelis Village

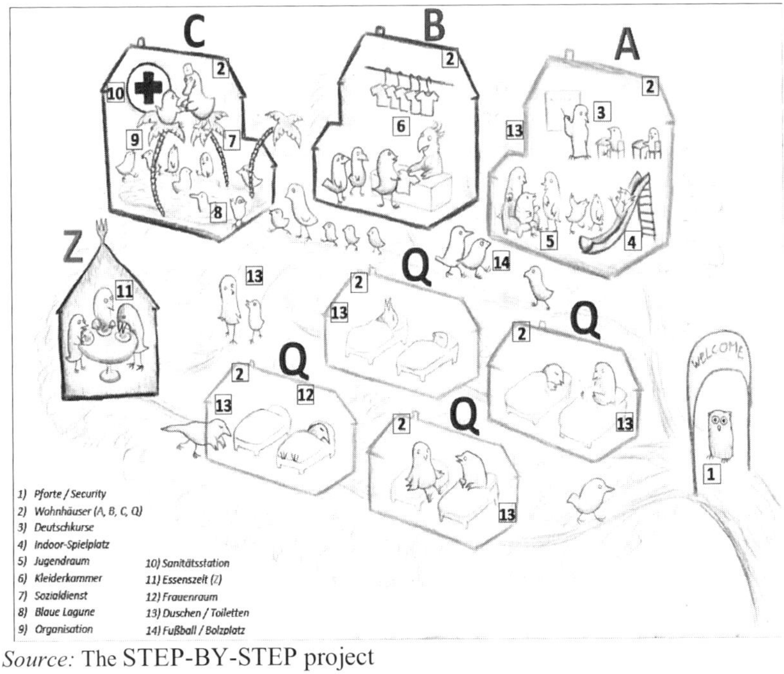

1) Pforte / Security
2) Wohnhäuser (A, B, C, Q)
3) Deutschkurse
4) Indoor-Spielplatz
5) Jugendraum
6) Kleiderkammer
7) Sozialdienst
8) Blaue Lagune
9) Organisation
10) Sanitätsstation
11) Essenszelt (?)
12) Frauenraum
13) Duschen / Toiletten
14) Fußball / Bolzplatz

Source: The STEP-BY-STEP project

Establish an atmosphere of interpersonal encounters and show empathy for the unimaginable burdens of man-made-disasters

As result of surviving experiences like traumatisation, torture or flight many refugees developed highly sensitive antenna perceiving even unconscious signals of others. Beyond language, traumatised persons perceive attitudes and feelings of people they meet in the receiving country. Thereby, it is highly important whether those people are empathetically interested in the atrocities of war, torture and flight or if they turn away or even react with rejection, sadistic impulses or dehumanisation. In continuous trainings and regular supervisions, provided for professionals and volunteers in the 'Michaelisdorf' those findings and their consequences for the interaction with refugees were discussed repeatedly.

Provide alternative relationship experiences strengthening resiliency in refugees

Psychoanalytic trauma research showed the vital importance of alternative relationship experiences especially concerning victims of man-made-disasters as war, persecution and torture. For instance, survivors of the Shoah newly exposed to sadistic and degrading situations in the camps of displaced persons often lost the last remnant of inner hope, which helped them to survive the concentration camps. As consequences of this loss, even suicides occurred regularly. Again, this important finding of trauma research was conveyed to all professionals and volunteers of the 'Michaelisdorf' repeatedly.

Convey meaningful activities instead of passive powerlessness

Before and during flight the residents of 'Michaelisdorf' experienced powerlessness, desperation and existential threat. Thus, all team members of STEP-BY-STEP together with the teams on-site tried to help the refugees to get out of passivity and motivate them towards an active participation. It was always important to encourage all residents to choose actively some of the activities from the weekly schedule. Everyone should at least be actively part of an offering for two hours a day ('getting something') as well as 'giving something back' for two hours a day by helping within the community (for example translating, gardening, paining rooms, helping within other activities).

Regain human dignity

Refugees are often victims of violence, humiliating live conditions and other degradations making them especially sensitive to new experiences of humiliation and powerlessness. Therefore, from a psychoanalytic perspective it is crucial to see refugees not as a homogenous group but rather as individuals having a specific trauma and live history. Moreover, everyone's different qualifications and potential resources should be appreciated. Accordingly, during the initial conversation in 'Michaelisdorf' the team found out the residents' profession, interests and skills in order to motivate this person to have an active attitude and 'give something back' to the community preventing a passive withdraw. Through the interest and uptake of specific skills and individual competences, the self-esteem of newly arrived refugees got strengthened. Being interested in the individual characteristics it became clear how highly diverse the residents of 'Michaelisdorf' were: an illiterate mason from Syria as well as an expert of English literature and a pianist from Damascus, a car mechanic from Eritrea and a hotel operator for the US army from Afghanistan.

Clinical Psychoanalytic Work within an Initial Reception Centre

To give an impression of the concrete psychoanalytic work based on the theoretical considerations implemented earlier, four of the STEP-BY-STEP offerings are explained: (a) the psychoanalytic-psychosocial consultation hour, (b) the therapeutic painting group for children, (c) the FIRST STEPS groups for pregnant women and mothers with infants, and (d) the groups for adolescents.

a) Weekly Psychoanalytic-Psychosocial Consultation Hour

In an initial reception center for refugees, it is highly important to be able to recognize severely traumatised people and provide mental and psychosocial emergency aid. STEP-BY-STEP is based on psychoanalytic and interdisciplinary trauma research.

During trauma, the natural protection against overwhelming stimulus is destroyed because of a sudden, unforeseeable, and dramatic experience that causes mortal danger and fear of death. The ego is exposed to a feeling of extreme powerlessness and the inability to control or manage the situation. It is flooded with panic and extreme physiological reactions, leading to a psychological and physiological state of shock. The traumatic experience destroys the empathic shield that the internalised relationship subjects (primary objects) form and the confidence in the continued presence of good relationships and the expectation of human empathy. In trauma, the memory of inner good people (good inner objects) as empathic mediators between the self and environment falls silent (Bohleber, 2010; Leuzinger-Bohleber, 2015).

During specific training sessions, the weekly case conferences, and team supervision, all medical, social, educational, and administrative professional teams of Michaelis Village and the STEP-BY-STEP team members were schooled to recognize traumatised refugees. Based on corresponding everyday observations (or specific information from the refugees themselves), vulnerable people were presented in the weekly psychosocial consultation hour. In particular, traumatised refugees received several psychoanalytically oriented crisis interventions, often in close collaboration with the Michaelis Village medical and social teams (Leuzinger-Bohleber, Tahiri & Hettich, 2017). If necessary, the refugee also received medication (prescribed by psychiatric colleagues in the village). The consultations were documented systematically but with careful consideration of data protection. All information was discussed during the weekly case conferences in order to jointly initiate "first steps" in the initial reception center. Furthermore, "second steps" (medical, psychotherapeutic, psychosocial, educational) were offered to support traumatized people after the transfer to long-term accommodation in the Darmstadt or Frankfurt area. Figure 2 shows the flowchart of this process.

Figure 2: Flowchart of the psychoanalytic consultation hour's process.

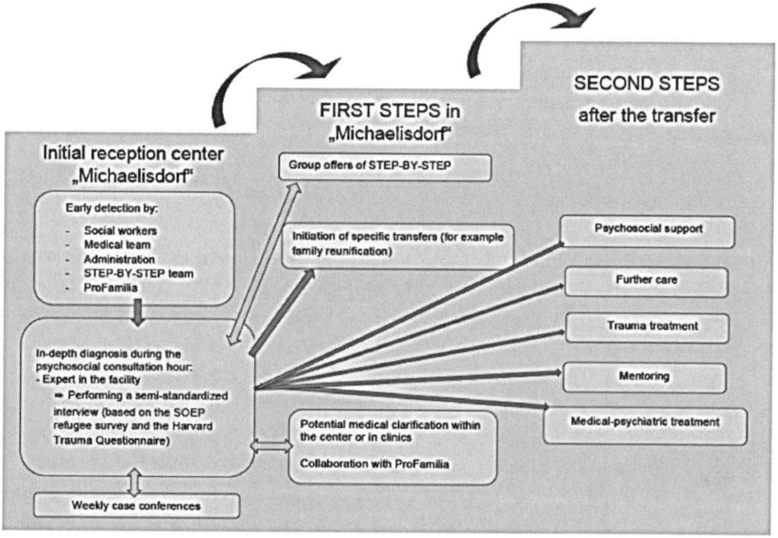

Source: The STEP-BY-STEP project

The following case study illustrates the specific clinical contribution that psychoanalysis can make in this context.

The Syrian Woman with the "Frozen Face"

A woman traveling alone and eight months pregnant was introduced to me during the consultation hour because she did not leave her room but would confusedly wander around at night. She hardly ate anything and was socially completely isolated. Mrs. M., dressed in black, sat down in silence. She seemed petrified to me—in an acute state of shock. She showed all the characteristics of a "frozen face." As often happened during crisis interventions in Michaelis Village, almost unbearable feelings spread in my countertransference. We were silent for a long time. The extreme feelings, such as emptiness, helplessness, powerlessness, and despair in the context of trauma, have been described by Laub (1997) as the "empty circle," by Kogan (2011) as a "black hole," and by Abraham and Torok (2001) as a bodily perception of being locked up in an inner crypt (see, e.g., Leuzinger-Bohleber & Hettich, 2018). Only after I recalled those metaphors did I feel that I could respond to the extreme trauma of the "black, petrified woman" sitting in front of me. "You have probably experienced something horrible ... maybe you want to tell me about it..." I finally said hesitantly. A young woman translated. For the first time, Mrs. M. looked directly at me—a long look—and suddenly, I saw that tears ran down her cheeks. She began to cry more heavily until she finally sobbed in despair and started to scream loudly. The translator was startled and hugged Mrs. M., telling me to stop asking her questions. "Let her cry, why should she not ... she must have had horrible experiences ... it's good, if she can cry," I said softly. Overwhelmed by tears, Mrs. M. finally told me in fragmented phrases that her husband had sent her into flight with three preschool children because the family felt acutely threatened by ISIS.

Her husband stayed at home with the four older children. She took a boat across the Mediterranean, and all three children drowned. Only she managed to reach Germany via the Balkan route. Her husband and other four children were now in Greece, but they could not travel any further. Thinking about the delivery of her new child frightened her; the child would lie "across." "I can well understand that you have terrible fear of giving birth after all you've experienced ... and that you feel absolutely left alone ... do you know anyone here in Germany?" It turned out that she had a sister in northern Germany who had been living in the country for a long time. We called her, and Mrs. M. talked to her for a long while, sobbing. Finally, I also talked to the sister and asked if she could accommodate Mrs. M. until the delivery and accompany her to the clinic. The sister agreed. With the help of all the Michaelisdorf teams, we managed to override bureaucratic rules that usually keep pregnant women in Darmstadt until after delivery. All of those responsible understood my psychoanalytically and empirically based declaration that it was crucial, after the traumatic loss of three children, for her to be accompanied by her own sister during the upcoming birth. Mrs. M. was transferred to northern Germany within a few days and, as I learned much later, gave birth to a healthy child. At the same time, the social workers examined the legal possibilities for arranging a family reunification and bringing her husband and the four older children to Germany. At the end of the conversation, Mrs. M. told me that she was very worried because she had learned that her sixteen-year-old daughter had left alone to avoid repatriation to Turkey. Despite this helpful crisis intervention, Mrs. M. and her family will need long-term social and psychotherapeutic care, which we hope will be offered within the newly established psychosocial centers.

b) Therapeutic Painting Group for Children

Another therapeutic offer was the weekly painting group, which supplemented the pedagogical groups for children as a form of interdisciplinary cooperation in STEP-BY-STEP. Psychoanalytic experiences with seriously burdened and traumatized children, as well as empirical studies, have impressively demonstrated how important it is for children to be able to put the overwhelming traumatic experiences, observations, and developing phantasies into images or words. This reduces the likelihood that the trauma is trapped in the body. Otherwise, the "embodied memories" ("unconscious" memories accumulated in the body; see Leuzinger-Bohleber, 2015) influence the children's thoughts, actions, and feelings, undetected and long lasting. Child psychologists and child therapists speak of the need to symbolise traumatising experiences, concretise them, and in the best case, communicate them verbally. Thus, the child is less alone with the unbearable, incomprehensible traumatisation suffered from man-made disasters.

Often, children are afraid to burden their parents and close family members with their traumatic experiences and try to behave as if nothing had happened in order to give their parents the impression that everything is all right. As a result, the psychologically unbearable experiences of traumatisation find another way to manifest. Psychic or psychosocial symptoms are among those possibilities. Traumatised children often suffer from nightmares, flashbacks, sleep and eating disorders, concentration difficulties, depressive moods, or various behavioral problems. During the therapeutic painting group, an experienced psychoanalytic child and adolescent therapist—along with STEP-BY-STEP staff and appropriate refugees (who served as translators)—provided a space for children to share their distressing experiences by painting, kneading clay, playing, or expressing themselves with other materials. For example, a six-year-old boy sculpted a person with a torn-off leg. In his home country, he had seen a suicide bomber at close range. With the help of clay figures, he was able at last to talk about his disturbing observations and related, recurring nightmares—a first step out of the psychological state of shock and away from being completely alone with the experience.

The child therapist was in close contact with her colleague, who offered the weekly psychosocial consultation hour, as well as with an experienced pediatrician and child therapist, who saw particularly needy children for weekly individual counseling as crisis interventions. Together, they often organised "second steps," such as long-term therapeutic or medical care for these children and their families after transfer to permanent accommodation in the Darmstadt or Frankfurt areas.

c) FIRST STEPS Group for Pregnant Women and Women with Babies

In the FIRST STEPS group, pregnant women and women with babies (up to one year) came together. Siblings were allowed to participate in the group. The group was conceptually based on the FIRST STEPS early prevention project of the Sigmund Freud Institute (SFI) and Anna Freud Institute (Burkhardt-Mußmann, 2015; Leuzinger-Bohleber & Lebiger-Vogel, 2016). Following this concept, the Michaelis Village group was also concerned with improving early environmental and relationship experiences and the developmental environments of infants. In addition, early mother–child relationships were supported in order to have a positive influence on the child's development. The group offer was intended to create a sheltered "safe space" that allowed women to get in touch with the group leaders and other mothers. The mothers experienced appreciation through the relationship experiences with the group leaders and so built trust. The group mostly worked without a language mediator. As a result, the focus was not on detailed discussions but on the interest in each other and the use of existing verbal and nonverbal possibilities. As an example, an Afghan woman used her tablet to express her fear and despair to a group leader. She said that after five months, she still had not received a decision on her asylum application from the Federal Office for Migration and Refugees and that she was very afraid of being sent back to Afghanistan. She showed the group leader a picture of a blood-spattered dead person and said "That's Afghanistan." Afterward, she took the group leader's hand and held it for a long time. In this situation, it became possible to share the enduring flood of anxiety and despair even with very limited verbal resources.

d) Psychoanalytic-Based Groups for Adolescents

Adolescents, in particular, intensively experience the processes of uprooting and identity crisis associated with flight, trauma, and migration. They are in a susceptible developmental phase, which is triggered by the physical changes of puberty. Adolescence in the context of migration has been described as a "double transformation requirement" (King, 2011). This is especially true for refugee adolescents: about 80% of refugees are adolescents and young men between twenty and thirty years of age. They often come from cultures that still bear many traits of "cold societies" (Lévi-Strauss, 1962) or traditionalist cultures. This means that young people transform from child to adult through a single ritual act. They are thereby directly accorded all the rights and duties that the traditionalist societies clearly dictate to them.

However, our Western "hot cultures" depend on the younger generation breaking new ground and questioning old structures in order to develop new ideas, think of innovative processes, and create alternative lifestyles. This often takes several years of chaotic phases and development. Consequently, for (Western) young people, separating from their parents and finding their own identity means a fascinating, powerful departure to a new world. At the same time, there is a loss of security, which was guaranteed to them by their position as a child in their parents' home. Fear of loneliness and abandonment may result and could be further intensified by (traumatic) flight experiences. Adolescent refugees from "cold cultures" often feel particularly lost, alone, and overwhelmed in Western societies.

Therefore, preventive offers, such as STEP-BY-STEP, have to deal with young people's need to be part of a peer group in order to maintain an emotional hold in the current uprooting and orientation phase. It is important to share the diverse experiences of being a foreigner and the desire to arrive in the host country.

Untreated, the feelings of being alone and thrown out of the family union, as well as living outside the familiar everyday life and the native culture, can make adolescents susceptible to radical demagogues. Time and again, reports show that Salafi extremists take advantage of the vulnerable mental and psychosocial situation of refugees to radicalize them, especially young refugees traveling alone. From the social-psychological, ethnological, and psychoanalytical perspectives, such reports must be taken seriously, because the internal and external situation of refugees and specifically traumatised adolescents may make them particularly vulnerable to such recruitments. Salafist preachers act with an intuitive accuracy about this vulnerability. They offer young people a sense of belonging, meaning, and security: the loneliness will disappear. Through the phantasised participation in a god-chosen community, the Ummah, the self-esteem of the adolescent is also raised narcissistically.

As Fonagy et al. (2014) have pointed out, many Western cultures have underestimated the evolutionary biological importance of adolescents' sense of belonging. The affiliation with a group offers a huge survival advantage: beyond the family association, above all, the social group ensures the individual's survival. Many observations from STEP-BY-STEP show that the search for affiliation to a particular ethnic or religious group, especially among young people traveling alone and late adolescents from various cultures, is remarkably often seen within the framework of an initial reception facility.

Further, the conversion to a fundamentalist form of Islam "redeems" youths from the adolescent developmental task of integrating the sexually mature body into the self-image and pre-Oedipal and Oedipal yearnings and conflicts. It is no longer necessary to develop a unique sexual identity as man or woman and to find a (heterosexual or homosexual) love object. This very demanding and conflictual mental task in today's Western world is often unresolvable for young people from more traditionalist cultures.

By contrast, ISIS fighter groups convey clear patriarchal ideas of gender relations (Schr ter, 2016). Instead of years of searching for an adult (sexual) identity in a foreign culture, the (adolescent) fighters, and the young women who leave to fight in Syria, grow very fast from a child to an adult, as in traditionalist societies. ISIS also enables the satisfaction of pre-genital instinctual renewals, which are revived in the early stages of adolescence, by dealing brutally with unbelievers. Those instinctual revivals are a social taboo in Western cultures and are subject to a demanding process of sublimation (verbal and fair combat).

Against this backdrop, the brutal films of beheadings or people being burned alive unconsciously offer a tremendous satisfaction of archaic drives. Moreover, the individual can act out his or her own suicidality as an omnipotent victory over the fear of death, experienced as the last triumph. As has been described, adolescent terrorists in a suicide bombing fight their own mortal dread insofar as they assure themselves that they will not be alone at the moment of death: their victim dies with them (E. Rolnik, personal communication based on clinical–psychoanalytical experiences with suicide bombers in Israel, 2014).

A further aspect of radicalisation processes in adolescence is, as empirical attachment research shows, that the adolescent identity-finding process is less about detachment than about a transformation of attachment relationships. In adolescence, the patterns of behaviour the child has developed in an active attachment system conflict with the quest for independence. The adolescent needs to find a new balance between the bonding processes and the search for autonomy.

So, it is especially those disorganised attached adolescents who are attracted by the clear black-and-white thinking: the precise distinction between right and wrong, believers and unbelievers, etc. In the sense of victimisation, these traumatised adolescents act out their unprocessed traumas and transform into action what they have passively suffered. To never again be a helpless, powerless victim is often a powerful unconscious source of motivation. They combat their former personal helplessness and despair in the helpless, fearful eyes of their victims. Because of these clinical and empirical findings on refugee adolescents, it is absolutely necessary to support them in their development of specific identity-finding processes characterized by trauma, flight, and persecution. It is important to recognise pathological transformations at an early stage and treat adolescents preventively and therapeutically (Leuzinger-Bohleber, 2016).

We understand the three STEP-BY-STEP youth groups against this conceptual background. In another publication, we tried to illustrate these considerations with examples from STEP-BY-STEP (see Leuzinger-Bohleber & Hettich, 2018).

Implementation of the STEP-BY-STEP Project

Continuation of the STEP-BY-STEP Project with Students of Social Work

In July 2017, the STEP-BY-STEP pilot project and its financial support ended. Colleagues from the University of Applied Science Darmstadt decided to continue the project on a voluntary basis with BA students of social work in context of the university's programme "Social Work Plus—Migration and Globalization", which prepares students for international work with refugees and migrants both in Germany and abroad. Students are required to spend an academic year abroad, including both a semester of study and an internship in a country outside the EU. The main idea of this year abroad is for students to experience the refugees' position as foreigners themselves, outside of their comfort zone, and to encourage a change of perspective and empathy with the wishes, needs, and challenges of refugees and migrants.

The teaching staff thought that a similar effect could be achieved by continuing the STEP-BY-STEP programme, with the additional benefit that students would be given the opportunity to prepare both theoretically and practically for the application of psychoanalytically based social work with refugees and migrants. Spontaneously, fourteen students in the first and second year of study agreed to take part, and we offered several groups once a week in Michaelis Village, as described above: a therapeutic painting group for children, a youth group, a mother and baby group, and an individual partnership with two young severely traumatised refugees.

Reflection on the students' experiences took place during a weekly supervision session at the university. As teaching staff, we applied a format, the "project module," that extends over the complete second year of study, from the beginning of October to the end of July. This project module includes three hours of theoretical work per week, 4.5 hours of practical application in the form of the internship (at Michaelis Village), and 1.5 hours of reflection and supervision.

In June of 2018, the Hessian State Parliament announced that Michaelis Village would close due to the diminishing numbers of refugees. There was great outrage over eliminating a facility with such a well-functioning network of professionals and volunteers, including active protest (online petitions, letters to the Minister of Social Affairs of the federal state of Hesse by several institutions and volunteers.) Nevertheless, Hesse held its position, arguing that STEP-BY-STEP had achieved its conceptual goals with the four psychosocial centers and that these had been sufficiently financed for five years. The establishment of the centres was an important step in the provision of service for refugees.

"Otto-Röhm-Straße" (Otto-Roehm-Street). Implementation of the STEP-BY-STEP Project in an initial Reception Centre[4]

The Darmstadt University of Applied Sciences and the Red Cross Darmstadt have been collaborated in order to provide psychosocial support for traumatized refugees, now working with the third cohort of social work students. The "Otto-Roehm-Street" is one of several reception centres for refugees in city of Darmstadt.

This initial reception center is another transition phase for refugees, where they stay for an indefinite period of time and regardless of their residency status, but not permanently. Due to the housing shortage and the scarcity of public funds of the city, the initial reception centre is located in an industrial area, where there are no other housing areas or public spaces, and refugees remain isolated from the city.

The initial reception centre "Otto-Roehm-Street" consists of 14 apartment block units, each with 9 three-room apartments. These three rooms are usually used as three separate apartments in one big apartment, so that sometimes three people or three smaller families live together in one apartment. The centre provides shelter for 924 people (Kooperation Asyl GbR, 2019). Unlike in other initial reception centres, in "Otto-Roehm-Street" there was a greater need for psychosocial support.

In the beginning there were almost no programmes for the residents, so the following weekly offers were much welcomed by the residents: a children's

---

[4] We thank the German Red Cross Darmstadt. Within the framework of the project "Strong Together" funded by the German Federal Ministry of Education and Research, the joint psychosocial support of refugees takes place in "Otto-Roehm-Street". C. Ziegler, R. Yilmaz (responsible for the team of Red Cross Darmstadt), K. L. Laezer (responsible for the team of the University of Applied Sciences Darmstadt), T. Babatunde, L. Adams, S. Alksne, V. Benetos, N. Anandasharma, A. Beck, J. Block, A. Erdes, M. Groß, C. Heidepeter, A. Melek, and S. Tresp (students of social work at the University of Applied Sciences Darmstadt).

group, three youth groups (one for female adolescents, one for male and female adolescents ages 10 to 16 and one for the ages 17 to 21), a mother and baby group, and individual partnerships with severely traumatised refugees. In the following we give a report on our experience with the adolescents.

Youth groups provide meaningful contacts and friendship

The youth groups in the Otto-Roehm-Street offer adolescent spaces for protection and opportunity (King, 2013) to the young people where they can overcome childlike self-images, try out new relationships and rearrange their striving for autonomy and social connectedness (Gerner, 2010).

Opening up the group to both genders aims at cultivating respect for diversity, respectful treatment of each other and equality. The regular and safe structure of the programs were of particular importance. This included inviting the adolescents personally each week in order to build direct relationships with them, their families and the other residents and to show them appreciation. "Knocking at their door", literally "picking them up" and "taking them by their hand" quickly became a ritual which the adolescents even initiated themselves.

Three phases could be identified in the youth groups. During the first phase, the programme was determined by a very fluctuating group. It was a surprising observation that the adolescents in "Otto-Roehm-Street" did not know each other at the beginning, even though the residents lived together on close premises and the participants in our target groups are in a similar age group. Apparently the small apartments and rooms hardly offer any opportunity to spend time together, and they did not meet outside of the apartments either. Transitioning into the second stage, the establishment of a core group could be observed. The participants became more engaged and active. A sense of trust could be observed towards the group instructors, but also between the participants. The adolescents got to know each other through the programme, showed support for each other now, and contributed creative ideas for activities. In addition to the core group, new participants joined each week, creating new constellations of interests each week. This phase was followed by the third phase, in which more activities took place in the social space of the city and the range of action becomes increasingly larger. The youth groups provided meaningful contacts that developed into friendships. The adolescents of "Otto-Roehm-Street" spend time together outside of the group offers now.

Youth groups as spaces for play

One of the favorite games in the youth group of the 10-16-year-olds was the game called "Murderers and Citizens". By drawing lots each player is either assigned the role of a citizen or the role of a murderer, who must "kill" the citizens by winking at them without attracting attention and must stay undetected in order to win the game. In order to win, the citizens have to try and identify all the murderers before they have killed all the citizens. After each "murder case", the person who is thought to have behaved suspiciously is accused by the players. And here it started to get interesting for the young people. It allowed them to assume a new role which they have to defend. They were challenged to try themselves in a creative way: Is my defence convincing? Does it comply with my own moral values? How do I feel when I have to lie as a "murderer"?

The game serves as an example on how age-related questions and challenges can be staged in a playful way within a protected group setting and how young people can try out a "creative-reflexive" way of dealing with these questions (Günther, Wischmann & Zölch, 2010).

Youth groups provide space for protection and opportunity for identity development

It was noticed that more boys than girls participated in the older youth group. Many female adolescents were home when the youth leaders knocked on the doors, but they didn't come along to the youth group. Apart from one female participant, the female adolescents were hesitating in responding to the personal invitation. Some of them were whispering in the apartment, wondering whether other female adolescents are attending the youth group. Despite assuring them that another girl participates regularly, none of the other female adolescents came out to the youth group. As the following remark by a male participant about his sister shows, the young women and men in "Otto-Roehm-Straße" seemed to come into conflict with their values gender roles and of hierarchy and loyalty. Referring to his sister he said, *"She won't come along, she would rather stay at home to help"*.

This remark comments on the aspect of "female solidarity" (Amini Renken, 2012), which we often observed. Amini Renken (2012) unterstands female solidarity as a generalisation of the mother-daughter relationship into a solidarity between women in general. For some female adolescents, the youth group for female adolescents was therefore an opportunity to get engaged with new spaces of opportunity for themselves beyond their family bonds and without getting into conflict with their family and gender values.

In the following we will outline typical conflicts of the adolescents in the "Otto-Roehm-Street" and thus highlight the need to establish space for protection and opportunity beyond the family bond. In our experience, it is important to acknowledge the adolescents' need for belonging (Fonagy et al., 2014) and to leave it open, how much they emphasise on individualistic and/or collectivist values, autonomy and/or social connectedness (Gerner, 2010).

Amina (17 years old from Somalia)

Amina from Somalia is the only female 17-year old participant in the youth group Plus (ages 17-21). She is a confident, open minded adolescent and speaks German very well. In the youth group she was well respected and was viewed as part of the core group. One day, the group met in the kitchen of the youth club to bake pizza together. On this day, a few male youths joined the group for the first time. The group dynamics therefore was different, more provocative, more judgmental, compared to the usual, rather calm dynamics of the core group.

At the beginning Amina was still happily cutting vegetables, but then she became more and more quiet. When she was finished topping her pizza, she distanced herself from the group by sitting down at a table separate from the others. She blocked off any attempt to get her back to the group table. Even before the pizza was ready, Amina went home. In the following weeks Amina came back and interacted as usual in the group. The youth worker was very confused by the situation, since she felt that before the pizza incident Amina had felt comfortable in the group and had enjoyed coming. On that day it had been quite the opposite. Amina had seemed as if she had felt restrained and her coping strategies had failed.

In the supervision session Amina's behaviour was understood as a creative solution. Going home she avoided letting the conflict break out openly, and looked for shelter at home. Amina was able to come back feeling strengthened in the following weeks. She could make use of the opportunities the youth group environment provided for her.

Rabea (13 years old from Syria)

Rabea is a 13-year old girl from Syria and only speaks Arabic. She has ten siblings and frequently some of them join her to go to the youth club (ages 10-16). The other youth already knew each other well, when Rabea came first to the youth group. Rabea was not really able to join in with them since she did not speak German very well. Quickly, a conflict arose between her and two other boys of the youth group: The boys insulted her in German, while it was evident by her facial expressions and gestures that she was insulting the two boys in Arabic. The following week, a group was playing outside and Rabea rode her bike through the group again and again and complained with aggressive gestures why the others were blocking her way. The boys took this as a provocation and a fight broke out. Even though the first two encounters with the youth group were marked by conflict, Rabea came back again the following week. At first, she wasn't able to participate because of the little German she knew, but then two girls who spoke Arabic were able to translate.

When Rabea was able to participate for the first time, a big smile showed up on her face.

In the following weeks Rabea happily took part in the youth group and showed interest. She gave the youth worker a bracelet she had made and invited her to her home for the breaking of the fast after Ramadan. But Rabea continued her aggressive behaviour. For example, one time, during a reaction game that Rabea was very good at, she pointed at herself and shouted, "GOOD!" over and over again. But when she had to draw cards herself (a negative move in this game) she started getting aggressive and yelled "HIT YOU!" at the others, making aggressive gestures. During another difficult situation one of her younger sisters was not allowed to participate because of the age limit. Rabea couldn't understand this, started complaining aggressively in Arabic and made a dramatic exit. Nevertheless, Rabea came back after 10 minutes and joined the game without any further comment.

During the supervision sessions the holding and containing function of the youth group for Rabea's 'breakthrough of emotions' and the implicit experience of alternative relationships with the youth worker became evident.

Abdal (18 years old from Syria)

Abdal is from Syria and is 18 years old. During one of the meetings the youth workers had prepared various drawing and painting materials, paper and tote bags to decorate. A while ago Abdal had mentioned that he did not enjoy artistic activities. To the youth workers' surprise, Abdal joined the activities with great enthusiasm on this day and it turned out he was very good and talented in drawing. He did not want to take his works of art back home though, because his parents would not appreciate art. He said that he was thinking a lot about his perspectives for the future and what could raise his chance for a residence permit. In this context, he mentioned that his parents perceived art as something "unnecessary".

The Abdal's scenario leads us back to the psychological distress and fragility of protected spaces related to flight and migration. The residents of "Otto-Roehm-Street" can quickly find themselves in a situation of uncertainty. The sudden presence of police and deportations are extremely distressing and frightening for the residents and affect professionals as well. In "Michaelis Village" and in "Otto-Roehm-Street" the social work students established a farewell ritual in each group at the end of each weekly meeting in order to ease sudden seperations at least a little.

Chronic lack of ressoures

Besides the chronic threat to the residents' permit to stay in Germany, there was a chronic lack of institutional equipment. For example, "Otto-Roehm-Street", with over 800 residents, had only two meeting rooms of about 25m^2, no playgrounds and no green spaces. The double role of the project agency as operator of the initial reception center and as provider of social services meant that the employed social workers of the agency primarily "administrated" the residents[5]. Therefore, our group offers filled in a gap with a relationship oriented social work approach. The meeting rooms were two adjoining rooms and were used for different functions. It happened that random people suddenly passed through the room while a group programme took place. Curtains that were sewn by the female adolescents group themselves were one way to address the problem. A short example demonstrates how the children and adolescents dealt with these shortages.

The fight for the pizza - The way out of passivity into activity

The youth workers had planned to bake pizza in the last meeting of the youth group ages 10-16 before Ramadan started, because it was an activity they had always loved. After the younger children realized that the pizza was made specifically for the youth, they tried to get into the kitchen with all kinds of tricks, in order to get a slice. Playing turned into fighting, to the point that the youth literally had to push the children out of the kitchen and the children tried to get into the kitchen again. It was a difficult situation for the youth leaders that was about to escalate and consequently hard to oversee. The older youth defended their pizza against the younger children and their siblings.

In the supervision sessions this situation made us realise that group offers for children and adolescents made a need arise that was not there before. When children and adolescents had not even known each other before, there hadn't been a need. Meanwhile the children, adolescents and their numerous siblings have found contact with each other in the group programmes and have developed their own wishes and could express their needs. We understood the fight for pizza as a playful struggle, a way out of passivity into activity that made desires, wishes and needs arise. The absence of any expectations (to which the local administrators had become accustomed) changed into demands, expectations and desires (which the administrators primarily interpreted as arrogance and excessive demands and put them in their place).

---

5   The staff to client ratio: one social worker for 80 refugees has to be considered as a "very good" ratio in comparison to other municipalities.

Conclusion: Psychoanalytic Supervision as the Core of Psychoanalytic Social Work

Summarising our experiences of social work with traumatised refugees in the framework of higher education of social work students at the Darmstadt University of Applied Sciences, the psychoanalytic supervision turned out to be core of the students' professionalisation as social workers.

As described in the first chapter, social workers might get into conflict with the institutions they work in when they strive for "the overarching principles of social work", which include "respect for the inherent worth and dignity of human beings, doing no harm, respect for diversity and upholding human rights and social justice" (IFSW, 2014). Establishing meaningful personal relationships with refugees in the "Otto-Roehm-Street" and relating to the refugees with empathy, the social work students got, from time to time, into moral and manifest conflicts with structural and administrative issues, e.g. other employed social workers who foremost had to "admnistrate" the refugees (staff to client ratio: one social worker for 80 refugees) and had no time to have a closer look at the individual needs of the refugees. It took time to establish a productive cooperation with all employed social workers and other actors like the security unit of "Otto-Roehm-Street". The social work students found themselves emotionally confronted with, what they perceived as "dehumanisation" and stigmatisation of the refugees, lack of resources, bureaucratic restrictions and other problems that have been described as typical challenges in this area of work (see Leuzinger-Bohleber & Hettich 2018; Bohleber & Leuzinger-Bohleber, 2016). Students had to deal with a constant fluctuation of refugees living at "Otto-Roehm-Street" (related to their status), language barriers, and the fact that more children and adolescents wanted to participate in the groups then they actually could take in. This included the demand of a lot of siblings who wanted to participate in the group offers as well. From a psychological point of view, students were confronted with feelings of being limited, feelings of frustration, anger, sadness and questions about psychodynamics of refugee families (including sibling and parent parentification, gender roles and cultural identity), child and adolescent development as well as dynamics of groups and organisations.

The psychoanalytic supervision deliberately aimed to promote the social workers' mentalising capacity and reflective functioning.

> Mentalising is the capacity to understand ourselves and others in terms of intentional mental states. It involves an awareness of mental states in oneself or in other people, particularly when it comes to explaining behaviour. That mental states influence behaviour is beyond question. Beliefs, wishes, feelings and thoughts, whether inside or outside our awareness, always determine what we

do. Mentalizing is often simplistically understood as synonymous with the capacity for empathy towards other people. In fact, mentalizing involves a spectrum of capacities. It is underpinned by four polarities involving relatively distinct neural circuits: (1) automatic–controlled, (2) internally–externally based, (3) mentalizing with regard to self and others, and (4) cognitive versus affective (Fonagy & Luyten, 2009). As such, mentalizing provides a comprehensive map of social cognition. (Fonagy & Campell, 2015: 237; Fonagy et al., 2002)

A first study of Hartmann et al. (2015) could show that teachers who received psychoanalytic case supervision every two weeks over two years achieved higher scores of "Reflective Functioning" scores, a measurement to assess the mentalizing capacity, as day-care teachers without supervision. Social work students reported as well about the improvement of their reflective functioning and mentalizing capacity. One of the social work students wrote about the supervision in her final report:

> During the practical phase at "Otto-Roehm-Street", I became aware again and again that the supervision in particular supported me in my work. I found it much easier to reflect on my role and thus to be in contact with the refugees in the youth group with the appropriate level of closeness and distance. In addition to self-reflection, I became aware of the positive and appreciative reflection of our social work with children and youth and specific difficult situations. This approach has helped me a lot in accepting situations and dealing with them well and quietly. (Sina Tresp, personal communication, 1 July 2019)

In the context of supervision, psychoanalytic thinking was helpful including its long tradition of scientific and clinical study of unconscious desires, conflicts, human aggression, destruction, creativity and generativity. In the supervision, students could recognise the subjective suffering of refugees against the background of their specific life stories and the surrounding circumstances. The supervision set in motion a process of understanding, and the terrible and incomprehensible facets of trauma could be held and contained in the supervision group. Psychoanalytical knowledge on trauma (as described above) asured students that they as professionals do not have to be afraid of the intense feelings that traumatized refugees evoke in them. Students and supervisor understood the feelings, imaginations, fantasies, as well as seemingly strange actions and symptoms that became apparent in the relationship between refugees and social work students in the reflection process of supervision. Supervision became a place where the social work students talked about their emotional involvement in dialogue with others, thought about what they have experienced, analysed and understood it in order to become and remain able to work as social workers.

The supervision improved the the social work students' ability to accept one's own limitations and the ambiguity of feelings. Coming back to the example with Rabea, the social work student could accept the adolescent with her conflicting actions and accepted that on the one hand Rabea gave her the self-made bracelet as a gift and on the other hand that Rabea attacked her, when she reacted aggressively towards other group members and the social work student. In the depressive position the social worker became able to endure and contain ambiguous feelings of fear/anger *and* hope over a longer period of time. Psychoanalytic supervision served the aim to protect the social work students by enhancing their reflective functioning, so that their humanity and empathy towards refugees were not worn down, but strengthened.

Recently, the UCL–Lancet Commission on Migration and Health gathered evidence from more then 300 studies and meta-analyses and came to the following conclusion, which also formulates an important goal for education of the next generation of professionals:

> Migration should be urgently treated as a core determinant of health and wellbeing and addressed as a global health priority of the 21st century. Migration and global health are both defining issues of our time. How the world addresses human mobility will determine public health and social cohesion for decades to come. (Abubakar et al., 2018)

Given the substantial problems that societies faces in response to the global refugee crisis and to migration, the authors consider their project and the commitment of many volunteers and students a mere drop in the endless ocean of pain, despair, and suffering of thousands of refugees who have escaped war, terror, and poverty in their home countries and are hoping for a better life in Europe and elsewhere.

References

Abraham, N. & Torok, M. (2001). Trauer oder Melancholie. Introjizieren-inkorporieren [Grief or melancholy. Introjection-incorporation]. *Psyche 55, 6, pp. 545–559.*
Abubakar, I., Aldridge, R.W., Devakumar, D., Orcutt, M., Burns, R., Barreto, M.L., Dhavan, P., Fouad, F.M., Groce, N., Guo, Y., Hargreaves, S., Knipper, M., Miranda, J.J., Madise, N., Kumar, B., Mosca, D., McGovern, T., Rubenstein, L., Sammonds, P., Sawyer, S.M., Sheikh, K., Tollman, S., Spiegel, P., Zimmerman, C. (2018). The UCL–Lancet Commission on Migration and Health: The health of a world on the move. In: *Lancet 392, pp. 2606–54.*
Arendt, H. (2007). We refugees. In: Kohn, J. & Feldman, R.H. (ed.): Hannah Arendt. *The Jewish writings.* New York: Schocken Books, pp. 264-274.
Arendt, H. (1989). Gäste aus dem Niemandsland [Guests from no man's land]. In: Geisel, Eike/Bittermann, Klaus (ed.): Arendt, Hannah. *Nach Ausschwitz. Essays und Kommentare,* Berlin.
Amini Renken, A. (2012). Adoleszenz und Migration: Eine empirische Untersuchung zu Identitätsbildungsprozessen junger Frauen mit iranischem Migrationshintergrund [Adolescence and Migration: An empirical study of the identity processes of young women with an Iranian migrant background]. *Oldenburger Beiträge zur Geschlechterforschung: Vol. 13.* Oldenburg: BIS-Verlag der Carl von Ossietzky Universität Oldenburg.
Bodenstab, J. (2015). *Dramen der Verlorenheit: Mutter-Tochter-Beziehungen in der Shoah* [Dramas of the lost: Mother-daughter relationships in the Shoah]. Göttingen: Vandenhoeck & Ruprecht.
Bohleber, W. (2010). *Destructiveness, Intersubjectivity and Trauma: The Identity Crisis of Modern Psychoanalysis.* London: Karnac.
Bohleber, W. Leuzinger-Bohleber, M. (2016). The Special Problem of Interpretation in the Treatment of Traumatized Patients. In: *Psychoanalytic Inquiry 36,* 1, pp. 60–76.
Burkhardt-Mußmann, C. (2015). *R   die Halt geben* [Rooms that give hold and support]. Frankfurt am Main: Brandes & Apsel.
Fonagy, P. & Campell, C. (2015). Bad Blood Revisited: Attachment and Psychoanalysis. *British Journal of Psychotherapy 31, 2, pp. 229–250.*
Fonagy, P., Cottrell, D., Phillips, J., Bevington, D., Glaser, D., Allison, E. (2014) *What Works for Whom?: A Critical Review of Treatments for Children and Adolescents.* New York: Guilford Publications.
Fonagy, P., Gergely, G., Jurist, E.L., Target, M. (2002). *Affect Regulation, Mentalization, and the Development of the Self.* New York: Other Press.
Gerner, S. (2010): Das ist halt einfach so 'ne Bindung: Familiäre Ablösungsprozesse junger Frauen im generationenübergreifenden Einwanderungskontext [It is simply a connection: family transfer processes for young women in the context of intergenerational

immigration]. In Riegel, Ch., Geisen, T. (ed.). *Jugend, Zugehörigkeit und Migration: Subjektpositionierung im Kontext von Jugendkultur, Ethnizitäts- und Geschlechterkonstruktionen.* Wiesbaden: VS Verl. für Sozialwissenschaften, pp. 227–246.

Günther, M., Wischmann, A., Zölch, J. (2010). Chancen und Risiken im Kontext von Migration und Adoleszenz: eine Fallstudie. Diskurs Kindheits- und Jugendforschung, Discourse [Opportunities and risks in the context of migration and adolescence: a case study. Discourse on childhood and youth research, discourse]. *Journal of Childhood and Adolescence Research, 5(1), pp. 21–32.*

Hartmann, L.K., Neubert, V., Laezer, K.L., Ackermann, P., Schreiber, M., Fischmann, T., Leuzinger-Bohleber, M. (2015). Mentalization and the Impact of Psychoanalytic Case Supervision. *Journal of the American Psychoanalytic Association Jun; 63, 3, NP20-2.*

IFSW, International Federation of Social Workers (2014). *Global definition of Social Work profession. Principles.* retrieved from: https://www.ifsw.org/what-is-social-work/global-definition-of-social-work/

Jovi , V. (2018). Working with Traumatized Refugees on the Balkan Route. *International Journal of Applied Psychoanalytic Studies 15, 3, pp. 187–201.*

King, V. (2011). Kultur, Familie und Adoleszenz—generationale und individuelle Wandlungen [Culture, family, and adolescence—generational and individual transformations]. In P. J. Uhlhaas (ed.): *Entwicklungspsychologie. Das adoleszente Gehirn* [Developmental psychology. The adolescent brain], Stuttgart: Kohlhammer, pp. 75–89.

King, V. (2013). *Die Entstehung des Neuen in der Adoleszenz: Individuation, Generativität und Geschlecht in modernisierten Gesellschaften [The Emergence of the New in Adolescence. Individuation, Generativity and Gender in Modernized Societies].* Wiesbaden: Springer VS.

Kogan, I. (2011): *Mit der Trauer k fen: Schmerz und Trauer in der Psychotherapie traumatisierter Menschen* [To fight with grief: Pain and grief in the psychotherapy of traumatized people]. Stuttgart: Klett-Cotta.

Kooperation Asyl GbR (2019). Erstwohnhäuser in der Otto-Röhm-Straße 39 [First houses on Otto-Röhm-Straße 39]. Retrieved from: http://www.kooperation-asyl.de

Krell, R., Peter S. & Soriano, E. (2011). Child Holocaust Survivors as Parents: A Transgenerational Perspective. *American Journal of Orthopsychiatry 74, 4, pp. 502–508.*

Kristeva, J. (1991). *Strangers to Ourselves.* New York: Columbia University Press.

Kristeva, J. (2016): *Was ist ein Fremder? Anmerkungen einer energischen Pessimistin. Kursbuch 185.* Hamburg: Murmann.

Laub, D. (1997). The Empty Circle: Children of Survivors and the Limits of Reconstruction. *Journal of the American Psychoanalytic Association 46, 2, pp. 507–529.*

Laub, D. (2005). Traumatic Shutdown of Narrative and Symbolization: A Death Instinct Derivative?. *Contemporary Psychoanalysis 41, 2, pp. 307–326.*

Leuzinger-Bohleber, M. (2015). *Finding the Body in the Mind: Psychoanalysis and Embodied Cognitive Science in Dialogue.* London: Karnac.

Leuzinger-Bohleber, M. (2016): From Free Speech to IS—Pathological Regression of Some Traumatized Adolescents from a Migrant Background in Germany. *International Journal of Applied Psychoanalytic Studies 13, 3, pp. 213–223.*

Leuzinger-Bohleber, M. & Lebiger-Vogel, J. (2016). *Migration, fr Elternschaft und die Weitergabe von Traumtisierungen. Das Intergrationsprojekt "ERSTE SCHRITTE"* [Migration, early parenting, and passing on trauma. The integration project "FIRST STEPS"]. Stuttgart: Klett Cotta.

Leuzinger-Bohleber, M., Rickmeyer, C., Tahırı, M., Hettich, N. & Fischmann, T. (2016a). Special Communication. What Can Psychoanalysis Contribute to the Current Refugee Crisis? Preliminary Reports from STEP-BY-STEP: A Psychoanalytic Pilot Project for Supporting Refugees in a 'First Reception Camp' and Crisis Interventions with Traumatized Refugees. *International Journal of Psychoanalysis 97, 4, pp. 1077–1093.*

Leuzinger-Bohleber, M., Rickmeyer, C., Lebiger-Vogel, J., Fritzemeyer, K., Tahiri, M. & Hettich, N. (2016b). Frühe Elternschaft bei traumatisierten Migranten und Geflüchteten und ihre transgenerativen Folgen—Psychoanalytische berlegungen zur Prävention [Early parenthood in traumatized migrants and refugees and their transgenerational consequences—Psychoanalytic considerations for prevention]. *Psyche 70, 9, pp. 949–976.*

Leuzinger-Bohleber, M., Tahiri, M. & Hettich, N. (2017). STEP-BY- STEP. *Psychotherapeut 62, 4, pp. 341–347.*

Leuzinger-Bohleber, M. & Parens, H. (2018). Editorial: Special issue on trauma, flight and migration. *International Journal of Applied Psychoanalytic Studies 15, 3, pp. 143–150.*

Leuzinger-Bohleber, M. & Hettich. N. (2018). What and How Can Psychoanalysis Contribute in Support of Refugees? Concepts, Clinical Experiences and Applications in the Project STEP-BY-STEP, a Pilot Project Supporting Refugees in the Initial Reception Center 'Michaelisdorf' (Michaelis-village) in Darmstadt, Germany. *International Journal of Applied Psychoanalytic Studies 15, 3, pp. 151–173.*

Leuzinger-Bohleber, M. & Laezer, K.L. (2019). Mobilizing empathy. How psychoanalysis and psychoanalytically based social work can contribute to the current refugee crisis. In: Habtemichael, K., Leitch, D. & Groterath, A. (ed.): *Migration & Refugees: Global Patterns and Local Contexts.* New York: Nova Science Academic Publishers, pp. 111-141.

Lévi-Strauss, C. (1962): *La pens e sauvage* [Wild thinking]. Paris: Plon.

Neumann, C. (2018). Intergenerational Transmission of Trauma Due to War and Displacement. *Socialnet.* Accessed November 11, 2018. http://www.socialnet.de/materialien/28166.php.

Parens, H. (2018). Being a Refugee—Reflections and Comments. *International Journal of Applied Psychoanalytic Studies. 15, 3, pp. 219–236.*

Pschiuk, L. (2018) Resilience and Posttraumatic Growth of Refugee Women: Impacts and Challenges. *Socialnet.* Accessed November 11, 2018. http://www.socialnet.de/materialien/28165.php.

Schröder, H., Klaus, Z. & Faulbaum, F. (2018). Gesundheit von Geflüchteten in Deutschland—Ergebnisse einer Befragung von Schutzsuchenden aus Syrien, Irak und Afghanistan. Die Versicherten-Umfrage des Wissenschaftlichen Instituts der AOK [Health of refugees in Germany—Results of a survey of refugees from Syria, Iraq, and Afghanistan. The health insurance survey of the Scientific Institute of AOK], *WIdO-monitor 2018 15, 1, pp. 1–20.*

Schr ter, S. (2016). *Gott r als der eigenen Halsschlagader: Fromme Muslime in Deutschland* [Closer to God than towards his own carotid artery: Devout Muslims in Germany]. Frankfurt am Main: Campus Verlag.

Varvin, S. (2017). Unsere Beziehung zu Flüchtlingen: Zwischen Mitgefühl und Dehumanisierung [Our relationship with refugees: Between compassion and dehumanization]. *Bulletin of the European Psychoanalytical Federation 71, pp. 11–30.*

Varvin, S. (2018). Refugees, Their Situation and Treatment Needs. *International Journal of Applied Psychoanalytic Studies 15, 3, pp. 174–186.*

The Service System for Victims of Human Trafficking in the City of Rome

Germana Cesarano, Angelika Groterath, Daniela Moretti

Background

The "Exploitation of prostitution" (sfruttamento della prostituzione) is a criminal offence in Italy since 1958, the year when the "Merlin law" came into power. This law is named after a woman, a socialist member of the Italian Parliament, whose efforts terminated the exploitation of sex workers.

The law banned brothels, which had been under the authority of the state before. The women were registered as prostitutes, and their documents contained indications on their profession, which made it impossible for them to find another job. Every 15 days they could be transferred into another brothel and they had no say in the matter. They were, indeed, slaves.

The "Merlin law" is still in use today. It does not prohibit prostitution, but it prohibits and punishes exploitation. With the end of the brothels, however, prostitution went on in private houses and in the streets, and the pimp emerged as a new "profession".

In the late '80s, a new type of prevention gained a footing in countries hit by the spreade of HIV/AIDS amongst of injecting drug users. New experimental projects turned the traditional walk-in model of counselling services upside down. Social and medical operators left their offices and clinics and went by cars and camper vans to reach out to the users in the streets. The "street units", or "outreach units", they formed were very successful in the fight against HIV/AIDS contamination. Against the background of this positive experience, an attempt was made to apply this outreach model to the services for sex workers also. The first street unit specifically for sex workers was created by the *Cooperativa Magliana '80*, in 1994 under the responsibility of one of the authors of this chapter (Cesarano & Camposeragna, 2006). Since then, Magliana '80 has been involved in street work with sex workers in Rome and so could observe developments in the phenomenon at close quarters.

In the '90s an almost uninterrupted increase in numbers of sex workers was recorded both for transgender sex workers of South American origin and for young girls from Eastern Europe. Eastern European countries were collapsing or on the edge of a civil war in these times, if not, as in former Yugoslavia, in the middle of a bloody conflict. Street prostitution spread across Rome and left or went beyond its classical milieus in the city. Little by little the picture changed: Italian women moved indoors, the drug addicted women moved to places like railway stations, and the streets were more and more occupied by foreign women with their history of long and endured pain and exploitation.

The girls from the war affected areas were often in charge of supporting their men and their families with the money they made as prostitutes. They reported about the lack of jobs, and also about deception and blackmail. In most cases the families at home were put at high risk when the women tried to escape.

The Law

The European Commission states:

> Since 1998, Italy has been at the forefront of the fight against trafficking in human beings and the protection of victims, both children and adults. The Italian model, which is still considered as a best practice in this field, was built on the principle that an effective anti-trafficking strategy should be based on a **victim rights-centred approach.** The main legal provisions regulating the national response to trafficking in persons were drafted in accordance with this principle and are: Article 18 of the National Law on Migration (Legislative Decree No 286 of 1998); Article 13 of the National Law against Trafficking in Human Beings (Law No 228 of 2003).
>
> European Commission (2019, November 10).

On the basis of these laws, Italy has developed a complex system for the assistance to victims of trafficking. Through article 18, the country gives them the opportunity to start a new life in Italy or in their country of origin. They can benefit from assisted voluntary return or from a special residence permit for social protection. This residence permit is envisaged in article 18 by the Legislative Decree No 286 of 1998: "The granting of this residence permit does not depend on reporting traffickers/exploiters to law enforcement agencies by the victim. The only necessary condition for the permit to be issued is to meet the requirements provided for by the law, participate in the "Article 18" assistance programme and complete it" (ibid).

Article 18 remains in force, but over the years new rules have been approved both to adapt to European regulations and to facilitate the emergence or detection of trafficked or immigrant people:

- The Legislative Decree No 142/2015, implementing the European Directive 2013/33 UE and Directive 2013/32 establishes the rules

relating to hospitality of citizens from non-EU countries and asylum seekers.
- DPCM 16/05/2016 defines the "Programma unico di emersione, assistenza e integrazione sociale" (integrated programme of emergence, assistance and social integration)

The Regione Lazio, which the City of Rome belongs to, has regulated its integrated programme / system of respective intervention and social services via the law L.R. 10 Agosto 2016, n. 11.

Article 18 makes it possible to work in a sort of joint venture on more levels in an important network of services from the social, the legal and the health area. The residence permit can be carried out at:

- The District Attorney's Office, when legal measures are underway in relation to violence or serious exploitation towards the foreign citizen.
- Local social services or NGOs that are accredited / being listed on the pertinent national register of the Ministry for Employment and Social Policies (National register).

Such a two-paths system is new and remarkable, if not unique in Europe. The 'judicial path' entails cooperation with law enforcement agencies; the 'social path' requires only the submission of a statement on behalf of the victim by an accredited NGO or by the social services of a local authority.

Both procedures can result in the issuance of a six-month humanitarian residence permit, which is renewable for one year and can be converted into a student or work residence permit. To be eligible for programmes of social protection, the person, no matter whether irregular or regular, must be in a situation of danger due to violence and exploitation, which must be certified by the police or by social workers of the municipality or accredited NGOs.

The first population benefiting from the regulations of article 18, were women from Eastern European countries, outside the EU in the late '90s. In the same period, the Italian and the Albanian government signed an agreement to prevent illegal migration and trafficking. The Albanian women dared to oppose their traffickers, and this made a difference in the relation between victims and traffickers. The system of slavery changed into forms of softer control.

The women were, for example, allowed to keep some money for themselves and to send it to the families. The traffickers then even became sort of agents for the women: they provided condoms, food, street places, car rides etc., and the women had to pay for these services.

The services of the City of Rome – the Roxanne project

With "Roxanne", the City of Rome was the first in Italy to create a programme of intervention against forced prostitution. A symbolic date, 8th of March, the International Women's day, was the launch date for the Roxanne project in 1998. The Services of the Roxanne project are:

1) Two street units in the metropolitan area, working five days per week in three different time slots (10/14, 14/20, 20/24). The team is comprised of psychologists, linguistic and cultural mediators, social workers, sociologists and anthropologists.
2) 12 guests in two different houses for emergency rescue and 12 guests in semi-autonomy. Semi-autonomy is for women who have a stay permit, Italian language skills at a b-level, and who can seek a job.
3) A front office for information, social and legal assistance.
4) A network of safe houses for emergencies (most of them in religious organisations / Catholic congregations).
5) A programme of education, training and job placement.

The intervention of the Roxanne project relies mainly upon four types of action; these are identification, emersion, orienting and reception, whereby emersion means to help people to be aware of the possibilities offered by Italian Law. The two street units have an average of 8,000 contacts with about 3,000/3,500 subjects per year. About 250/300 persons per year show up at the orientation and reception desk at the front office; and out of these 50 are involved in protection programmes. Since 1999, 611 women have been accepted and 70% of these completed the programme. The average length of stay in the programme is four years.

The role of the NGOs

Some services, such as the street units, the front office and the safe houses' management, are delegated to the "third sector", to accredited organisations that are registered in a register of national associations. Such recognition is granted only to associations that can show they have worked and continue to work in the respective sector. Magliana '80 is one of the third sector organisations in charge of Roxanne intervention in Rome on behalf of the municipality. The following examples of real activities relate to the Magliana '80 experience. However, even if the services are contracted out, the municipality retains ownership of the project.

The network

A particularly interesting feature of the Italian system is the service network. Such networks are constructed and maintained at national and local levels. They facilitate the intervention enormously. The primary goal of the intervention is to make escape from the condition of exploitation possible and to make, in a next step, the integration into Italian society easier. The network includes actors from the legal and the social sectors, but also representatives of the health system. In Italy everybody has the right to healthcare. In the late 90s, pressure by different groups and activists, as they would be called today, triggered the Italian government to give access to the public health system to Non-EU citizens without residency permits also. They can access health services through the STP card (STP = temporarily present foreigner).

As the Roxanne project and the network established by and around it were very efficient, the Municipality of Rome stabilised the project's future in 2004, guaranteeing funds from the regular municipal budget for services.

Real activities

In the streets and in the front office:

The outreach units contact people who prostitute themselves on roads or indoors, whether they are victims of trafficking or not. The staff distributes prevention material such as good quality lubricants and condoms, information material on sexually transmitted diseases and local services, especially health services. They bring along sweets and fresh water in summer or hot drinks in winter and they offer a moment to listen to the personal stories of the people they meet. They often speak about their kids, their family, of some situation of abuse or violence. As a German student on a traineeship put it, deeply impressed: "They are even able to conduct a therapeutic consultation in the midst of the night in the Roman Banlieue in front of a rubbish container!"[1]

The staff also gives them leaflets with the phone number of the front office and any information they ask for. In the street, contact is fast to avoid interfering with the job or calling the attention of the pimps. It happens quite often that while the women are talking with the staff, they receive a phone call, and "somebody" asks who these people are and what they want. The first rule is to not put them in danger, to understand the situation and to act and react accordingly.

---

1 Henriette Lewek, personal communication in 2011.

In the front office, a multidisciplinary team is working that is formed of a social assistant, by social workers, psychologists, legal consultants and cultural and linguistic mediators. Their interventions are based upon:

- A trust agreement between the victim and the anti-trafficking system, negotiable at any time.
- Inclusion paths respectful of the cultures of origin and the migratory project of the single person.
- The presence and cooperation of cultural mediators that facilitate contact and dialogue.

The interview is the main instrument in use in this work, but the interview is specific for each problem and for each person. Through years of experience the team has defined a series of items in order to help the person who does not speak Italian. Many of them went through traumatic experiences during the journey, or in the hell of Libya, or with clients, or pimps, or escaping from police. They are scared and stressed, and they do not know about this new place, its law, its values, and the support workers do not necessarily know anything about their world.[2] During the interview the staff must collect and give information but must also leave space to take care of the person, his/her fears, his/her pain.

In the interview process they follow a list of items that are useful or necessary to write a relevant description of the person, without forgetting the mandatory information needed when somebody is asking for a stay permit. The criteria of identification are described in the European laws. During the individual case assessment, which can also be requested without an appointment, all information regarding the access to services or how to get out from exploitation, is given to the person. If she/he is in a situation of serious threat she/he can be sent to reception shelters immediately.

In the reception shelters and the other houses:

Reception shelters, where interdisciplinary teams are at work, can welcome people brought by the police, in case of emergency. However, the normal proceeding contains an interview with the Roxanne director (one of the authors of this chapter, Moretti), and a second interview with the reception shelter responsible. The municipality, in the shape of the Roxanne director, empowers the association that runs the shelter, to take care of the victim. By this the reintegration and rehabilitation path is prepared. An individual case assessment

---

2   The Romans wrote on their maps of Africa and other lands outside the borders of the Roman Empire "Hic sunt leones", "Here are lions". Sometimes we ask ourselves how much we have expanded our knowledge.

is carried out to refer the person to the health care services, to an Italian language and culture class and to the education system. Mobile phones are not available at first until a new number is activated, in order to avoid contact with the exploiter or those close to him.

During the first years of the Roxanne project the houses were populated with girls from different countries. The communication language was Italian and this facilitated the learning of the language. Moreover, many of them already had some education and the integration process was smoother. Among the shelters' guests, Nigerian women hardly asked to access the reintegration and rehabilitation process until their debt was repaid and they were set free from the *juju*[3] curse.

Some figures about prostitution in Rome

It is impossible to provide exact figures on the number of prostitutes in Rome's streets. The last "census" (by NGOs and a Hotline phone number service) found 3452 individuals. Despite some Italian politician's declarations about an invasion from Africa, 38 % out of all these were European, with 75% Romanians and 17% Albanians as the largest groups. Only 36.7 % were Africans (mostly from Nigeria). Transgender prostitution was counted at 16%, mostly coming from South-America and 2.3 % out of these 3452 persons were Italians.

The persons who gained access to reintegration and rehabilitation programmes, however, were and are mostly Nigerian women. Their presence makes pidgin English the most widely spoken language in shelters and that has a negative impact on the individual success in educational programmes, in particular because of major gaps in the knowledge of Italian. Moreover, most of them having only had a poor education, their stay in the shelters lasts longer. Indeed, at the beginning, the average stay in safe houses was about 18 months, and similarly in second accommodation homes, the period of the total stay today goes over 48 months.

---

3   Juju is a traditional religion or rather a part of witchcraft in West Africa.

Figure 1: People hosted by Roxanne's project (source: Progetto Roxanne)

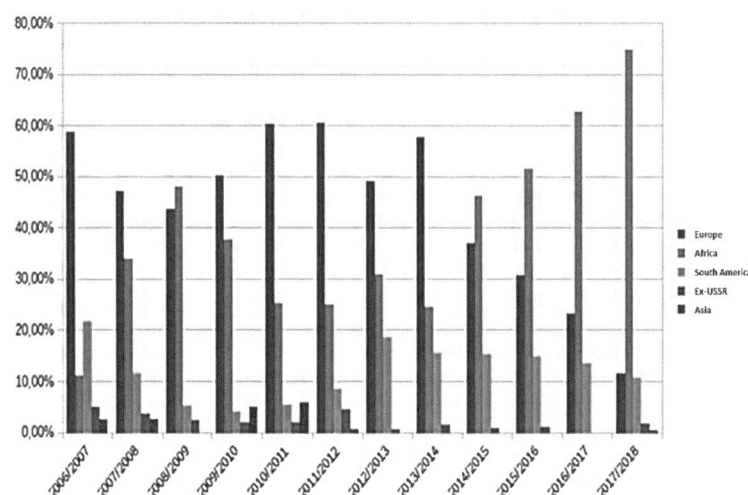

Source: Unpublished statistics Progetto Roxanne; to be published by Carchedi, Francesco, in Edizioni Bordeaux

Figure 2: Rumenian and Nigerian people hosted by Roxanne' project

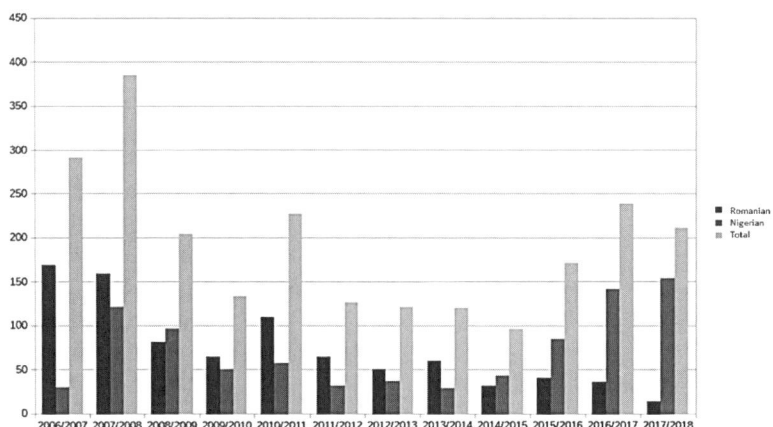

Source: Unpublished statistics Progetto Roxanne; to be published by Carchedi, Francesco, in Edizioni Bordeaux.

Some actors of Roxanne's network

In the Lazio region there is a well-developed network of 13 associations that manages different services, funded with national grants. This project allows transgender people, minors and women with children to access the reception system, also dealing with cases of severe labour exploitation.

Recently a protocol among Lazio Region and Municipality of Rome has been signed in order to deepen the cooperation between services even if, regrettably, this cooperation must be renewed with a new project every year. The network, that has been put together in the first years of the Roxanne Project, has been expanded and well-structured, also thanks to new actors. The intervention system now operates as a multi-agency network:

- Health Services: ASL (Local Health Unite), hospitals, general practitioners for health services accessible to both women in the programme and not.
- Law Enforcement: Police (Polizia di stato squadra mobile seconda sezione/ Nuclei operativi dei Carabinieri/ Polizia Locale di Roma Capitale) collect reports and carry out investigations for the victim's protection.
- Public Prosecutors Office and Central Immigration Office in the Police Station for the release, the renewal or conversion of the protection/residence permit or assisted returns in their home countries.
- Other Municipality of Rome Services: shelters for vulnerable individuals and women with children, Child Protection Office and Foreign Unaccompanied Child Reception Centres (MiSNA).
- UN and NGO: UN IOM for UN mainly, and NGOs such as Save the Children and IRC/International Rescue Committee.
- Health Organisations: such as the NIHMP San Gallicano (National Institute for Health, Migration and Poverty).
- Faith Based Organisations: many of these organizations have outreach units and reception centres, such as Churches, Caritas, S. Egidio Community.
- Juvenile Justice Services: Juvenile Court, Penal Institutions, Social Services.

The first Roxanne project's network was:

Figure 1: First Roxanne project's network

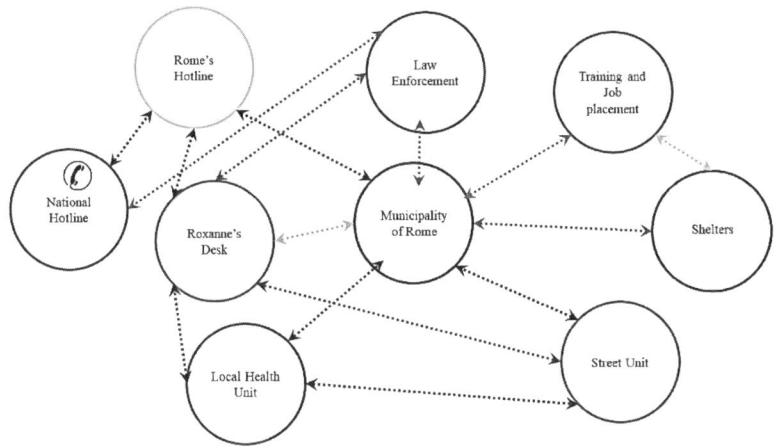

Source: Authors

Today the network has developed:

Figure 2: Roxanne project's network nowadays

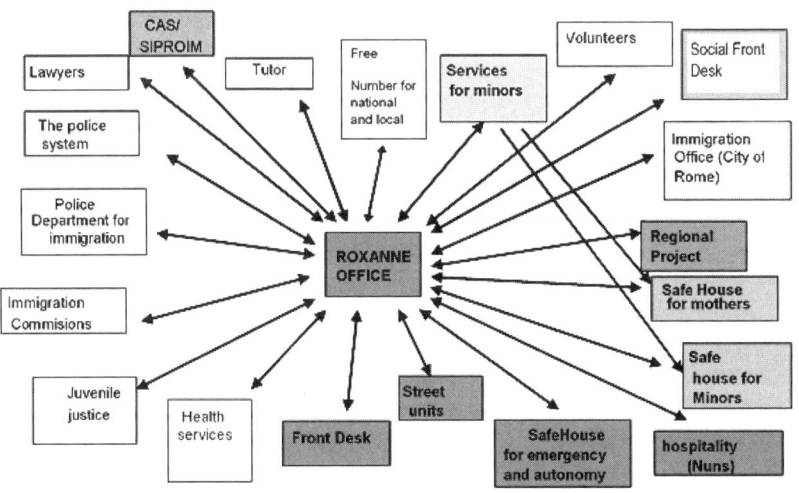

Source: Authors

Today, for most of the women it is easier to gain access to assistance programmes than before. Another possibility that article 18 offers instead is the *assisted voluntary return*, which allows people to go back to their country with financial assistance and the support to start a job. Only few of the women, however, choose this option.

Over the past few years the network around Roxanne has tried to strengthen the partnership with the institutions by creating round-tables on anti-trafficking laws and procedures, mostly with the Immigration Office, Police and the Public Prosecutor's Office in Rome. Contacts with the Ambassador of Nigeria in Rome are underway to facilitate ID release and to discuss how to manage trafficking between Europe and Nigeria. Moreover, discussions on the development of the trafficking issue and how to strengthen protection, reception and integration of the victims, with particular regard to minors, single pregnant women and single-parent families, are held in cooperation with partners and voluntary sector organisations in order to provide new resources and to improve both financial possibilities and services. Also, the shelter's intervention plan for users is being revised because it needs to take into account the educational aspect as well as the protection of the victims. Therefore, the presence of cultural mediators and a team that is able to work in a multicultural environment is essential. To sum up, we are trying to:

- Facilitate the release of residence permits according to art.18 (Consolidated Immigration Act 286/1998) for social protection.
- Deepen the cooperation among territorial commissions, asylum seekers, Prosecutor's Office, Prefecture and anti-trafficking services by signing operational and understanding protocols.
- Start collaboration with European countries.
- Start collaborations with the countries of origin, and in particular Nigeria, to raise as a role model the women who got free, instead of a rich 'Madame' coming back to recruit new victims, by giving protection and material support to needy families.

Finally, it is possible to fight back against the trafficking of human beings by improving cooperation across the network, to fight criminal organisations with the police along with voluntary sector organisations involving European actors, and the countries of origin to develop particular policies in order to deter girls from migrating illegally and improving cooperation with the country of origin for economic development.

Prostitution will not be defeated unless serious policies aimed at educating clients are going to be put in action to cut the demand. To many, prostitution is the world's oldest profession. Our job is to defeat exploitation and allow people to choose.

Suggested readings

Carchedi F., Orfano I. (Eds) (2007) *La tratta di Persone in Italia. Volume 1: Evoluzione del fenomeno ed ambiti di sfruttamento [Trafficking of human beings in Italy. Volume 1: its development and stettings of exploitation].* Milano, Franco Angeli.

Caritas-CNCA (2013) *Punto e a Capo sulla Tratta. I Rapporto di ricerca sulla tratta di persone e grave sfruttamento. Anticipazioni. [Back at the start of human trafficking. First research report on the trafficking and severe exploitation of human beings. Previews].* Available at: https://www.caritas.it/caritasitaliana/allegati/3430/SINTESI_Rapporto_Tratta2013.pdf

Cesarano G, Camposeragna A, (2006) Prevenzione dell'infezione dell'HIV nel lavoro di unità di strada e analisi delle tipologie di utenza [Prevention of HIV infections in the street social work and analysis of the types of users]. In A. Colucci, A.M. Luzi, P. Gallo, F. Starace. L. Cafaro & G. Rezza (Eds) *Congress proceedings: La ricerca psicologica, neuropsichiatrica e sociale nell'infezione da HIV e nell'AIDS [Psychological, neuropsychiatric, and social research in the field of HIV related infections and AIDS]*, ISTISAN Report 06/20. Available at: http://www.antoniocasella.eu/archila/ISS_ricerca_psicologica_neuropsichiatrica_HIV_AIDS_2004.pdf

CNCA, (2003). *Libro nero sulla prostituzione e la tratta. [The black book on prostitution and human trafficking].* La Meridiana Edizioni, Molfetta, Italy.

Costella P., Orfano I., Rosi E. (2005) *Tratta degli esseri umani. Rapporto del Gruppo di Esperti nominato dalla Commissione Europea, CE. [Trafficking of human beings. Expert reports designated by the European Commission].* Il Centro Stampa, Roma, Italy.

European Commission (2019) *November 10: Together Against Trafficking in Human Beings, Member States, Italy – 1. GENERAL INFORMATION.* Retrieved from https://ec.europa.eu/anti-trafficking/member-states/italy-1-general-information_en;

Fachile S., F. Nicodemi, M. Nibali, G. Altieri (2007). *La tratta di persone, le norme di tutela delle vittime e di contrasto alla criminalità [Trafficking oif human beings, regulations for victims' protection and contrast to organised crime]* Franco Angeli ed., Milano.

Magliana '80-ISS (2008) *Donne in strada e salute: sperimentazione di modelli efficaci di accesso alla diagnosi per donne straniere e prostitute. Report Finale Convenzione con ISS [Women working in the streets and health: experimentation of effective models of access to diagnosis for foreign women and prostitutes. Final report of the agreement between Magliana 80 and ISS].* Roma.

Mancini D. (2008) *Traffico di migranti e tratta di persone, tutela dei diritti umani e azioni di contrasto [Trafficking of migrants and of human beings, protection of human rights and contrasting actions]* Franco Angeli, Milano.

National Referral mechanism (2004) *Joining efforts to protect the right of trafficked persons. A practical handbook OCSE- ODHR 2004.* Available at: https://www.osce.org/odihr/13967?download=true

Prina F. (2007). *La tratta di Persone in Italia, vol. 3: il sistema degli interventi a favore delle vittime [The trafficking of human beings. Volume 3: the system of interventions in favour of the victims].* Franco Angeli, Milano.

Roxanne Progect sitography:

https://www.comune.roma.it/pcr/it/servizio_roxanne.page
http://www.associazionerising.eu/Roxanne-per-ilte-alla-tratta/
http://espresso.repubblica.it/attualita/2019/07/25/news/1-400-adolescenti-prostitute-schiave-il-dossier-di-save-the-children-sulle-vittime-di-tratta-1.337314

Indicators for identification of victims of trafficking in human beings

Sofija Georgievska

Introduction

Trafficking of humans is a serious and complex international problem; it is third in terms of criminal business after the drugs and arms trade, and one of the increasing forms of organised crime on global level, which is present in countries with bad economic conditions, even in developed countries. The countries of South Eastern Europe, which have been in a period of transition for many years, are especially affected by this problem. Most of them are countries of origin, transit and destination of the victims of trafficking as a result of existing sexual exploitation, forced labour or service in various sectors. One of these serious problems is the trafficking of humans.

North Macedonia, unlike the other countries of the region, was previously a country of transit and destination of victims, foreign subjects traded primarily for sexual exploitation. This problem has been treated successfully by the Government of the Republic of North Macedonia.

Declaring itself as a country of transit and destination, North Macedonia risks the possibility of other problems in the field of human trafficking being neglected i.e. the problem of internal trafficking in women and children, its connection to the transnational trafficking as well as the human trafficking with other social problems such as: prostitution, illegal work, begging, homelessness etc. The Republic of North Macedonia is an exceptionally poor country, with around 39% unemployment, of which the majority are young people. There are also numerous child beggars and homeless people. It has all the preconditions for the appearance of internal trafficking of humans. The groups at most risk are: minors, the youth of the institutions for children without parents or parental care, the children and the youth of the Roma community, the children on the streets, and youth from the rural areas. This raises the the question as to whether, despite the high risk in North Macedonia, there is no internal trafficking in humans or that human trafficking does exist but there are there no records made by the competent struc-tures of the country.

According to official reports from the state institutions of the Republic of North Macedonia, there is no internal human trafficking. According to the reports of the national NGOs and international organisations in North Macedonia, this problem does exist, and it is increasing. The question as to which of these diametrically opposite claims is a reflection of the real condition of this problem in North Macedonia is a question of great significance for the prevention of human trafficking and the planning of modes to fight against human trafficking.

We must firmly emphasise that both of the claims are an arbitrary estimate on the current situation, not grounded in objective data on the phenomenon or the appropriate methodology for evaluation of the social answers on this phenomenon. We claim this because in North Macedonia there has been no research on human trafficking. The only more detailed research on this phenomenon is the research made during the STOP programme by the International Organisation for Migration, which confirmed the notion that there is no relevant data on the real state of human trafficking in North Macedonia. The lack of objective information may lead to an unjustified ignoring of the appearance of the relevant factors in the country, and an escalation of the country's difficulties in prevention and elimination of the problem. The best manner to provide objective information on the state of internal human trafficking in the Republic of North Macedonia is through carry-ing out research based on scientific methodology, including professionals from relevant governmental institutions, NGOs and international organisa-tions that have been working in the field of the issue.

The phenomenon of human trafficking

Human trafficking is not only a contemporary phenomenon. Contrarily, trafficking in women has been present since the nineteenth century in Western Europe, whereby women were transported to European colonies in order to be used for forced prostitution. That is how the term "white slavery" came about that caused an international campaign that resulted in the first international agreement, signed in Paris in 1904. In 1904 the first United Nations Convention on preventing human trafficking and exploitation by prostitution was adopted[1].

On an international level, the human trafficking has been a current issue in the last decades of the twentieth century, or more precisely in the 90s. It resulted in intensive efforts by the international community to provide adequate mechanisms for the fight against this social ill. Proof for that are the numerous significant activities of international organisations, as well as other organisations such as: the United Nations, the European Union, the Council of Europe, the Organisation for Security and Cooperation, the Stability Pact, etc.

Although the phenomenon is partially known, the proportion it took on in recent years is not correctly acknowledged. Supposedly, around four million

---

[1] Report by U.S. Department of State (2004), Report by UNICEF (2004)

people a year are victims of human trafficking and most of them are women and children, although there is a great number of men and children targeted by the traffickers for labour exploitation along with other forms of exploitation. The latest report of MOT on forced labour indicates that it was estimated that 2.5 million people became victims of human trafficking and one third of them were sold for profit[2]. Although the hidden nature of organised crime aggravates achieving reliable and complete data, human trafficking is considered as one of the three top criminal activities and sources of financing of the organised crime on global level, along with the drugs and the arms trade. According to the report of the European Union (2004) on the state of the organised crime on a global scale, human trafficking is a business which is worth from 8.5 to 12 billion euros a year. According to MOT, the profit that has been generated through the labour exploitation of trafficked women, men and children is 32 billion American dollars a year[3].

Unlike other kinds of illegal business, human trafficking is mainly based on activities that, in the most brutal way, violate the human rights of the victims and their human dignity.

Phases of human trafficking

Human trafficking is a process that consists of three phases:

1. Recruitment
2. Transition
3. Exploitation.

Recruitment

Recruitment means offering a job inside the country or abroad (mostly low-paid jobs such as: cleaners, waitresses, housekeepers, dancers, building labourers, agricultural workers, textile industry and catering services, etc.).

The potential victim can be recruited in any phase of the trafficking process: in the country of origin, the country of transit or the country of destination. Typically the victims of internal trafficking are recruited within the framework of their own country and afterwards they are led to other destinations, where they additionally become victims of sexual exploitation, forced labour or other kinds of exploitation. The recruitment of the victims of trafficking out of the country to other countries usually takes place in their

---

[2] Manual for journalists on trafficking in humans: League of Women Voters of Montenegro
[3] MOT- Global Alliance against Forced Labour, 2005, p. 46

home countries, and afterwards they become a subject of trade in one or more countries.

The most common methods for recruitment of victims are:

- Compulsion by kidnapping or trade (usually children suffer);
- Deceit and kidnapping followed by promise for legal employment or marriage;
- Deceit by giving false information, for instance, that the subject can work illegally without explaining the risks.

Recruiting can be done in many ways, including: individual recruiters who work in the neighbourhood; networks that can involve family members and friends; media advertising of legal/semi-legal mediators, including the agencies that offer work, studying or work abroad

Transport

Transfer and transport of the sold humans means organising transport and transfer of the subjects who are supposed to be sold from one place to another within the frameworks of the country or across the borders of countries.

The traffickers transport the victims out of their place of origin (in their home country or abroad), in order to alienate them from their community, families and friends, and to isolate them so they can keep them under control easily. During transport, the victim can be sold to one trafficker and then to another without having the slightest idea of what is happening; and he/she can also be constantly moved without his/her permission. During the journey, the victim is not aware of what situation he/she will be part of at the place of destination, or he/she is exploited by the trader and instantly moved to another place.

Recent reports indicate that internal trafficking is becoming more frequent. According to the UNDP, "the number of foreign women has decreased, and the number of internally sold women victims of human trafficking has increased in the Western Balkan countries (Albania, Bosnia and Herzegovina, North Macedonia, Serbia and Montenegro, including Kosovo). Especially in Kosovo, there are a great number of victims of internal trafficking[4].

4   UNDP- 2005, p. 63

Exploitation

The forms of exploitation that are related human trafficking, such as sexual exploitation, slavery or practices like slavery, the removal of organs, have been defined in many international documents[5].

During the exploitation process, the victims of human trafficking completely depend on the traders, who they must obey. Fear of abuse or their vulnerability under the law is a key element of exploitation. In this phase there is a total realisation of the traders' goals i.e. exploitation of the victims for financial profit.

It must be emphasised that in reality the three phases are partially overlapping. There are some cases that consist of several phases of transit and destination because the victims very often are sold more than once. Contrarily, in other cases there can be several phases of transit (in the same country) or transit countries. In all of the phases of human trafficking, the human rights of the victim are violated.

Victims of human trafficking

The most common victims of trafficking are women, children and male migrants.

Trafficking in women

Although the most common form of the trafficking in women is sexual exploitation, which is well known and discussed in public, trafficking in women is a wider problem that occurs in three basic forms:

- Trafficking in women in order to achieve sexual exploitation,
- Trafficking in women in order to achieve labour exploitation,
- Trafficking in women in order to achieve for marriage.

When discussing trafficking of women for sexual exploitation, one must make a difference between trafficking in women and prostitution. The basic difference is that the trafficking in women means slavery i.e. full absence of freedom of movement and discretion where women are possessed by the person who bought them and do not have the privilege to decide whether they want to be involved in prostitution or not i.e. they cannot leave their 'owner'. However, with prostitution, regardless of how many forms of exploitation prostitution involves, the person involved has the privilege to possess the

[5] Defining of basic terms

earned money and her body, to move freely, with the freedom of choice as to whether she is going to be involved in prostitution or not, etc.

Female victims of human trafficking can be any woman who was fraudulently forced to work as a prostitute, along with the women who chose to be prostitutes but later were involved in the human trafficking chain and became slaves.

Trafficking in children

While trafficking of women has tended to be for sexual and labour exploitation reasons, the trafficking of children includes exploiting them to carry out criminal acts and other antisocial behaviours (for instance, begging, child pornography), along with trafficking in for adoption, organs, etc.

Trafficking in migrants

Trafficking in migrants is closely connected to people smuggling, and it consists of various forms of forced labour exploitation.

Because of the complexity of this kind of crime all the actors involved in the fight against human trafficking are faced with many specificities and difficulties. The first and basic question is defining the phenomenon and its forms by which difficulties appear connected to the identification of the persons (whether it is irregular work, illegal migration, prostitution, etc.), which is a basic difficulty for the services that do the identification. Secondly, the victims of human trafficking are not in position to testify because of the risk of reprisals against them or their families and/or because of the traumatic experiences of violence they have had; all of this hinders the investigation and persecution of the traders. Human trafficking as a phenomenon is not manifested everywhere in the same way. The local conditions and the specific situation determine who is most endangered, how the traders work and which forms of exploitation are most common. Because of that, in the fight against this crime the multiagency approach is most significant - coordination and the cooperation with all national and international subjects involved in the fight against human trafficking. The multiagency approach means the recognised "good practice" that enables victims to get the necessary support for their recovery and stabilisation, and at the same time a better chance for success in the investigation of the criminal act. In the meantime, like any other form of criminality, the acknowledgement of the national and the international legislature on the fight against human trafficking is very significant for handling the complex problems.

Human trafficking and the effectual legislature

Adopted international documents

The beginning of the twenty-first century was marked by the signing of the United Nations Convention against transnational organised crime with the protocol for prevention, end and punishment of human trafficking especially women and children, and the protocol against illegal migrant smuggling by land, air or sea, as significant step in the promotion of the international instruments in the fight against transnational organised crime, through the stronger international cooperation and the reign of law.

The protocol against human trafficking completes the convention and its goal to prevent and fight against human trafficking, to provide protection and help for the victims, as well as promotion of the coordination. It is the first international document that requires the countries to include in their legislature human trafficking as a special criminal act.

In parallel with this, within the framework of the operative group for human trafficking is the Stability Pact, which Republic of North Macedonia is a signatory to:

- the Declaration of the countries of South Eastern Europe against human trafficking - 13 December 2000 in Palermo,
- attestation for the contribution of the legislature about the status of trafficking victims- 11 December 2002 in Tirana, and
- attestation for the contribution for the protection of the victims/witnesses of trafficking in children- 10 December 2003 in Sofia.

These attestations have a purpose to facilitate the national activities in the legislature on implementation of the duties given by the Palermo Convention and the Protocol. According to the Ministry of Justice, the attestation for contribution for protection of the victims/witnesses of trafficking in children- 10 December 2003 in Sofia is considered as relevant.

After the signing in 2001 and the ratification of the Stabilisation and Association Agreement with the European Union in 2004, the Republic of North Macedonia took on serious responsibilities in the field of justice and internal affairs, steps that lead to the harmonisation of the legislature of Republic of North Macedonia in the function of the efficient cooperation in the fight against transnational organised crime.

Harmonising of the criminal legislature of Republic of North Macedonia with the international standards

Taking into consideration that the Palermo Convention along with the protocol emphasises the necessity of consistency and efficient legal framework as an essential precondition for effectiveness of the calculated instruments, the strategic goal of the government for the last year was tackling organised crime.

Reforms of the criminal legislature

In this field, the top priorities of the Ministry of Justice most recently were the activities for reforms of the criminal legislature as part of of building the legal framework for more efficient prevention and ending the acts connected to organised crime.

So, in the material part of the criminal legislature, in February 2002 the Criminal Code was changed with the explicit insertion of a new criminal act in Article 418-a "Trafficking in Humans".

In its primary version of Paragraph 1 of this criminal act there was included:

> "The one who by force and serious threats brings under delusion or other kinds of force, abduction, fraud, misuse of his status or pregnancy, weakness or physical/mental incapability of some other person, or giving and receiving money or other goods in order to achieve consent of other person- the one recruits, transports, buys, sells, hides and accepts persons in order to exploit them by prostitution or other forms of sexual exploitation, pornography, forced labour or servitude, slavery, forced marriages, forced fertilization, illegal adoption or similar actions, as well as illegal implantation of human organs."

Within the framework of the international expertise that in 2000 conducted the project of the Council of Europe, named "Reforms of the criminal legislature in the fight against trafficking in humans", it was confirmed that the inclusion of "trafficking in humans" in the Criminal Code of the Republic of North Macedonia corresponds and outgrows the standards of Article 3 of the Protocol, within the framework of this criminal act that refers to inclusion of the acts of "confiscation or destruction of the passports in favor of trafficking in humans" as well as "use or facilitating other to use the sexual services from the victim of trafficking in humans".

It is significant to mention that the acts of recruiting, transport, transit, buying, selling, sheltering or accepting children or minors in favor of exploitation is punishable; Paragraph 5 includes the act of "use or facilitating other to use the sexual services from a child or a minor, which is considered as victim of trafficking in humans".

In the Palermo Protocol there is a request to the countries members to incriminate the attempt, the complicity and the organisation of the criminal acts in human trafficking. These regulations are fully incorporated and applicable in accordance with the General Part of the Criminal Code.

Despite all the changes and supplements to the legislature since 2002, the process of harmonisation of the criminal legislature continued till 2004 when the changes and supplements to the Criminal Code and the Criminal Law Act were made.

The Criminal Code

Along with the changes and the supplements to the Criminal Code in March 2004, more were made with the inclusion of Article 418-a: addition of new acts for implementation in Paragraph 1 and introducing two Paragraphs 6 and 7 that refer to the punishment of legal entities and confiscation of the instruments by which the crime was committed.

Also, in Article 418-b a new criminal act was instituted: Organisation and inducement for the acts, in accordance with Article 5 of the Palermo Convention. The Convention introduces the term 'organised criminal group'. The Criminal Code does not have this term, but the terms group and gang are defined equally.

According to the Protocol against the smuggling of migrants, in Article 418-b the criminal act of migrant smuggling was introduced. By the introduction of human trafficking in the criminal legislature of the Republic of North Macedonia, by its courts and prosecutor's offices, numerous cases of human trafficking proceeded.

The activities for treating human trafficking as a form of organised crime must not be reduced to the inclusion of Articles 418-a and 418-b only, without the incorporation of the other legal instruments of the Palermo Convention.

Changes and supplements to the Criminal Code:

In the changes and the supplements to the Criminal Code the following instruments of the Palermo Convention that were relevant for efficiency of the activities for treating trafficking in humans were implemented:

Criminal responsibility of the legal entities according to the conditions in Article 28-a of the Criminal Code, which creates a legal basis for sanctions of the acts by which the legal entities participated in the organised criminal actions, including human trafficking. This regulation is part of Article 10 of the Palermo Convention.

Confiscation of property gained by committing a criminal act and international cooperation on enforcement of property confiscation. This regulation is part of Articles 12 and 13 of the Palermo Convention.

Especially significant are the regulations of the Palermo Protocol and the Protocol against trafficking in humans, by which are defined the rights of the victims of trafficking in humans: The European Union Attestation for contribution of the legislature about the status of the trafficking victims in 2001 and the Attestation for contribution for protection of the victims/witnesses of trafficking in children in 10 December 2003 in Sofia. By those two attestations are determined the rights of the victims of trafficking in humans to: legal help; information on the relevant lawsuits and other procedure; medical and psychological help and health care; privacy and identity protection and the right to compensation for the damages done to the victims of human trafficking.

The criminal legislature of the Republic of North Macedonia corresponds with these regulations: the right to compensation for the damages done to the victims of trafficking in humans is guaranteed by the Criminal Law Act, by which the rights of the damaged person and the regulations on legal property requests are determined.

The Criminal Law Act

As a function of a more efficient realisation of the legal property requests there is Article 101, Paragraph 2 from the Changes and Supplements Law and the Criminal Act Law in accordance with: "The verdict by which the defendant is charged guilty, the court decides fully or partially about the legal property request".

The right to legal help is guaranteed by the regulations of the Criminal Law Act and they refer to the rights and the responsibilities of the witness and the damaged person in the criminal act. As a function of the implementation of the right to identity and privacy protection of the victims of human trafficking, in the changes and the supplements made to the Criminal Law Act in October 2004 there is the addition of the new Chapter XIX-a: Protection of witnesses, collaborators of justice and victims. According to these regulations, process and inprocess measures for the protection of witnesses and collaborators of justice and victims are determined. Process measures are determined in Article 270-a:

During the process, the public prosecutor or the investigative judge or the president of the council take measures for effective protection of witnesses and collaborators of justice and victims if they appear as witnesses in the process, when there is danger of their exposure to sabre-rattling, threats of revenge or threats to their lives, if their health of physical integrity is endangered or if they need any kind of protection.

The protection of the subjects in Paragraph (1) of this Article is conducted in a special manner by interrogations and participation in the process.

In the cases of Paragraph (1) of this Article, the witness is examined only in the presence of the public prosecutor and the investigative judge or the president of the council, on territory that guarantees protection of his identity. There are exceptions only when the witness together with the council decides that the hearing be done through the court or by the use of technical or other means of communication. A copy of the record consisting of the witness's statement, without his signature, is given to the defendant and his advocate who are allowed to question the witness in writing through the court.

Witness Protection Law

The inprocess measures for witness protection are taken according to Article 270-b by being included in the witness protection programme. In the function of this regulation, the Ministry of Justice prepared the proposal on passing the Witness Protection Law that was passed by the Government and the Parliament in 2005.

By Article 1, Paragraph 2 of the Witness Protection Law the subjects of protection are defined as: witnesses, victims and collaborators of justice; and in Article 26 measures for protection are defined as: identity protection, providing personal protection, change of dwelling-place and change of the protected witness's identity.

In Article 12 of this law it is determined that the Department for Witness Protection by the Ministry of Internal Affairs as a competent body for enforcement of these measures, excluding the "identity protection"; and in Article 5, the Council for Witness Protection is a competent body for decisions on inclusion in the witness protection programme, as well as the measure for "protection by change of identity".

Within the framework of the Transit Centre for Protection of Victims of Trafficking in Humans by the Ministry of Internal Affairs offers: psychosocial and health care, and support for the victims of trafficking in humans. There is also the necessity for regulation of the right for temporary residence of the victims of human trafficking, guaranteed by the Protocol and the Declarations signed by Republic of North Macedonia.

National strategy and National action plan for the fight against human trafficking and illegal migration

In order to be actively included in the efforts of the International Community for the prevention of and fight against human trafficking, the Republic of North Macedonia in 2000 formed the National Commission for Fighting Against Trafficking in Humans and Illegal Migration.

The Commission passed the National Programme for Fighting Against Trafficking in Humans. The programme includes activities for the reduction of the economic and the social factors that impact on the significant percentage of those affected by human trafficking, including:

- Identification of the rate of domestic violence;
- Inducement for cooperation between the governmental institutions and the non-governmental sector for participation in research projects for the trafficking in human issue;
- Promotion of projects for implementation of economic integration of groups at risk.

The National Commission has a task to follow and analyse the state of trafficking in humans and illegal migration, and to coordinate the activities of the authorised institutions, the international[6] and the non-governmental organisations that are included in solving the issues in this field.

In 2003, the Secretariat for Fighting against HumanTrafficking was established. It is a body that functions within the framework of the National Commission, in which representatives participate from the international, the non-governmental and the governmental institutions. Within the framework of the National Commission the Subgroup for Fighting against Trafficking in Children was also established.

In 2005, the National Commission prepared a National Strategic Action Plan for the fight against human trafficking and illegal migration. The integral parts of the strategy and the National Action Plan are: prevention, identification, help, support, protection, reintegration of the victims, competent criminal persecution, international cooperation, education of the institutional capacities, coordination, unique information system, and informative awareness raising material for influencing public opinion.

During its regular meeting on 21 March 2006, the Government of Republic of North Macedonia passed the strategy and the National Action Plan.

---

[6] OSCE, IOM, UNDP, ICMPD, USAID, UNICEF, the programs of the US Embassy- ICITAP and OPDAT

National Referral Mechanism for the fight against trafficking in women and juveniles [7]

The Ministry of Labour and Social Policy in September 2005 conducted the National Referral Mechanism (NRM) programme supported by the mis-sion of OSCE in Skopje. The project enabled the institution and operation of a National Referral Mechanism (NRM) in order to strengthen the country's capacity in providing adequate identification, help and protection, based on the international human rights of all the victims of trafficking in humans, especially minors, regardless of nationality, ethnicity, age and sex.

Since September 2005, within the framework of the Ministry of Labour and Social Policy there is the office of the National Referral Mechanism of the victims of trafficking in humans.

The NRM office has a coordinative role in the process of requiring and organising all kinds of help and protection for the victims of human trafficking. The basic roles of the NRM office are:

- The improvement of the current process of identification of victims of human trafficking, based on the human rights standard.
- Providing information on the available medical, psychosocial and legal services, as well as providing help for the victims of human trafficking.
- Development of standard operative procedures in favour of the NRM function.
- Promotion of the cooperation between the institutions of the country and the non-governmental organisations.
- Raising public awareness, to change the perception of human trafficking and to accept it as a violation of human rights, through informative campaigns.

The Guidebook for treatment and protection of the victims of human trafficking who live in the Republic of North Macedonia, is in progress. This document will consist of the standard procedures that will be done by the authorised institutitons.

Promotion of international criminal law cooperation

In the latest changes and the supplements to the Criminal Code, there were added solutions on the promotion of international criminal law cooperation, relevant and efficient for the fight against human trafficking. In this sense, in

---

7 Project- National Referral Mechanism, January- September 2006

the changes and the supplements to the Criminal Code, in Article 502 on regulation of the international legal help, it includes the supremation of the regulations of the Palermo Convention on international legal cooperation. So, accordingly it was introduced as the legal basis for:

- Hearing witnesses and expert witnesses by means of video link and video conference, and the opportunity for the country to participate in these actions, according to Article 18, Paragraph 18 of the Palermo Convention.
- International investigations according to Article 19 of the Palermo Convention.

Adoption of the proposed laws will contribute to the realisation of the obligations in the part of the agreement that refers to justice and internal affairs. In the same time, by finalising the legislative activities on 27 September 2004, The Parliament of the Republic of North Macedonia passed an Act for Ratification of the Convention with the Protocols, by which this first international instrument according to the North Macedonian Constitution becomes a constituent part of the legal system and plays a great part in the prevention of this kind of criminal act.

The Ministry of Justice disseminated the Palermo Convention with the Protocol. In 2002, in cooperation with the United Nations, representatives of the relevant ministries, judges, and public prosecutors from the Republic of North Macedonia the pre-ratification analysis was done, and as a result the "United Nations Convention against Transnational Crime with the Protocols" was published. The conclusions and the recommendations in this publication immediately contributed to the modeling of the criminal legislature.

The Republic of North Macedonia participates in the work of the European Council Committee for the fight against human trafficking, and has a mandate to prepare a Proposal for the European Convention for the fight against human trafficking. Last December, during the last session of the Committee, the Convention Proposal was approved by 29 member countries of the Council of Europe, including the Republic of North Macedonia

Recommendations and conclusion

- There is an urgent necessity to begin the realisation of the programme activities from the National Action Plan for the Fight Against Human Trafficking and the Action Plan for the Fight against Trafficking in Children, which consist of activities for: prevention, protection of the

victims, persecution of the traffickers, and education of professionals and volunteers who work in this field;
- Especially urgent is the realisation of the programmes for protection of children victims or potential victims;
- In the realisation of these activities the common participation of the governmental institutions, the domestic NGOs and the international institutions is necessary;
- Support for the activities of the NGO sector by the Government, the international organisations and the embassies of other countries in Northern Macedonia must be continued and strengthened;
- There is a necessity for better efficiency in the resolving of cases of human trafficking;
- There is the necessity for a national database for the recording of cases of human trafficking;
- There is a necessity for adjustment to the current criteria for identification of the changes of the phenomenon, and unified criteria for all the subjects whose responsibility is the identification of the victims of trafficking;
- An obligatory memorandum for cooperation between the governmental, the non-governmental and the international institutions must be established;
- There is a necessity for the organised training of experts from social work centres, policemen, educators from institutions for social protection, the competent services, teachers in educational institutions and volunteers from NGOs;
- The prevention of the phenomenon requires education of children, youth and students;
- There is a necessity for the establishment of a system for supervision of professionals and volunteers who directly work with victims of trafficking (the operators of the SOS telephone lines, the psychosocial workers, the medical cadres, the lawyers);
- There is a necessity for a systematic education of prevention of stress and weariness of the professionals who have been working for a long period of time with victims, because of the danger of "burnout";
- The establishment of mechanisms for monitoring the work and evaluation of the results of all the organisations included in the fight against human trafficking;
- There is a necessity for research on the phenomenon of trafficking for labour exploitation, because it is one of the most hidden forms for which there is a lack of information. Even human trafficking experts have insufficient information;

- There is a need to open day-care centres for resocialisation of victims and to work with their families (in Skopje and the cities where this phenomenon is most prevalent).

References

Criminal Code (1996). Government gazette of Republic of Macedonia no. 37/96

Criminal Law Act (1997). Government gazette of Republic of Macedonia no. 15/97

Criminal Code (2004). Government gazette of Republic of Macedonia no. 19/04

Croatian Government, national committee for the suppression of human trafficking (2005) *Nacionalni program za suzbivanje trgovanja ljudima* [National programme for the suppresson of human trafficking], Zagreb, available at https://vlada.gov.hr/UserDocsImages/2016/Sjednice/Arhiva/57%20-%2004.%20to%C4%8Dka%20a.pdf

Nikoli -Ristanovi , V., Ćopi , S., Milivojevi , S., Simeunovi -Pati , B., & Mihi , B. (2004). *Trgovina ljudima u Srbiji. Beograd: Viktimološko društvo Srbije [Trafficking in people in Serbia]*. OSCE:Belgrade

Surtees R. (2005). *International Organization for Migration (IOM). Second Annual Report on Victims of Trafficking in South-Eastern Europe*

UNICEF (2004), Guidelines for Protection of the Rights of Child Victims of Trafficking, May 2003 updated in April 2005

U.S. Department of State (2004) Macedonia 2006 TIER (www.state.gov/g/tip/rls/tiprpt/2005/46614.htm)

U.S. Department of State (2005) Trafficking In Persons

United States Department of State, (2006). *U.S. Department of State 2006 Trafficking in Persons Report - Macedonia*, available at: https://www.refworld.org/docid/4680d89b29.html

United States Department of States, (2019). *U.S. Department of State 2019 Trafficking in Persons Report - Macedonia*, available at https://www.state.gov/wp-content/uploads/2019/06/2019-Trafficking-in-Persons-Report.pdf

Witness Protection Law (2005), *Government gazette of Republic of Macedonia* 38/05, 58/05 –available at: http://www.pravo.org.mk

The challenge of recovering trafficked and smuggled humans: new integration proposals starting from analysis of the old protection system for asylum seekers (SPRAR) in Sicily

Giuseppe Mannino, Eleonora Maria Cuccia, Marta Schiera, Erika Faraci

Introduction

Since the 1990s, Italy has changed from being a country of emigration to a country of immigration, with dramatically increasing numbers of immigrants. While immigrants in the world double every 35 years, in Italy this growth takes place every 10 years (Bissolo & Fazzi, 2005).
At the beginning of 2019 over 5 million foreign nationals (ninety-seven thousand more than the previous year), were resident in Italy, equal to 8.5% of the total residents.
The migratory flows in the Mediterranean Sea are decreasing. However, human trafficking and smuggling thrives, and mortality is on the rise. Criminal organisations control the migration flows, and consider it a fruitful business, estimated in 10 billion USD per year from Africa to Europe (Lacz-ko, 2017). Criminal organisations are able to drag money from desperate people willing to reach wealthy countries, they put their lives at risk, organising dangerous trips across the sea or through the mainland, that often end in deaths.
A 2018 UNHCR report indicates that 139,300 people arrived in Europe in 2018, of which 116,647 through the Mediterranean, the lowest number of the last five years. Despite this drastic decline, 2,275 people died or are missing, an alarming number. The reduction of search and rescue capacities, together with an uncoordinated or unpredictable response to those reaching land, led to an increase in the mortality rate, since people continued to flee their countries due to conflict, violations of human rights, persecution and poverty.
The refugees, compared to other categories of migrants, question the control of national borders and with that the principle of sovereignty of the states: They not only arrive without being welcome in Europe, they also ask for protection, which requires the expediture of financial resources by host countries (Ambrosini, 2014, p. 90).
The Geneva Convention, signed on 28 July 1951, defines the refugee as "The one who, (...) fearing of being persecuted for reasons of race, religion, nationality, belonging to a certain social group or for his/her political opin-

ions, is located outside the country of citizenship and cannot or does not want, because of this fear, to make use of the protection of this country; or that, not having citizenship and being outside the country of usual residence, as a result of such events, cannot or does not want to return to it for the above-mentioned fear." Once the status of international protection has been acknowledged, the beneficiary has an intermediate position between an EU citizen and a foreign resident with non-EU citizenship (Codini et al., 2011, p. 63).

The current 'refugee problem' is related to the conditions that can favour an effective integration between the different ethno-cultural-social components, avoiding or reducing the conflictuality which derives from the competition for the (supposedly) scarce resources (Inch, 2007, p. 20).

Integration is a two-way dynamic process, involving both refugees and the host community. Integration, however, is the result of two components: the willingness of the local community to "integrate" ethnic minorities, adopting socially acceptable behaviours (e.g. hospitality, tolerance) and specific initiatives (e.g. programmes of welcome) aimed at encouraging their fitting into the social stucture; and the willingness of immigrants to enter into the social environment and to interpret the territorial context as a "place of adoption". Integration requires their willingness to adapt their lifestyle to the new circumstances and the willingness of the host society to adapt their institutions.

The attitude is different when the refugees do not intend to remain in the country where they arrived (Dublin Regulation). Despite the EU's attempts to make the rules more coherent through the Dublin system, there are substantial differences between the Member States in relation to the procedures for the recognition of status and with regard to the living conditions of refugees after recognition of international protection.

These differences are reflected in several aspects, including the time needed to examine applications, housing conditions, health care and the possibility of integration after the status recognition (Cellini, 2017, pp. 952-953).

Integration is a "long-term" process because it often starts on arrival in a country and continues even when a refugee has become an active member of that society from a legal, social, economic, educational and cultural point of view. Integration is thus related to the sense of community, i.e. the perception of similarity with others, a recognised interdependence and the willingness to undertake to maintain it. In particular, the sense of shared emotional connection unites the members of a community and reinforces their bond. (Mannino, 2013, pp. 77-78).

In Italy, since 2002, asylum seekers and refugees have been hosted in the local services of the national system of protection of asylum seekers and refugees. Each service offered its users, for a period of about six months, activities of "integrated reception", which included: knowledge of the territory, support for access to health care, vocational training, school services and legal assistance (Catarci, 2012, p. 77; Anci et al. 2014, 2016).

After the first reception, mostly related to emergency situations (such as disembarkment on southern Italian coasts, after dangerous journeys through the Meditarranean Sea), the S.P.R.A.R., the "second level reception system for adults and for all unaccompanied foreign minors", was aimed at stabilising refugees' and asylum seekers' life conditions. In this way, they facilitated migrants' autonomy and social inclusion, through services such as: job placement, housing, access to local services, courses in Italian, school enrolment for minors, social and health courses, job training (Shirrippa, 2017).

We briefly present here the results of an inquiry, granted by the European Refugee Fund 2008 – 2013, whose aim it was to shed a light on the quality of the integration process involving migrants and asylum seekers in Italy. The study was carried out in the S.P.R.A.R. in Sicily, in 2017 (before the changes due to the "Security Decree", Law 132/2018, that provided for more rigid procedures in terms of permit to stay approvals).

The data were collected through the administration of a 60-item questionnaire formed by five sections: database (item 1-15), work situation (item 16-23), housing situation (item 24-26), leisure (item 27-32) and integration projects (item 33-60). Fifty asylum seekers and adult refugees, from the S.P.R.A.R.s in the area of Palermo and Agrigento, 49 males and one female, aged 21-40 years, participated in our study.

Most of the subjects were younger than 31 years (78%), had a low secondary school degree (63%), and were unmarried (72%).

As for the months spent waiting for the territorial commission interview, which would confirm their status as refugees/asylum seekers, only 6% met the commission in the first six months, all the others waited for it 9, 12 months or more.

Thirty percent of the sample had asylum seeker status, i.e. still awaiting a response from the Commission or the Court. It should be noted that the status of "asylum seeker" is psychologically destabilising because it simultaneously represents the potential for security and the potential for expulsion; 36% waited for the answer on their status for more than 12 months and 22% waited from 9 to 12 months.

More than 50% have been in Italy for more than 2 years, only 28% have a job, 64% still live in a S.P.R.A.R., and 40% have been living there for more than 2 years which is an excessive extension of the residence in SPRAR allowed by law, far beyond the already lengthy waiting time for permit documents (6-12 months).

Most of the participants in the study (79%) affirm that they were involved in an integration project: Italian language course (69%), support in job search (35%), access to medical care (82%). Most of them (79%) affirm that the integration project they were involved in was of good quality. However, a huge percentage, 96%, of refugees and asylum seekers said they had a lot of free time, 58% more than 8-10 hours per day, mostly spent with other refugees/asylum seekers and/or family members.

The results highlight that the S.P.R.A.R.'s main aim, "welcoming and integration", was hardly reached. Our 50 subjects recruited for the study gave us a picture where a meaningful effort was made, for example involving them in several activities aimed at improving the quality of socialisation and integration. However, they still spent a lot of time in the company of their relatives or other refuges/asylum seekers, without a stable job, often waiting for a long time for the documents necessary to look for a job. They are stuck in space and in time (Vacchiano, 2005; Hass, 2017). These data challenge the main aim of reception: revealing persons without a job, with a lot of free time spent in the sole company of other migrants/refugees reflect for us an enclave inside a social environment it has no strong relationship with.

It is therefore important to point out that the majority of refugees and asylum seekers on the S.P.R.A.R. circuit have not received considerable and professional help for integration, instead only medical health and basic care, the fullfilment of other needs being unattended. The S.P.R.A.R. system seems to have produced only an assistentialistic mechanism. In this way, refugees and asylum seekers become dependent on the facilities, also because of the low number of refugees and asylum seekers working, many of them with no regular contracts.

It must be noted that full employment can be certainly hampered by the life history of these people, by the traumas they suffered during the journey, as well as by their difficulties in learning a new language.

However, as noted in one of the contributions in this volume (Pschiuk et al. 2020), it is necessary to conceive new models of integration, based on resilience and empowerment: an integrated, active, resilient migrant can represent a resource also for the economy of the the host nation. Most of the migrants arriving in Europe (estimated about 80%) are very young, they could spend their entire working life carrying out productive activities reenforcing the human resources of the local enterprises. (QuiFinanza, 2017).

In conclusion, the analysis that we presented in this contribution helped us to point out that an efficient reception system should focus on pragmatic measures to help migrants/refugees to access the social life in the host country. Beyond support and assistance for primary needs, what seems to be a crucial action is to prepare the migrants/refugees to enter the labour market, as well as to prepare the local enterprises to welcome this human resource coming from abroad.

Although this conclusion seems to be quite plain and rational, this is not happening currently all over Europe, as the contemporary political scenario seems to move in an opposite direction than social integration of migrants/refugees.

For example, in Italy, the previous right-wing oriented government (June 2018 – September 2019), put in place several regulations intended to limit the reception practices, from cutting financial support to the reception centres, to opposing the NGOs actions in the Mediterranean Sea, including using military force. Although this right-wing government was replaced by another coalition, the decrees that were promulgated in the last months are still in force. A noticeable consequence is that the irregular migrants must be transferred to special shelters or CAS, while those entitled to international protection or unaccompanied minors can still access the S.P.R.A.R. project. As a result of this decree, the time spent at the detention centres for repatriation (CPR) increased to 180 days.

Humanitarian protection will no longer be guaranteed by police and territorial committees or by courts. Instead, a residence permit is introduced for some "special cases", for certain categories of people: victims of domestic violence or serious exploitation of work, for those who need medical treatment because they are in a serious state of health compromise; for people from a country that is in a situation of "contingent and exceptional calamity", and finally for victims of social criminal systems (such as women victims of trafficking).

Furthermore, the "security" law has redesigned, in an administrative-beaurocratic fashion, the composition of the territorial commissions for the recognition of international protection, and the social professional component, whose role is essential in case management, has been eliminated.

It is clear that this set of "security" regulations, dismantling the previous system whose stated goal was to integrate the migrant (although with limitations in its effectiveness), emphasising the emotional equivalence between migrants and social menace, questioning the migrants' right to be welcome in a foreign land, has a high probability to enhance tension between migrants/refugees and the host communities, the former may feel rejected, the latter may feel invaded.

We believe that we need to consider more practices, spaces, forms and ways of creating inclusive societies through the creation of forms of intercultural relationships that generate new ways of thinking and new ways of individual and social behaviour.

Interculture is a process in which everyone renounces something in the name of shared values to be found together: "To be himself, everyone needs the other" (Ratzinger, 1994, p. 24). The most important feature of intercul-tural education is, therefore, to promote mutual exchange: "You do not as-similate the other by forcing them to betray their origins, the same way you do not accept to defend customs that harm human integrity (for example, genital mutilation or violence against women and children)" (Santerini, 2017).

Within the scope of interculturality, one of the finalities is the meaning of European citizenship: "Citizenship, in the broadest sense of the term, indi-cates a right and also a responsibility to participate, together with others, in the social and economic life and public affairs of the community" (White Paper on Intercultural Dialogue, 2008, p. 29). Citizenship is an indispensable element for intercultural dialogue. We can certainly say that education for democratic citizenship is fundamental for the functioning of a free, tolerant, open, inclusive society for social cohesion, mutual understanding, solidarity, intercultural and religious dialogue and equality between women and men (ibid., p. 30).

From problem to opportunity

Migrants are people who are looking for a better future for themselves and their families, hoping to find it in Europe. No one could agree to the two ex-treme solutions, a total rejection versus an unconditional openness, which seem to be two opposite ideological positions none of them based on reality test. Nobody can affirm that the migration flows can be solved simply building walls, nor can affirm that migrant people are welcome at any rate. Reception without integration is a temporary humanitarian acceptance without a real pragmatic effort to stabilise and verify the undertaken solutions. Integration without acceptance is an implicit tolerance towards people who have arrived illegally, waiting for a "sanatorium" law that allows them to gain a regular status (Ambrosini 2015, p. 81). On the other hand, exclusion solutions are not cost-effective either, in particular for ageing countries, Italy, for example, which is getting older demographically and productively.

The key to the management of such a social change is a strong political will, interconnected with a cultural change giving up on clichés ("Italians first"), xenophobic formulas ("Italy for Italians") or hypocritical statements ("let us help them at home"). Both of them should be aware that the relationships between different people are the origin and the opportunity for the complexity in which we live. A homogeneous world never existed and never will. Migration management is a test of our ability to live in complexity. Intercultural dialogue is the task for every citizen who wants to live peacefully with others, no matter which nationality or ethnicity they are. Interculture can be a powerful tool, perhaps the only one capable of generating sensitive citizens, able to live together aware of a common destiny. It is necessary to build a renewed international reception system based on evidence of real integration and interculturality both of the host country and of the subjects hosted.

The European White Paper on Intercultural Dialogue states: 'Traditional approaches to managing cultural diversity are no longer appropriate for societies that know an unprecedented and ever-developing level of diversity [...].

A new strategy is needed to achieve inclusive societies, that of intercultural dialogue" (Conseil de l' Europe 2008, p. 9).

The intercultural method is the only way that allows dialogue between people, different in age, gender, social status, place of birth and ethnicity. The world is made by equal subjects for rights but different for customs and habits. At the base of the intercultural project lies a moral horizon and, therefore, the need for education. Interculturality can therefore be defined as the set of psychic, relational and institutional processes concerning exchanges and the dynamic relationship between cultures, understood as complex totalities, and between people.

Education in intercultural relations is based on grasping the plurality of the resources of the elements within a culture: values, customs, beliefs, eating or sexual habits. It works with people, each in its own specific and unrepeatable diversity, but embedded in a reference environment that in turn is a bearer of resources and diversity.

Interesting research ("From refugees to workers") by Martín of the Interdisciplinary Research Group on Immigration, of the Pompeu Fabra university in Barcelona, has analysed the policies implemented in Italy, Germany, France, Netherlands, Austria, Denmark, Spain, Sweden and the United Kingdom. He was able to observe how the policies aimed at bringing asylum seekers who arrived in Europe into the labour world since 2014 to date have been able to offer the identity of a worker to refugees, thus making them citizens, bringing as a further result a collective economic convenience.

McKinsey Global Institute's report (2016) highlights some interesting estimates in this regard: good management of the 2.3 million asylum seekers and refugees who arrived in Europe between 2015 and 2016 would have contributed to GDP totalling EUR 60 or 70 billion by 2025: "Migration is a key feature of our increasingly interconnected world. It has also become a flashpoint for debate in many countries, which underscores the importance of understanding the patterns of global migration and the economic impact that is created when people move across the world's borders" (p.9).

The job offer is just an example of offering meaning, building common sense, using meaning-wise and meaning-generating relational forms. We think that the forms of the relationship organise the forms of thought and behaviour (Mannino, 2013).

The human mind is definable as an individual epiphenomenon that originates from a psychic-relational-social matrix. Its products are individual expressions in a procedural relationship with the social world interacting with the internal world in an alternation of roles, between container and content, meaning and significance.

The human mind is the transpersonal and transgenerational product of a multi-composed mental matrix, articulated on different levels: biological, genetic, ethnic, anthropological, transgenerationale, social, institutional, political, environmental: a mental, eco-bio-psycho-social-cultural matrix, made up of passages, constructions, exchanges and sense making. A process of transmission, exchange and construction of information and mutual influence that takes place in a given context, between two or more people, groups, institutions that relate, and narrating each other, generate new realities and shared meanings. (Mannino & Faraci, 2017). We would like to recall a statement from 2184 years ago. In 165 BC Terenzio stated: "*Homo sum nihil humani a me alienum puto* (I am human, and I think nothing human is alien to me)".

Psychopathology is the saturation of thought. Health is flexibility, unsaturation. (Lo Coco et al., 2018). So, it makes sense to ask what are the social forms of unsaturation? We know well the saturation of thought: fundamentalism, mafias, absence of culture, presence of saturated culture. So, the real possibility of transforming the phenomenon comes from a deep, clinical, psychodynamic work in the social process of interpretation and cultural signification. Neurons develop and create synapses based on 'environmental' learning, in Eco-Bio-Psycho-Socio-cultural mental matrix.

European countries sometimes seem to refuse to manage something they interpret solely as a problem, ignoring the aspect of a huge resource of life and development which is well known to the criminal organisations. Unfortunately, criminal organisations have understood this very well and are able to exploit the peculiar characteristics of eco-bio-psycho-socio-cultural thinking, but they are generating immutability, mental saturation for their illegal purposes (Mannino et al., 2015).

The insaturating and transformative generative possibility of each saturation is an individual-social psychodynamic semiotic process, a hermeneutic process of re-interpretation, mental, cultural, value, religious re-signification. The forms of the relationship organise the forms of thought, behaviour and regenerate new forms of human relationship.

References

Ambrosini M, (2010), *Richiesti e respinti. L'immigrazione in Italia. Come e perché.* [Required and rejected. Immigration to Italy. How and why]. Milano, Italy: Il Saggiatore,

Ambrosini, M., (2014), *Non passa lo straniero? Le politiche migratorie tra sovranità nazionale e diritti umani* [Will the stranger pass? The migratory policies between national sovereignty and human rights]. Assisi, Italy: Cittadella,.

Anci, Italian Caritas, Novialia, Fondazione Migrantes, & Sprar (2014). *Report on International protection in Italy*, Roma, Italy: Digitalia Lab,.

Anci, Italian Caritas, Novialia, Fondazione Migrantes, central service of Sprar, & UNHCR, (2016), *Report on International protection in Italy*, Roma, Italy: Digitalia Lab.

Bissolo, G., & Fazzi, L., (2005), *Costruire l'integrazione sociosanitaria. Attori, strumenti, metodi* [Building the socio-sanitary integration. Actors, tools, methods]. Roma, Italy: Carocci.

Catarci M., (2012), Conceptions and strategies on integration across refugee services in Italy, *Journal of educational, cultural and psychological studies*, 1, 75-107.

Cellini M., (2017), Filling the gap of the Dublin System: a soft cosmopolitan approach, *Journal of contemporary European Reserch*,1, 952-953

Codini, E., Fossati, A., & Frego Luppi, S., (2011), *Manuale di diritto dei servizi sociali* [Handbook of Social services law], Torino, Italy: Giappichelli.

Haas B.M., (2017), Citizens-in-Waiting, Deportees-in-Waiting: Power, Temporality, and Suffering in the U.S. Asylum System, *Ethos*, 1, 75-97.

Pollice, F. (2007). Popoli in fuga. Geografia delle migrazioni forzata. [Fleeing peoples. Geographs of forced migrations], Napoli, Italy: Cuen,.

Kaminsky, P., (2017) *Scant data hinders fight against smuggling*. MINDS Global Spotlight, 2 June. Available from https://www.mindsglobalspotlight.com/@globalperspective/2017/06/02/32093/scant-data-hinders-fight-against-smuggling

Lo Coco G, Mannino G, Salerno L, Oieni V, Di Fratello C, Profita G, Gullo S. (2018). The Italian Version of the Inventory of Interpersonal Problems (IIP-32): Psychometric Properties and Factor Structure in Clinical and Non-clinical Groups. *Frontiers in Psychology*, 9, 1-12, ISSN: 1664-1078, doi: https://doi.org/10.3389/fpsyg.2018.00341

Mannino G, Caronia V. (2017). Time, Well-Being, and Happiness: A Preliminary Explorative Study. World Futures, World Futures 73(2) 318-333,

Mannino, G., Giunta S., Buccafusca, S., Cannizzaro, G., & Lo Verso G.,(2014), Le strategie comunicative di Cosa Nostra: una ricerca empirica [the communative strategies of Cosa Nostra: an empirical research] Narrare i Gruppi, 9(1-2), 35-53,

Mannino G, Giunta S., Buccafusca S., Cannizzaro G., & Lo Verso G. (2015). Communication Strategies in Cosa Nostra: An Empirical Research. World Futures, 71, 153-172, doi: 10.1080/02604027.2015.1113 770

Mannino G, Montefiori V., Faraci E., Pillitteri R., Iacolino C., Pellerone M., & Giunta S. (2017). Subjective Perception of Time: Research Applied on Dynamic Psychology. World Futures, 73, 285-302, doi: 10.1080/02604027.2017.1333850

Mannino, G., & Schiera, M. (2017). La famiglia omogenitoriale oggi: pregiudizio per lo sviluppo del minore? Un'analisi della letteratura dal 2000 al 2015 [Same sex parents today: a prejudice for child development? A literature review from 200 to 2015]. *Maltrattamento e abuso all'infanzia*, 19, 87-103

Mannino, G. (2013). Anima, cultura, psiche. Relazioni generative [Soul, culture, psyche. Generative relations]. Milano, Italy: Franco Angeli

Mannino, G., & Faraci, E., (2017) Morphogenesis of work. Application to the psychological well-being and psychosocial health. *Rivista Internazionale di Scienze Sociali,* 3, 315-334

Mannino, G., Giunta, S., Montefiori, V., Tamanza, G., Iacolino, C., Novara, C., Pillitteri, R, La Fiura, G., & Bernardone, A. (2019) Healthy Lifestyle, Well-being, Physical Activity, Sport, and Scholastic/academic Performance: Interactions and Connections, *World Futures*.

Mannino, G., & Giunta, S. (2015). Psychodynamics of the Mafia Phenomenon: Psychological–Clinical Research on Environmental Tapping and White-Collar Crime, *World Futures*, 71(5-8), 185-201.

Martìn I., (2014), Perché offrire impiego ai rifugiati può essere un vantaggio per tutti [Why offering employment to refugees could be an advantage for all], Qui Finanza, N.P., December 22, 2017, https://quifinanza.it/lavoro/perche-offrire-lavoro-ai-rifugiati-potrebbe-essere-un-vantaggio-per-tutti/162598

McKinsey Global Institute (MGI), (2016), People on the move: Global migration's impact and opportunity, https://www.mckinsey.it/file/7291/download?token=evhrnzGh

OECD/EU (2018), Settling In 2018: Indicators of Immigrant Integration, , Paris/European Union, Brussels: OECD Publishing.

Pschiuk, L., Langher, V., Marinelli, G., & Groterath, A., (2020). Resilience and Posttraumatic Growth of Refugee Women – One Study and Two [Types of] Results. In A. Groterath, V. Langher, & G. Marinelli (Eds) *Flight and Migration from Africa to Europe. Contributions of*

Psychology and Social Work, Opladen, Germany: Barbara Budrich Publishers.

Schirripa, V., (2017). Lo "Sprar" come bottega di saperi professionali. [The Sprar reception system: a forge of new professional profiles.] *Studium Educationis*, 3, 87-90.

Study and Research Center IDOS/Immigration Statistical Dossier, (2014). Immigration statistical Dossier 2014. From discrimination to rights, Pomezia, Italy, Consorzio Age.

Vacchiano F. (2005). Cittadini sospesi: violenza e istitzioni nell'esperienza dei richiedenti asilo in Italia [Suspended citizens: Violence and institutions in the experience of the asylum seekers in Italy], *Antropologia*, 5, 95

Migration and family: a neglected nexus?

David Schiefer

Introduction

There is no doubt that the family is one of the most important social units in an individual's life. It consists of a group of individuals who are not only genetically related but also (at least in functional families) characterised by close emotional ties and mutual social and economic support. Whatever position a person has within the family (a daughter, a brother, a mother, etc.), much of his or her thinking, feeling, and behaviour is targeted towards the well-being and welfare of his or her family, but also towards norms, obligations and expectations imposed to him or her by the relatives.

Having that in mind, one can assume that family also plays an important role in an individual's migration decision and behavior. However, scholars, policy-makers and the wider public have for a long time viewed migration as a rather individual behaviour: It is individuals who migrate to seek better economic living conditions (e.g., start a job) in the country of destination, as international students, refugees or sojourners, and family-related migration is at best a subsequent phenomenon. Migration and family as a joint complex has most often been looked at with regard to the societal integration of migrant families who live as a whole in the country of destination. This individualised and in a way nationalistic perspective on migration that strongly differentiates between 'here' and 'there' with regard to migrants' lives (see Wimmer & Schiller, 2002 with regard to the term 'methodological nationalism' in migration research) overlooks that (a) family already plays a central role in migration decisions and behavior and that (b) the lives of those who moved to a destination country are often still shaped by their embeddedness in their family network in the country of origin. The latter has been discussed in the literature under the term *transnationalism* (with regard to social networks across national borders, e.g. Vertovec, 2009) or *transnational families* (e.g., Bryceson & Vuorela 2002).

Migration as a family project

The importance of family for migration is reflected both in administrative statistics and empirical studies. In Germany, one of the European countries with the largest recent inflow of immigrants, data of the Central Register of Foreign Nationals show that among foreign nationals living in Germany with a temporary residence permit around one third holds a permit that is based on family reasons (e.g., family reunion, see Statistisches Bundesamt, 2019).[1] Moreover, if one does not look at the legal categories of residence permits but on individual's subjective migration motives, the importance of family becomes even more evident. Data from the German Micro Census 2017 show, for example, that family-related reasons (family reunion, family formation) are the most prevalent reasons for migrants to move to Germany, regardless of the continent they originate from (Statistisches Bundesamt, 2018).

Family is a central migration motive also for immigrants from African countries. Figure 1 depicts data from the German Socio-Economic-Panel, a representative survey that includes also immigrants (see Goebel et al., 2019).

In the 2015 sample, participants with migration background (at least one parent was born outside of Germany) were asked to state the main reason to migrate to Germany. As can be taken from the figure, family-related reasons (partnership or other family reasons or economic reasons with regard to their children) were, taken together, the strongest drivers of migration. The meaning of family for migration decisions and behaviour is not only reflected in empirical data but also taken into account by various theoretical approaches. One prominent approach is the value-expectancy-model of migration (see De Jong & Fawcett, 1981). It originates from the early conceptualisation of migration as a behaviour that is based on the interplay of contextual factors (e.g., economic conditions) and individual cost-benefit-evaluations (rational choice approach, see, e.g., Haug, 2008). According to this approach, individuals strive to maximize gain on several highly-valued dimensions. An action, in this case migration, is performed when it is expected to be followed by a highly-valued consequence. According to De Jong and Fawcett (1981) such highly-valued consequences can be wealth, comfort, or autonomy, but

---

[1] The Central Register of Foreign Nationals is one of German public administration's largest data bases. Every non-German citizen residing in Germany for more than three months is registered there. The register comprises, among other, information on the type and length of residence permit a foreign individual holds. In the data base, temporary residence permits can be differentiated between different migration reasons the permit is based on (e.g., work-related, humanitarian protection, family-reunion). However, those migrants who do not need a residence permit (e.g., EU-citizens) or who hold a permanent residence permit cannot be distinguished by migration reasons.

also affiliation, e.g., living close to family and friends or being included in a social group.

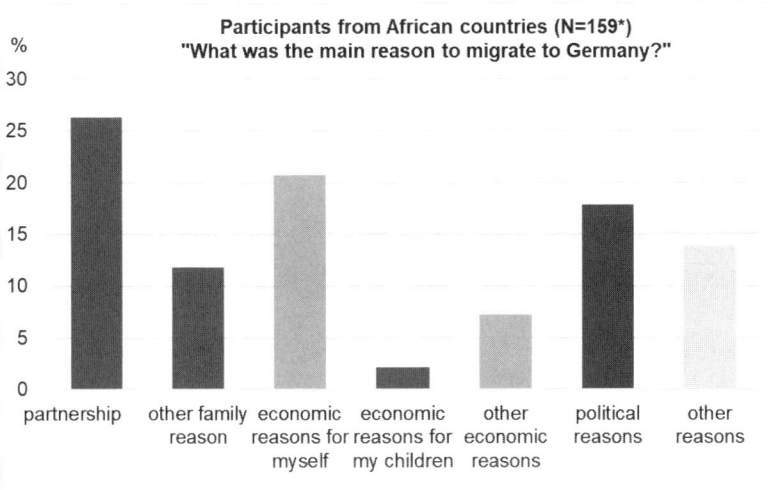

Figure 1: Migration Motives of immigrants in Germany

Note: *Participants from African countries that responded to the question. Largest five national groups: Morocco (N=41), Tunisia (N=24), Nigeria (N=19), Egypt (N=12), Ghana (N=8). Data are weighted.
Source: German Institute for Economic Research, Socio-Economic Panel (SOEP) 2015

A further development of this rational-choice approach, the New Economics of Labor Migration Theory (Stark, 1991), assumes that it is not the individual benefit that is at the core of migration decisions but the benefit of the household, i.e. the family, the individual is a member of. "Migration is therefore in essence a family strategy" (Haug, 2008), and migration decisions emerge from the interaction of family members. This explains, for example, the large amount of financial remittances that is sent by immigrants in receiving countries to their relatives in their countries of origin (e.g., Tiemoko, 2004; Taylor, 1999). Harbison (1981), in turn, presented a theoretical model that emphasizes the role of family for migration even more. It assumes that individuals' migration decision processes are shaped by the economic, physical, and sociocultural environment, but the family functions as a mediator. It transmits societal values to its offspring and assigns societal kinship rights and obligations to its members. It is furthermore the subsistence unit the individual relies on and therefore links contextual economic conditions (e.g. unemployment rate) to the individual family member, e.g., by choosing him or her to migrate as one strategy to secure the family income (Harbison, 1981).

The above described theoretical explanations of migration behavior, however, cannot explain why individuals still decide to migrate to another country even though circumstances (e.g., the labor market opportunities in the country of origin) have changed positively over time or the subsistence of his or her family is meanwhile well secured. This is where social network approaches to the understanding of migration come into play which again point to the importance of family: Once migrants have settled in a country of destination, they can stimulate further migration to this country through the social networks to their home country, especially their family ties. They provide the 'left-behind' with information about opportunities in the destination countries, with financial and logistic support for the move, and render assistance during the first time of settlement. This makes further migration more likely and can establish self-sustaining migration patterns between countries (Boyd, 1989; Massey, Alarcón, Durand, & González, 1987). Such follow-up migration processes apply to labor migration or family reunion but also to forced migration. Scholz (2013), for example, found that for refugees, family networks are one of the main reasons to choose Germany as the country where to seek humanitarian protection.

Family related-migration: forms and patterns

The family does not only play an important role for migration decisions of individuals, family-related migration itself also shows certain forms and patterns. Pries (2011) distinguishes between different types of family-induced migration. A person, for example, might migrate individually but for family-reasons, e.g., to start a job in the country of destination to support the family back home. Others accompany their spouse to another country or (and this is the more prevalent case) migrate to reunite with their spouse or their children in the country of destination. Yet others migrate to marry someone in the destination country and found a family there. Taken all together, these forms of migration constitute a major part of international migration movements (Pries 2011).

Faist (1997) as well as Haug (2000) postulate different migration stages that are associated with social networks between sending and receiving countries. Initially, a few individuals migrate to another country. For them, migration comes at highest costs and lowest benefits, because they do not have support networks in the receiving country, yet. Once they have settled in, they lower the costs for family members or other persons from the community of origin which stimulates increasing migration flows. Eventually, this increase levels off over time and remains on a certain level as the migration potential in the countries of origin decreases.

Whereas this (somewhat ideal-typical, c.f. De Haas, 2010) migration pattern still has the characteristic of a 'one-way-road', especially family-related migration can also have a circular character: Migrants can return to their family back home on a regular base for several months, or family members move to a relative abroad for a certain period of time and then return back home. Family members might even switch their role as the breadwinner who works abroad. Massey, Alarcón, Durand, and González (1987), for example, who studied migration from Mexico to the United States, found different migration strategies Mexican families pursue to secure economic subsistence. They all have in common that family members who migrate to the United States (temporarily, recurrently or permanently) still maintain close ties to their families back home and move back and forth on a regular base. To take another example, in Senegal of the 1960s, young bachelor men were chosen by the head of the family to move to France. These young men were expected to return to Senegal after about ten years to marry a woman. They then continued their lives in France with regular visits to their spouse and children in Senegal until they eventually returned for good (Beauchamin, Caarls & Mazzucato, 2013). Such migration patterns challenge the dichotomous perspective on international migration as a single act of moving from a 'country of origin' to a 'country of destination', which is still prominent in public debates on migration as well as in migration statistics.[2]

Family migration can also follow certain trajectories, which can be strategically planned. For example, a family member (e.g. the father or a child) migrates first, and once he or she is settled in the country of destination, his or her relatives try to follow. This is commonly found among refugee families, where the often dangerous flight is first undertaken by the most resilient family member.

After migration: transnational family arrangements

Once migrants have arrived in a country of destination they develop new social relations, try to access the labor market, learn the language and settle in. Nevertheless, they often keep strong social ties and remain embedded in social networks in the country of origin. This regards especially to the ties to family member. Such family relations across national borders are discussed in the

---

2 Migration flow statistics, for example, usually do not differentiate between initial entries and re-entries.

literature under the term *transnational family*. Although this term still lacks a clear and consensual definition, it generally describes families whose members are (at least partly) separated across national borders and often across large geographical distances, yet still form a socially and emotionally close unit. They maintain regular close contacts (e.g. by mail, phone) and visit each other regularly. The person living abroad often supports his or her family financially through remittances, but also communicates knowledge, experiences and (changed) cultural values, which has been described as the social form of remittances (Levitt, 1998). Most importantly, despite the sometimes large geographical distance the family members still have a strong personal and emotional meaning for each other. They share in each other's lives but also negotiate values and normative expectations or even raise their children across distance (e.g., Ducu, Nedelcu & Telegdi-Csetri, 2018). The person living abroad can also still be strongly attached to his or her home region und thus somewhat live 'between here and there'. In that sense, Bryceson and Vuorela (2002) define transnational families as "[...] families that live some or most of the time separated from each other, yet hold together and create something that can be seen as a feeling of collective welfare and unity, namely 'familyhood', even across national borders" (p. 3). This concept of multi-local family arrangements has challenged traditional (Western) sociological and psychological family concepts which view a family as a permanent unit of parents and children living together in the same household.

Strong transnational family ties can have a determining impact on migrants' lives in the country of destination. In many cases, for example, they face an additional financial burden due to the remittances they are expected to send to their families back home. This piles the pressure of accessing the labour marked as quick as possible, which in turn can be in conflict with the need to invest further month or years of education and training in order to adapt to the local job market and gain a sustainable position in it (Schiefer, 2017; Datta et al., 2007). Moreover, having close relatives back home can impact migrants' efforts to settle in the destination country in different ways. On the one hand, it can motivate them to learn the language and take effort to find a decent job in order to provide for the family back home (or prepare for their reunion in the country of destination). On the other hand, the separation from them can also be an emotional and cognitive strain (especially when the economic and physical security of the left-behind is threatened) which impedes such efforts. Furthermore, transnational family arrangements can bear conflict potential within the family itself. For example, if a migrant makes the experience of living on his or her own for the first time in a culturally new environment, this can change his or her values, goals and life style which then might become difficult to bring in accordance with normative expectations he or she is exposed to from the family back home.

One aspect of transnational family arrangements that has received much attention in the literature is the separation of children from their parents. Several studies show that both children and parents often suffer from this separation emotionally. This regards especially to mothers, which is often explained by gender norms: Women are often assigned to the role of the primary caregiver. Thus, if a woman lives abroad separated from her children, she more likely than men feels guilty for and stressed by not being able to fulfil that role with regard to their left-behind children (e.g., Bernard Landolt & Goldring, 2009; Robila, 2010). However, the degree to which separation causes psychological distress among parents and children also depends on individual, contextual and cultural factors (Mazzucato et al., 2015, see also the next chapter). Sometimes, reunion of parents and children is not even the preferred option in transnational family arrangements (Mazzucato et al., 2013).

Migration from Africa: the role of family

Family-related migration is also an important aspect of migration movements within and across African countries and from Africa to Europe. Family members living and working abroad is a common practice to improve the family's living conditions (Mazzucato et al., 2013; 2015). Being successful in a country of the Global North can even be associated with high social status and prestige in the sending countries.

One aspect that facilitates migration from African countries is the family structure. Of course, there is not *the* single 'African' family system. The way kin relations are structured and roles are ascribed, and the kind of shared normative regulations vary across countries, rural and urban regions, and ethnic groups. Moreover, family systems have undergone tremendous change during the last decades. Yet, kinship relations still play a strong role for the social life across African societies (Alber, Häberlein & Martin, 2010; Mazzucato et al., 2015). Several family characteristics that are still common today originate from what is usually subsumed under the term 'extended family systems'. In contrast to the nuclear family concept (a family consists of parents and their children living together), this family system is more broad, including other members of the matri- and patrilineal family line (e.g., aunts, uncles or cousins) and even persons who are not blood-related. In that sense a family is more a social construction than a mere biologically determined unit.

At least two characteristics of such broader family systems have been discussed to enhance migration of its members. Firstly, the broader family network is highly important, among other aspect, for the insurance of economic subsistence, especially when the state does not provide respective support systems (Sauer et al., 2018). Moreover, such families are often hierarchically organized and social control is high, with central decisions for the welfare of the kinship group made by authority figures such as family elders (Kok, 2010; Fleischer, 2017). This can result in individual family members being chosen to migrate in order to contribute to the economic welfare of the family, and pressure to support the family from abroad via remittances is high (e.g.: Fleischer, 2007, for the case of Cameroon).

Secondly, in such extended family systems the co-residence of spouses and their biological children has traditionally been far less the norm than in nuclear family systems. Spouses traditionally lived (and often still live) in separate homes with less frequent conjugal interaction. Furthermore, putting children in foster homes within the extended family network has long been and often still is a common practice. This form of child raising is traditionally viewed as a natural part of the family system in which the direct biological link between parents and their children is less important than the belonging to the extended family as a whole (Alber, Häberlein & Martin, 2010; Mazzucato et al., 2015).

Although this multi-site residence of spouses and children has become less frequent in many regions and among many groups in recent decades (see Alber, Häberlein & Martin, 2010), it can be assumed that geographical separation of close family members, e.g., through international migration, is still viewed as more normative und thus less emotionally distressing than it is the case in nuclear family systems (see Poeza & Mazzucato, 2014). Extended family system, so to speak, lower the "costs" of migration of individual family members.

A study that has investigated migration within African families extensively is the *Migration from Africa to Europe (MAFE)* project (see Beauchamin, 2012). What renders this study unique is the survey design: Families were interviewed in sending countries (Senegal, Ghana, Congo) as well as in receiving European countries (Belgium, France, Italy, Spain, United Kingdom, The Netherlands). This study design makes it possible to investigate patterns of out-, return-, and circular migration, consequences of migration for those living abroad and those left behind, as well as transnational family-arrangements from a multi-national and multi-contextual perspective. The surveys were conducted between 2008 and 2010. Among other findings, between 43,5 percent (Ghana) and 63,2 percent (Congo) of the households surveyed in the sending countries reported being in contact with a member of the core or extended family abroad, mostly in the Global North. The majority of these contacts, however, were not with close relatives such as spouses or children but with members of the extended family (Mazzucato et al., 2013). If family members lived abroad, contacts (e.g. via phone) were rather frequent with the majority of survey participants reporting weekly or monthly contacts (*Ibidem 13-14*).

Among the immigrant participants surveyed in European countries a considerable number reported living in transnational family arrangements (at least one member of the nuclear family lives in another country). Importantly, however, the numbers differed substantially between both sending and receiving national contexts. Whereas on average around 44 percent of the Senegalese participants in Europe reported that, it was only around 23 percent of the Congolese and 17 percent of the Ghanaian participants living in Europe. The case of immigrants from Senegal also serves as a good example for differences between receiving countries: Whereas 66 percent of the Senegalese participants in Italy reported living in transnational family arrangements, this regarded only to 23 percent of the Senegalese participants in France (Mazzucato et al., 2013).

A central economic feature of transnational family arrangements is the practice of sending remittances (e.g., Tiemoko, 2004). In the MAFE-survey, around half of the households in Senegal, Ghana, and Congo confirmed to receive financial support from family members abroad. Importantly, such support is not only provided by core family members abroad (spouses or children) but also substantially by more distant kin (Mazzucato et al., 2013).

Tiemoko (2004) reports similar numbers based on a survey among returned migrants in Côte d'Ivoire and Ghana. Depending on the sample[3], between 42 and 91 percent of the participants reported that they had regular contact[4] with their relatives during their time abroad. Between 47 and 76 percent reported having sent remittances to their families.

Taken together, these studies document how frequent transnational family arrangements can be in African countries and the respective destination countries, but also show differences between them. Such differences can be traced back to variations in migration histories in the sending countries, migration policies in the receiving countries but also culture-specific family structures and values that favor family-reunion or transnational family arrangements to a higher or lower degree (see Beauchemin et al., 2013, for the case of Senegal).

---

3 The data comprise two (non-representative samples) in both countries: one comprises highly skilled participants (university degree and managerial/professional job position prior to emigration), the other comprises a more heterogeneous sample in terms of education and occupational status (Tiemoko, 2004).
4 The frequency of contact was differentiated into "regular", "irregular" and "none".

Do migration policies meet the requirements of family-related migration?

As the previous chapters discussed, in many, if not the majority of cases migration across the globe is not an individual endeavor but is grounded in family structures, familial living arrangements and subsistence strategies. However, is this important driver of migration also reflected in immigration regulations of destination countries?

Despite all national variations, a general answer can be: In theory yes, in practice only to a limited extend. Several international conventions including those concerning migration (e.g., the Migrant Worker Convention (Supplementary Provisions) passed by the International Labor Organization in 1975) incorporate the right for family union based on the view of family as a superior good that need to be protected. Yet, they do that with different explicitness (Kraler, 2010).

Accordingly, all EU-countries have regulations that determine which non-EU citizens are allowed to accompany or follow their family members that hold a work-based or other kind of residence permit in a destination country, and under what conditions family reunification is granted.[5] In Germany, for example, a residence permit for the purpose of family-reunification (e.g., reunification of spouses) requires, among other criteria, the prove that the subsistence of the accompanying or subsequently migrating family member is secured, that there is sufficient accommodation (in terms of space) and that the subsequently migrating person has a minimum knowledge of German (Grote, 2017).

There exist a number of exceptions and additional regulations which under certain conditions lower the administrative barriers for certain groups (e.g. relatives of grantees of humanitarian protection under the Geneva refugee convention or of holders of the so-called EU Blue Card[6]). Yet, in many cases the requirements are difficult to fulfill for the couples or families (Kraler, 2010). In addition, the application process can take very long, especially for refugee families, due to long waiting periods in embassies in the countries of origin or in third countries (Grote, 2017).

Even though family reunification might not always be the primary goal for transnational families, at least the possibility to visit each other, also in the countries of destination, is important for the family cohesion and the well-being of family members. In the European Union, short-term visits of non-EU

---

5 In the course of increasing migration pressure to EU countries and a political shift towards the right in some EU-member states such regulations have become more restrictive in recent years (Kraler 2010, Mazzucato/Schans/Caarls/Beauchemin 2013).

6 See https://ec.europa.eu/immigration/blue-card/essential-information_en (last access 08/20/2019).

citizens are principally possible via the so-called Schengen-Visa. It allows visitors to enter the European Union for up to 90 days[7]. While this could be a key regulation for transnational families from all over the world, rejections rates of such EU-short-term visa applications are considerably high.

Figure 2 shows the rejection rates for applications from African countries in 2018. As can be seen, the rates are remarkably high in numerous countries. For example, every second application for an EU-short-term visa filed by a Nigerian citizens was rejected.

The crucial barrier here is again the set of conditions a person is required to fulfill in order to be granted such a visa. Some criteria, such as the proof of a travel health insurance and the ability to bear all travel and living costs (or a declaration of financial commitment by a host) are rather clear-cut. However, other criteria are more vague, in particular the proof of the person's willingness to return to his or her home country. Whether this willingness is considered plausible depends much more on the judgement of the respective authority than other criteria. Critics of the Schengen member states' issuing practices therefore claim that there are no clear criteria for a plausible willingness to return, yet a non-plausible return intention is supposed to be the main reason for visa rejections among the authorities (for Germany see, e.g., Ataman, 2010; Dağdelen et al., 2017).

---

7 https://ec.europa.eu/home-affairs/what-we-do/policies/borders-and-visas/visa-policy/schengen_visa_en (last access 08/20/2019).

Figure 2: Rejection rates of EU-short-term visa 2018 by African countries

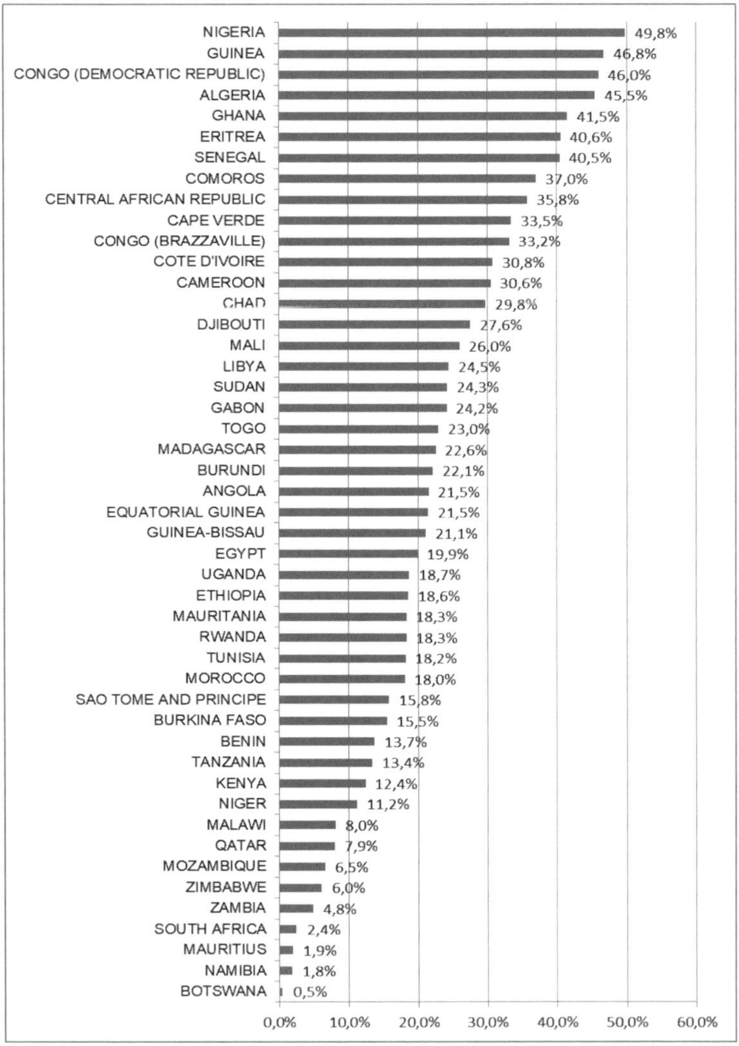

Note: Percentage of uniform short-stay visa applications (single and multiple entry visa and visa with limited territorial validity) that have been rejected by the consulates of EU-member states. African countries with less than 1000 visa applications to the EU in 2018 are not depicted.
Source: European Commission, Schengen Visa Statistics.

Summary and conclusion: Is the awareness of family-related migration still too low?

When people think of immigrants, they usually have in mind an individual who leaves his or her country for various reasons and attempts to permanently settle down in another, e.g., European country. The present chapter points out, that this view is skewed in at least three ways. Firstly, migration is often a 'family project' in the sense that the individual act of migration takes place against the background of familial considerations, decisions and respective expectations towards the migrating person. Secondly, migration is not a decision to live 'here' or 'there'. It rather can be temporal, permanent, recurring or circular, especially when considering the importance of transnational family relations.

Thirdly, even if migration is permanent, an individual's life in the country of origin does not end after his or her journey to the new country. Especially the importance of family for an individual's thinking, feeling, and behavior results in regional and cultural self-localisations and identities that transcend national borders. Contrary to this, public discourses in host countries are often permeated by the assumption that once a person migrated, it is only the life in the destination country that matters to him or her and that this is all he or she as well as the society has to care for. The fact that a person's life continues to take place across national borders is somewhat perceived as if the person has not fully 'arrived' yet. However, whether this is the case, e.g., whether transnational family arrangements discourage migrants to settle down and participate in the receiving society is still to be investigated empirically.

Current migration policies, in turn, impede family migration in several ways. First of all, they set high restrictions for family reunification or mutual visits that are often rather difficult to fulfill. Furthermore, by granting family reunification only to spouses or to biological parents and their (under-aged) children, such regulations are grounded in a nuclear family concept. Thus, migration policies are neither consistent with the realities of family systems that go beyond this narrow definition of family nor do they sufficiently meet the requirements of transnational families, especially in terms of short-term visits. This, in turn, increases the likelihood that migrants find other, irregular ways of joining their family members in destination countries or support their relatives financially from abroad.

References

Alber, E., Häberlein, T., & Martin, J. (2010). Changing Webs of Kinship: Spotlights on West Africa. *Africa Spectrum*, 45(3), 43-67.

Ataman, F. (2010). Rein kommt nur, wer auch wieder geht [Only those who leave again are allowed to come in]. In: Tagesspiegel Online (24 October). Available at: https://www.tagesspiegel.de/politik/rein-kommt-nur-wer-auch-wieder-geht/1890424.html (Accessed: 28 August 2019).

Beauchemin, C. (2012). Migrations between Africa and Europe: Rationale for a Survey Design. MAFE-Project. Methodological note number: 5.

Beauchemin, C., Caarls, K., & Mazzucato, V. (2013). Senegalese Migrants between Here and There: An Overview of Family Patterns. MAFE-Project. Working paper number: 33.

Bernhard, J. K., Landolt, P., & Goldring, L. (2009). Transnationalizing Families: Canadian Immigration Policy and the Spatial Fragmentation of Caregiving among Latin American Newcomers 1. *International Migration*, 47(2), 3-31.

Boyd, M. (1989). Family and personal networks in international migration: recent developments and new agendas, *International Migration Review*, 23(3), 638-70.

Bryceson, D., & Vuorela, U. (2002). *The transnational family: New European frontiers and global networks*. Oxford, New York: Berg Publishers.

Dağdelen, S., Gehrcke, W., Korte, J., Groth, A., Hänsel, H., H ger, I., Hunko, A., Jelpke, U., et al. (2017). Minor interpellation: Visa issuance in 2016, Document 18/11083 of the German Federal Parliament, Berlin: Germany.

Datta, K., McIlwaine, C., Wills, J., Evans, Y., Herbert, J., & May, J. (2007). The new development finance or exploiting migrant labour?: remittance sending among low-paid migrant workers in London. *International Development Planning Review*, 29(1), 43-67.

De Haas, H. (2010). The internal dynamics of migration processes: A theoretical inquiry. *Journal of ethnic and migration studies*, 36(10), 1587-1617.

De Jong, G. F., & Fawcett, J. T. (1981). Motivations for Migration: An Assessment and a Value-Expectancy Research Model. In G. F. De Jong & R. W. Gardner, (Eds.), *Migration Decision Making. Multidisciplinary Approaches to Microlevel Studies in Developed and Developing Countries*, New York: Pergamon, (pp. 13-58).

Ducu, V., Nedelcu, M., & Telegdi-Csetri, Á. (Eds.). (2018). *Childhood and parenting in transnational settings*, Cham, Switzerland: Springer.

Faist, T. (1997). The Crucial Meso-Level. In T. G. Hammar, K. Brochmann,

K. Tamas & T. Faist (Eds.), *International Migration, Immobility and Development*, Oxford, New York: Berg, (pp. 187-217).
Fleischer, A. (2007). Family, obligations, and migration: The role of kinship in Cameroon, *Demographic Research*, 16, 413-440.
Goebel, J., Grabka, M. M., Liebig, S., Kroh, M., Richter, D., Schröder, C., & Schupp, J. (2019). The German Socio-economic Panel (SOEP). *Journal of Economics and Statistics*, 239(2), 345-360.
Grote, J. (2017). Family Reunification of third-country nationals in *Germany. Focus-Study by the German National Contact Point for the European Migration Network (EMN)*, Working Paper 73 of the Federal Office for Migration and Refugees, Nürnberg, Germany.
Harbison, S. F. (1981). Family structure and family strategy in migration decision making. In G. F. De Jong & R. W. Gardner (Eds.), *Migration Decision Making. Multidisciplinary Approaches to Microlevel Studies in Developed and Developing Countries*, New York: Pergamon, p. 225-51.
Haug, S. (2008). Migration networks and migration decision-making. *Journal of Ethnic and Migration Studies*, 34(4), 585-605.
Haug, S. (2000). S*oziales Kapital, Migrationsentscheidungen und Kettenmigrationsprozesse. Das Beispiel der italienischen Migranten in Deutschland* [Social capital, migration decisions and chain migration processes. The example of Italian migrants in Germany]. Working paper 13 of the Department of Sociology, Leipzig, Germany: University of Leipzig.
Kok, J. (2010). The family factor in migration decisions. In J. Lucassen, L. Lucassen & P. Manning (Eds.), *Migration History in World History: Multidisciplinary approaches*, (pp. 215-250). Leiden, The Netherlands: Koninklijke Brill NV.
Kraler, A. (2010). *Civic Stratification, Gender and Family Migration Policies in Europe*, Vienna: International Centre for Migration Policy Development (ICMPD).
Levitt, P. (1998). Social remittances: Migration driven local-level forms of cultural diffusion. *International migration review*, 32(4), 926-948.
Massey, D. S., Alarcón, R., Durand, J., & González, H. (1987*). Return to Aztlan: The social process of international migration from Western Mexico* (Vol. 1). Univ of California Press.
Mazzucato, V., Cebotari, V., Veale, A., White, A., Grassi, M., & Vivet, J. (2015). International parental migration and the psychological well-being of children in Ghana, Nigeria, and Angola. *Social Science & Medicine*, 132, 215-224.
Mazzucato, V., Schans, D., Caarls, K., & Beauchemin, C. (2013). *Migrant Families between Africa and Europe: Comparing Ghanaian, Congolese and Senegalese Migration Flows*, MAFE Working Paper

30, Paris: France.
Mazzucato, V., Schans, D., Caarls, K., & Beauchemin, C. (2015). Transnational Families Between Africa and Europe, *International migration review*, 49(1), 142-172.
Poeze, M., & Mazzucato, V. (2014). Ghanaian Children in Transnational Families: Understanding the Experiences of Left-Behind Children through Local Parenting Norms. In L. Baldassar, & L.Merla (eds.): *Transnational Families: Migration and the Circulation of Care* (pp. 149–169). London, UK: Routledge.
Pries, L. (2011). Familiäre Migration in Zeiten der Globalisierung [Family and migration in times of globalization], in: V. Fischer, & M. Springer (Eds.): *Handbuch Migration und Familie. Grundlagen für die Soziale Arbeit mit Familien* [Handbook migration and family. Principles of social work with families] (p. 23-35). Schwalbach am Taunus, Germany: Wochenschau Verlag,.
Robila, M. (2011). Parental migration and children's outcomes in Romania. *Journal of Child and Family Studies*, 20(3), 326-333.
Sauer, L., Diabaté, S., Gabel, S., Halfar, Y., Kraus, E., K., & Wenzel, L. (2018): *Doing transnational family im Kontext von Flucht und Krisenmigration: Stand der Forschung* [Doing transnational family in the context of forced migration and crisis management: State of research]. Working Paper 3/2018. Wiesbaden, Germany: Federal Institute for Population Research.
Schiefer, D. (2017). *Wie gelingt Integration? Asylsuchende über ihre Lebenslagen und Teilhabeperspektiven in Deutschland* [How might integration succeed? Asylum seekers about their life situations and participation perspectives in Germany], Berlin: SVR Research Unit and Robert Bosch Foundation. Policy-brief number: 2017/4.
Scholz, A. (2013). *Warum Deutschland? Einflussfaktoren bei der Zielstaatssuche von Asylbewerbern – Ergebnisse einer Expertenbefragung* [Why Germany? Influencing factors on the destination choices of asylum seekers. Results of an expert survey], Forschungsbericht 19, Bundesamt für Migration und Flüchtlinge, Nürnberg, Germany.
Stark, O. (1991). *The Migration of Labour*. Oxford, UK: Blackwell.
Statistisches Bundesamt (2018). *Bevölkerung und Erwerbstätigkeit. Bevölkerung mit Migrationshintergrund. Ergebnisse des Mikrozensus 2017* [Population and employment. Population with migration background. Results of the Micro Census 2017], Fachserie 1, Reihe 2.2, Wiesbaden, Germany.
Statistisches Bundesamt (2019). *Bevölkerung und Erwerbstätigkeit. Ausländische Bevölkerung. Ergebnisse des Ausländerzentralregisters* [Population and employment. Foreign population. Results of the

Central Register of Foreign Nationals]. Fachserie 1, Reihe 2, Wiesbaden, Germany.

Taylor, J.E. (1999). The new economics of labour migration and the role of remittances in the migration process, *International Migration*, 37, 63–88.

Tiemoko, R. (2004). Migration, return and socio-economic change in West Africa: the role of family. *Population, space and place*, 10(2), 155-174.

Vertovec, S. (2009). *Transnationalism*. London and New York: Routledge.

Wimmer, A., & Glick Schiller, N. (2002). Methodological nationalism and beyond: nation–state building, migration and the social sciences. *Global networks*, 2(4), 301-334.

Fabian Kessl
Walter Lorenz
Hans-Uwe Otto
Sue White (eds.)

European Social Work – A Compendium

2020. 453 pp. • Hardcover • 89,00 € (D) • 91,50 € (A)
ISBN 978-3-8474-0147-6 • eISBN 978-3-8474-0817-8

The publication takes account of the fundamental developments transforming social work in Europe at the beginning of the 21st century. A European standard of social work has already emerged, but models for future European social work are absent. Therefore the compendium gives an overview of the current transformation process for the first time, discusses the visible and invisible changes and maps out where social work is positioned in the emerging post-welfare states.

www.barbara-budrich.net

Ingrid Jungwirth
Carola Bauschke-Urban (eds.)

Gender and Diversity Studies

European Perspectives

2019. 326 pp • Pb. • 39,90 € (D) • 41,10 € (A)
ISBN 978-3-8474-0549-8 • eISBN 978-3-8474-0948-9

What concepts of 'gender' and 'diversity' emerge in the different regions and pertinent research and practical fields? On the back drop of current European developments – from the deregulation of economy, a shrinking welfare state to the dissolution and reinforcement of borders – the book examines the development of Gender and Diversity Studies in different European regions as well as beyond and focuses on central fields of theoretical reflection, empirical research and practical implementation policies and politics.

www.shop.budrich.de

Marianne Kneuer
Helen V. Milner (eds.)

Political Science and Digitalization – Global Perspectives

2019 • 290 pp. • Hardcover • 60,00 € (D) • US$85.00, GBP 53.00
ISBN 978-3-8474-2332-4 • eISBN 978-3-8474-1488-9

Digitalization is not only a new research subject for political science, but a transformative force for the discipline in terms of teaching and learning as well as research methods and publishing. This volume provides the first account of the influence of digitalization on the discipline of political science including contributions from 20 different countries. It presents a regional stocktaking of the challenges and opportunities of digitalization in most world regions.

Marianne Kneuer is Professor for Political Science and Director of the Institute of Social Sciences and Co-founder of the Center for digital Change at the University of Hildesheim, Germany.

Helen V. Milner is B.C. Forbes Professor of Politics and International Affairs at Princeton University as well as Director of the Niehaus Center for Globalization and Governance at Princeton's Woodrow Wilson School, USA.

www.barbara-budrich.net